A Tale of Two Murders

D0011079

Narrative
Credibility
Microhistory
Pass position down

A Tale of Two Murders

Passion and Power in Seventeenth-Century France

JAMES R. FARR

- math
- essay

Talbott - JLD
G - Will Arnet
Mom - Mary Steamburgen-eque
Dad - Ted Danson-eque

DUKE UNIVERSITY PRESS

DURHAM AND LONDON

2005

© 2005 *Duke University Press*

All rights reserved

Printed in the United States of America

on acid-free paper ♾

Designed by Amy Ruth Buchanan. Typeset
in Quadraat by Tseng Information Systems, Inc.
Library of Congress Cataloging-in-Publication
Data appear on the last printed page
of this book.

For Danielle

Contents

"Jiroo"
↳pronunciation (handwritten annotation)

Preface

Justice is "public vengeance, not private."[1] So pronounced Pierre de Saumaise, the Seigneur de Chasans, one of the key players in a *cause célèbre* that
shook Burgundy in the mid-seventeenth century. This book is about that historical episode. It centers on the murder trial of a distinguished and powerful man, Philippe Giroux, a *président*, or presiding judge, at Burgundy's Parlement, the highest court of appeal in the province. The trial was not simply
of provincial importance, however, for it came to involve the most powerful
men in France, among them Henri II de Bourbon, the prince of Condé; the
prime minister Cardinal Richelieu; and the king himself, Louis XIII. Because
of the powerful figures who became entangled in this affair, it dramatically
illuminates the intricate web of power relations of the time, and so demon-
strates how power and influence were exerted in concrete, lived situations.
One goal of mine, therefore, is to show the reader how power worked, both
formally through the law and informally through patron-client relations. I
also hope that this story exposes something more subtle and perhaps even
more profound about the nature of seventeenth-century political culture:
the deep contradictions upon which the social, judicial, and political systems rested. Saumaise's pronouncement about the public nature of justice
was only partly true, in fact, for families driven by private interests guided by
social imperatives captured the judicial system at a time when impartial law
and disinterested justice—what we call the rule of law—were crystallizing
as essential theoretical attributes of governing public polities.

The genesis of this book was an accident. While researching an earlier book, *Authority and Sexuality in Early Modern Burgundy (1550–1730)* (New York, 1995), I stumbled upon the record of a trial that I initially, and mistakenly, assumed to have been for the crime of adultery. I quickly discovered that it was about murder (and adultery only incidentally), and that it involved many of the most powerful families in Burgundy. I set the Giroux affair aside to complete the other book, but generous grants from the John Simon Guggenheim Foundation and the American Council of Learned Societies provided me the time and support to return to the Giroux affair and to complete this book. As I explored the fundamental issues at the heart of this study, I had the opportunity to share some of my preliminary conclusions with colleagues at other institutions. Steven Kaplan invited me on two occasions to present papers at Cornell University—first as part of the lecture series for the Humanities Center and the Program in French Studies, and then in the international colloquium that he chaired with Christian Jouhaud on "La Légitimation des acteurs sociaux comme sujets politiques (XVIᵉ–XVIIIᵉ siècles)." Likewise, Guido Ruggiero extended several opportunities to me to present my ideas on the law, first in the Cooper Lecture Series at the University of Miami, and subsequently at the International Conference on Honor and the Renaissance in Capo d'Istria, Slovenia. Jeff Watt graciously did the same, offering a venue in the lecturer series at my alma mater, the University of Mississippi, as did Peter Wallace in the lecturer series at Hartwick College. On two occasions I presented aspects of my interpretation of the Giroux affair to the Wabash Valley French History Group and received valuable commentary from John Lynn, David Kammerling Smith, Brad Brown, Paul Hanson, and Dean Ferguson. Most recently I learned a great deal from Peter Lake and his graduate students at Princeton University, especially John Hintermeier, having been invited to present a paper there on the Giroux affair in the Early Modern European Lecture Series. I offer my most heartfelt thanks to all these colleagues.

Most of the research for this book was done in the Archives Départementales de la Côte d'Or in Dijon and in the Bibliothèque Municipale de Dijon. Having become something of a denizen of those repositories given that my first two books were researched in them, I again owe a great debt of gratitude to all of the staff—above all Martine Chauney of the Bibliothèque Municipale—in those two efficiently organized and wonderfully stocked institutions. It has been a joy to mature as a scholar amid such helpful people and stimulating surroundings.

My thanks also go to those who read the manuscript and suggested improvements—my colleague at Purdue University John Lauritz Larson and above all Elliott Gorn of Brown University. And finally I thank my wife, Danielle. She has read the manuscript, and heard me talk about the characters in it so much, that she must feel that she knows them nearly as well as I do. Many an hour have we passed immersed in this episode of so long ago, still gripped by its passionate characters and tragic unfolding. It is to her that this book is dedicated.

Principal Characters

PIERRE BAILLET: Président at the Chambres des Comptes, a royal financial court in Dijon, husband of Marie Fyot, and first cousin of Philippe Giroux.

PIERRE BOREL, called DEVILLIERS: Trusted servant of Philippe Giroux.

HENRI II DE BOURBON, PRINCE OF CONDÉ: A royal prince, cousin of the king, and governor of Burgundy.

MARGUERITE BRULART: Mother of Marie Le Goux de La Berchere (and thus Philippe Giroux's mother-in-law), wife of the premier président Jean-Baptiste Le Goux de La Berchere.

CLAUDE BRYOT, called LA VALEUR: Servant of Philippe Giroux and key witness for the prosecution.

JEANNE BURGAT: Mother of Pierre Baillet.

DENIS CARTAUT, called SAINT DENIS: Trusted manservant of Philippe Giroux.

ELEANORE CORDIER: Servant of Philippe Giroux and governess of Giroux's son, Henri.

DEVILLIERS: Nickname of Pierre Borel, trusted servant of Philippe Giroux.

MARIE FYOT: Wife of Pierre Baillet, daughter of the distinguished François Fyot, lord of Barain, and reputed lover of Philippe Giroux.

BENOÎT GIROUX: Président à mortier in the Parlement until 1636, father of Philippe Giroux.

PHILIPPE GIROUX: One of seven (eight after 1638) présidents à mortier, or presiding judges at the Parlement of Dijon, the sovereign court of final appeal in the province of Burgundy.

MARIE LE GOUX DE LA BERCHERE: Wife of Philippe Giroux, daughter of Jean-Baptiste Le Goux de La Berchere (premier président of the Parlement of Dijon until 1631), and sister of Pierre (premier président from 1631).

ANTOINE JACQUOT: One of two commissioners leading the prosecution in the suspected murder of Pierre Baillet after the dismissal of Lantin.

JEAN-BAPTISTE LANTIN: *Conseiller* (advising judge) in the Parlement, first commissioner in the prosecution of the suspected murder of Pierre Baillet, dismissed in March 1640.

LA VALEUR: Nickname of Claude Bryot, servant of Philippe Giroux and key witness for the prosecution.

MICHEL MILLIÈRE: One of two commissioners leading the prosecution in the suspected murder of Pierre Baillet after the dismissal of Lantin.

FRANÇOISE PAILLEY: Wife of Denis Cartaut, called Saint Denis.

LAZARE RHODOT: Philippe Giroux's private physician.

SAINT DENIS: Nickname of Denis Cartaut, trusted manservant of Philippe Giroux.

PIERRE SAUMAISE DE CHASANS: *Conseiller* (advising judge) in the Parlement, archenemy of Philippe Giroux.

PIERRE DE XAINTONGE: Royal advocate general in the Parlement of Dijon, charged with organizing the prosecution of the suspected murder of Pierre Baillet.

Prologue

Looking Back

In midsummer of 1676, at the peak of Louis XIV's power in France and throughout Europe, a once-beautiful sixty-eight-year-old woman named Marie Fyot gazed upon a convicted murderer being led through the streets of Paris on her way to her execution. Executions were public events, and to catch a glimpse of the criminal on her way from the jailhouse to the stake, thousands of Parisians lined narrow cobbled streets, stood perched on rooftops, leaned from railings of balconies, and peered through the windows of the typical three- and four-story stone, plaster, and timber dwellings that housed the half-million people inhabiting France's great capital. A frail, petite woman sat hunched in the tumbrel that trundled slowly over the bridge spanning the Seine and rolled lugubriously along Paris's right bank toward the Place de Grève. She was flanked on one side by a priest who accompanied her to hear her final confession. On her other side stood her executioner.

The convicted murderer was an illustrious lady, and the spectacle of bringing down someone so high made for good theater. But for Marie Fyot, watching the baleful procession must have brought back painful memories from her own past. On this day, 17 July, one week past her sixty-eighth birthday, the once-beautiful Marie Fyot gazed upon the murderer Marie-Madeleine Dreux d'Aubray, the marquise of Brinvilliers, as the felon inexorably approached the stake where she was to be burned alive. The marquise was sentenced to suffer such a painful fate (and according to legal procedure at the time an unusual one) because she had been convicted of murder by poison, a crime made all the more heinous because the victims had been her husband and her two sons. Marie Fyot must have thought, recalling her own past many years ago, that she could have suffered the same fate. This is the story of what she might have remembered on that summer day during the reign of the Sun King.

CHAPTER I

Tales of Two Murders

Historians try to determine what happened in the past. Drawing upon evidence left to us, we try to get the story straight, for there lies historical "truth." This book is about two alleged murders in 1638 in Dijon, France. Much of the evidence used to write the narrative is drawn from the criminal trial that occurred between 1639 and 1643 to identify the culprit or culprits and to prove his, her, or their guilt. Hundreds of documents were produced—depositions of witnesses, interrogations of the accused, legal briefs of interested parties, and so on—each with a story to tell pertaining to the alleged murders. Often these documents, like any story, would have a narrative, a plot, a claim to credibility. What challenges the historian's obligation to get the story straight, however, is the palpable dishonesty of many of these documents, a large number of which flatly contradict one another. Many people, in other words, were obviously lying. The historian's task, much like the judges' of the time, is to determine what happened, but as historians we must go further and answer why—why did the judges reach the decision they did, and why does it matter to us in the twenty-first century? What follows in these pages is an attempt to accomplish these tasks— to get the story straight as much as is possible, and to explain why doing so matters.

Let us begin with a narrative about the alleged murders pieced together from a variety of sources, notably some depositions of witnesses called by the prosecuting authorities. Several witnesses said this: around 8 in the eve-

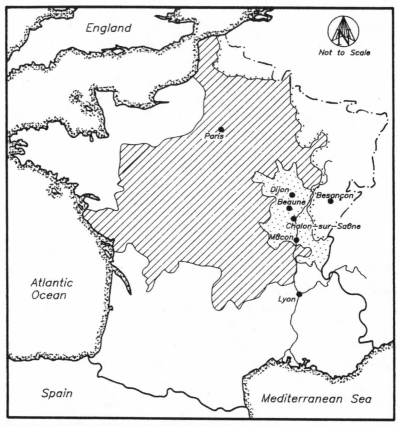

England

Not to Scale

Paris

Dijon
Beaune
Besançon
Chalon-sur-Saône
Mâcon

Atlantic
Ocean

Lyon

Spain

Mediterranean Sea

LEGEND:

Jurisdiction of Parlement of Paris

Jurisdiction of Parlement of Burgundy

Border of France (18th C.)

Border of France (1610)

Adapted by Matt Riebsomer

Territorial jurisdictions of the Parlements of Burgundy and Paris,
sixteenth and eighteenth centuries. From James R. Farr, *Authority and
Sexuality in Early Modern Burgundy (1550–1730)*, copyright 1995 and
used by permission of Oxford University Press, Inc.

ning on Monday, 6 September 1638, the servant Suzanne Odinelle opened the front door to admit a visitor to her master's impressive, multistory stone mansion in Dijon. This was the home of the nobleman Philippe Giroux. The visitor was Giroux's first cousin on his mother's side, a fellow nobleman named Pierre Baillet. Accompanied by his valet, Philibert Neugot, Baillet was escorted into the house—and to his death, for Baillet and his valet were never seen alive again.

Despite the close relation of host and guest, we hear from witnesses that this was no friendly visit; Baillet and Neugot came well armed. Baillet wore two daggers sheathed to the belt that also held a rapier swinging from his waist. Neugot carried two daggers and two swords. This was peculiar attire for a social visit, and Baillet was no soldier. He was a presiding judge, a président, at the royal financial court, the Chambre des Comptes, seated in Dijon, Burgundy's capital. Baillet possessed an office and a title, along with the social rank and the honor that came with them and placed him near the summit of society. His cousin Philippe Giroux was even more exalted, owning the office of presiding judge at the royal judicial court of Burgundy, the Parlement.

Baillet had been invited to his cousin's house, according to other witnesses, to patch up differences between them. They had a powerful incentive to do so, because family solidarity formed the base of power in this hierarchical age, and the "House of Giroux," as we will see, was unquestionably an increasingly powerful one. Though blood ties were what bound society, those between Baillet and Giroux were being sorely tested. Many people suspected—and told the court—that Baillet's wife Marie, a beautiful woman from the esteemed and powerful noble family of Fyot, was Giroux's mistress.

Perhaps jealousy and stained honor prompted Baillet to finger Giroux as the culprit in a political scandal that had erupted two years previously. In the mid-1630s France and its royal dynasty the Bourbons were deeply involved in the Thirty Years' War, squaring off against their historic enemy, the house of Habsburg. The Habsburgs' possessions spanned Europe, engulfing in their dominion the kingdom of Spain (which included much of the Americas), Sicily and the southern half of Italy, part of the Low Countries (present-day Belgium), and the German Holy Roman Empire. Part of the territory that came with the Empire was the County of Burgundy (today the

Franche-Comté), just to the east of the French province and former Duchy of Burgundy. This meant that Dijon was very much a frontier town, scarcely twenty miles from the border, and as the war between Habsburg and Bourbon heated up, French Burgundy and Dijon were put on a war footing.

The governor of the province of Burgundy, Henri II de Bourbon, the prince of Condé, was entrusted with the military campaigns against the imperial Habsburg forces in the area. After a bungled siege of the town of Dôle in 1636, about thirty miles southeast of Dijon, Condé was reminded of his military debacle by some unnamed person who smeared the prince's name and military prowess by printing and then plastering scores of one-page broadsides on the walls lining the public streets and market squares of Dijon. Condé, incensed at such effrontery, was allegedly informed by Baillet that the author of these infamous sheets was Philippe Giroux. Giroux of course denied this, and was certain that Baillet had been the source of the libel. Condé found Giroux's guilt impossible to believe: Giroux had been one of the prince's closest, hand-picked clients. In fact, as we will see in chapter 5 when we examine the House of Giroux, the rise to wealth, power, and influence of the Giroux clan owed largely to the favor of this prince of the blood, King Louis XIII's first cousin and second in line to the throne.

Giroux's patron-client bond with Condé was secure enough to weather that storm, but Philippe — guilty or not of the libel — certainly had good reason to despise his cousin for nearly wrecking a political and social career that had vaulted Philippe near the top of society no less than it placed him close to the center of the power structure in Burgundy. If political betrayal was not enough reason for Giroux to hate Baillet, according to witnesses his passion for his cousin's wife was so great that in the view of more than one person, if her husband were out of the way he would marry her. Moreover, rumors about town had supposedly reached Baillet's ear that a conspiracy to murder him was afoot.

So when Baillet received the invitation to come to Giroux's house, as this version of the story had it, he received it warily, and came armed. Could his cousin be the one conspiring to murder him? It was a staggering (and dubious?) prospect that a close family member would contemplate parricide, a heinous offense punishable by hideous forms of execution: burning at the stake or breaking on the wheel. Would Giroux risk that for revenge and for the love of another man's wife? Whatever Baillet's premonitions, many wit-

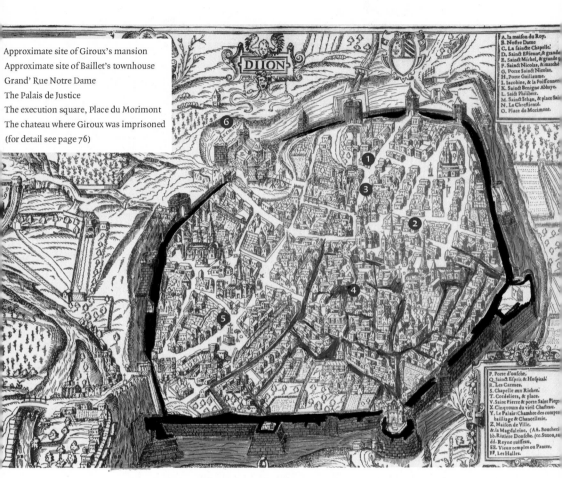

Approximate site of Giroux's mansion
Approximate site of Baillet's townhouse
Grand' Rue Notre Dame
The Palais de Justice
The execution square, Place du Morimont
The chateau where Giroux was imprisoned
(for detail see page 76)

A. la maison du Roy.
B. Noftre Dame
C. La fainête Chapelle.
D. Sainêt Eftienne, & grande
E. Sainêt Michel, & grande
F. Sainêt Nicolas, & marché
X. Sainêt Nicolas, & marché
G. Porte Sainêt Nicolas.
H. Porte Guillaume.
L. Iacobins, & la Poiffonner
K. Sainêt Benigne Abbaye.
L. Sainêt Philibert.
M. Sainêt Iehan, & place Sai
N. La Chreftienté.
O. Place du Morimont.

P. Porte d'ousche.
Q. Sainêt Efprit & Hofpital
R. Les Carmes.
S. Chapelle aux Riches.
T. Cordeliers, & place.
V. Saint Pierre & porte Saint Piet
X. Cinq tours du vieil Chafteau
Y. Le Palais-Chambre des compte
   bailliage & Chancellerie.
Z. Maifon de Ville,
   & la Magdaleine. (AA. Boucheri
bb. Riuiere Douîche. (cc. Suzon, to
dd. Reyne ruiffeau,
EE. Vieux remples ou Pantee,
FF. Les Halles.

A map of Dijon drawn by Euvrard Bredin in 1573.

nesses could be found to testify that he and his valet set off for Giroux's house after supper on 6 September 1638.

It was tradition in this Burgundian town of twenty thousand souls that during the warm month of September outdoor activity would be prolonged after nightfall by householders and shopkeepers affixing linen torches to the outside walls by their doors. Craftsmen could now slide their workbenches into the street and extend their workday. During the day hordes of beggars crouched and slumped in the streets and marketplaces awaiting the charity of passers-by, but now after nightfall they had been swept out of the city, through the town gates which were closed behind them, thrown on the other side of Dijon's walls to either wander down a road to another town or monastery or await the opening of the gates in the morning and flow like a running tide back into the city. With the beggars now banished, servants with nothing to do but await the call from masters or mistresses loitered in place of the beggars, standing on street corners or leaning casually against the walls of dwellings and shops that rose two, three, sometimes four stories straight up from the edge of the street. It was not just craftsmen and servants who clustered and chatted out of doors on these warm September evenings, but men and women of more respectable social station as well. Notaries, lawyers, ladies-in-waiting, all gathered and gossiped about the news of the day, or perhaps about the quality and quantity of the impending grape harvest of this renowned wine-producing region.

The scores of linen torches threw enough light upon the street for many people to catch at least a glimpse of Baillet and Neugot, which they later told the court. As befitting his social rank, Baillet strode down the street wearing a smart, high-collared doublet; beneath a stylish, broad-brimmed hat crowned with a decorative cord, locks curled to his shoulders from a wig, an accessory only recently become fashionable. To project style and status from head to toe (as everyone save the lowliest did), the president was shod in leather boots that hugged the calf but flared just above the knee. Pedestrians like Baillet avoided the middle of the street, since in the absence of underground sewers, human, animal, and household wastes followed the slope of the street toward an open gutter in its center which, predictably, was clogged with filth. If Baillet and Neugot had to carefully pick their way through the foul-smelling streets of the city, they also had to be attentive to warnings of "Garde de l'eau!" (literally "Watch out for the water!," or as we might say today, "Look out below!") shouted from upstairs windows just before buckets of waste were pitched into the street. Still, Baillet cut a fashionable figure and, followed by his valet Philibert Neugot, it is hardly surprising that more than a few people claimed to recognize who they were.

From Baillet's townhouse to Giroux's was but a ten-minute walk. Once the two men were shown in, some witnesses later reported, the servant Odinelle, obeying the customary practice of hospitality, directed Baillet's valet to the kitchen to join the other servants and there await his master, and then escorted Baillet upstairs to Giroux's chamber. If this account is accurate, the house must have seemed curiously empty and quiet to Baillet, since none of Giroux's many servants could be seen scuttling about the household as one might normally expect in the early evening. For reasons that would shortly become all too clear to him, all the domestic servants, one of them later said, had been ordered by Giroux's trusted manservant, Denis Cartaut, to either go to bed or remain in the kitchen. The only servants permitted anywhere else in the house this evening were Cartaut, nicknamed Saint Denis, and Pierre Borel, called Devilliers. Alongside their master, they awaited the entrance of Baillet into Giroux's chamber.

At this point a key witness picks up the story. This is the servant Claude Bryot, nicknamed La Valeur, who claimed later to have been an eyewitness. He was a youth in his early twenties who had grown up in the Giroux household, his mother having been the wet nurse of Philippe Giroux. What conversation there was during Baillet's visit we do not know—La Valeur reports nothing about it, but he does vividly describe what he supposedly saw and what he claims Devilliers told him later. As Baillet prepared to leave, he turned his back on Giroux. Baillet heard movement behind him, but he must have assumed that Giroux was approaching to show him to the door. Too late he realized that his cousin had other designs: Giroux suddenly seized Baillet, throwing his arm around his neck. While Baillet was momentarily restrained, Giroux reached for the dagger at his belt, unsheathed it, and then buried it in Baillet's back. As the victim lurched forward he cried out, and Saint Denis then leaped upon him, his knife flashing in the candlelit room. Alerted by the cries for help and the thumping on the wooden floor, Neugot bolted headlong to his master's aid. Already as suspicious as his master that this visit boded ill, he raced upstairs and down the corridor toward Giroux's chamber. He burst into the room, and no sooner had he seen his master sprawled on a blood-soaked floor than he was set upon by Saint Denis, still carrying his bloody dagger. Giroux's henchman quickly found his mark in Neugot's stomach. Neugot, badly wounded but still with much fight left in him, furiously lashed out at his attackers, disarming Saint Denis with one blow that sent his dagger flying from his grasp; another slashed the arm of Giroux, who brandished a dagger in one hand and a rapier in the other. With blood pouring from his gut, however, Neugot was fatally weakened. He was finally overmatched as Devilliers, seeing Saint Denis and Giroux momentarily thrown back on their heels, joined the fray. Devilliers and Neugot tumbled about the room, blood splattering the bed curtains and pooling on the floor. Saint Denis then snatched a knife from a table and jumped on Neugot's back. Clutching his hair in his fist, he snapped Neugot's head back and slit his throat.

As Neugot's body slumped to the floor, an unwelcome and unexpected visitor was seen peering in by the door. It was La Valeur, who despite Saint Denis's orders later claimed to have wandered away from the kitchen to fetch some water when he heard noises upstairs. He reported that he heard the voice of a man being choked, pleading, crying out for help, and pounding his boots against the wooden floor in his struggle to free himself. Running to investigate, he looked into his master's chamber as Giroux, Saint Denis, and Devilliers had just dispatched Neugot. Spying La Valeur, Giroux thundered, "God damn that rogue!" Saint Denis wanted to kill the intruder on the spot, but Devilliers convinced Giroux and Saint Denis that La Valeur could help them to dispose of the bodies and clean up the mess.

As the three assassins were deliberating the fate of La Valeur, the frightened youth ran from the house and into the walled courtyard behind it, where he tried to hide. Giroux and Saint Denis followed in hot pursuit. Saint Denis saw La Valeur duck into a shed and pointed out the fugitive's hiding place to Giroux. Giroux then approached La Valeur. The master tried to coax his servant out with gentle words, imploring him not to be afraid and to come back with him to the room. La Valeur refused. Terrified and trembling, he shrieked that he was scared to come out because Saint Denis had threatened to kill him. He then told Giroux that if anyone tried to come into the shed to get him he would run out the other door that opened onto the neighbor's courtyard. From there, La Valeur threatened, he would run to the neighbor's house and tell everyone there everything. Giroux responded with further blasphemous curses, and then, realizing that this would accomplish little, collected himself and spoke more gently to his servant, who was still beside himself with fear. He promised La Valeur that no harm would come to him, and that no one would know anything about what had just happened. La Valeur added that Giroux also promised to give him 400£, a huge sum to a servant, and arrange a marriage between La Valeur and the daughter of the tax collector of Marigny (the principal fiefdom and country estate of the Giroux family). With these enticements, which Giroux assured La Valeur would make him content for the rest of his life, La Valeur was lured out of his hiding place and back to the room where the murders had been committed.

When La Valeur entered the room he saw blood everywhere, pooling under the bodies of Baillet and Neugot and running in rivulets under the bed. Giroux stood before the enormous fireplace that spanned half the room, pale, visibly frightened, with blood smeared on his clothing and slippers. Still clutching a dagger in one hand and rapier in the other, he wiped the blood dripping from his sword on some linen. He then turned on La Valeur, grabbed him by the neck with the dagger still in hand, and swore, "By the death of God, if I hadn't given you my word, I'd run you through!" Fearing for his life, La Valeur struggled to free himself, and as the two tumbled backward and fell against a wardrobe, La Valeur retrieved the pistol he carried in his pocket and aimed it point blank at Giroux's face (one might wonder why he had not drawn it when he was trapped in the shed). He screamed that if Giroux touched him and did not keep his word he would kill him.

Giroux backed down and ordered the three servants to get the bodies out of the room. La Valeur, still shaken and clutching his pistol, said he would not touch the dead men, so Giroux ordered him to carry a torch and lead the macabre procession out of the house. Saint Denis ran ahead and checked to make sure that no lights were on in the neighbor's house. Then he, Devilliers, and Giroux dragged the bodies of Pierre Baillet and Philibert Neugot out of the room, through the corridor, down the stairs, and out the back door into the courtyard. The hastily improvised plan was to bury the bodies in a cellar at the back of the courtyard, but the men soon realized that the earth there was too hard for them to make sufficient headway before dawn. So they abandoned that plan in favor of disposing of the bodies in the privy. There they figured that quicklime would decompose the corpses rapidly, and that the stench of decaying flesh would be masked in the meantime by the normal odors of household and human waste. So as La Valeur led the way, carrying a torch, the three men dragged the bloody bodies to the outhouse, where they then tried to stuff them through the holes into the waste pit below. Neugot, presumably a man of smaller stature and girth than his master Baillet, slid through and plunged head first into this inglorious grave. Baillet, however, got lodged halfway, and so the assassins had to pull his body back out of the hole, remove the seat entirely, and then pitch Baillet fully clothed and booted into the latrine alongside his servant.

By now it was around midnight, and as Saint Denis and Devilliers departed, La Valeur was put to cleaning up the room. As his master screamed, "You damned bugger, make sure that it's so clean that no one could recognize that anything happened here!," the hapless servant worked till dawn. The furniture had little blood splattered on it, but the bed curtains, linens, and floor were a mess. He mopped up the floor with the linens, and blotted and scrubbed it with ashes. Then, gathering up a boot, still spurred, that had been torn off and a sword that had fallen during the armed struggle earlier in the evening, he threw the whole pile into the privy atop the bodies of Baillet and Neugot.

We know from a variety of sources that the next day Giroux left Dijon for the town of Rennes in Brittany to attend to litigation in the Parlement there, and that he took Devilliers and La Valeur with him. La Valeur only returned to Dijon in February. A year later, La Valeur later reported, he was spirited away by Giroux's father Benoît to the Giroux estate of Marigny. There he remained for four or five months. Then Benoît told him, "It is better for you and for us if we send you away to Avignon," a city far to the south of Burgundy. Giroux initially placed La Valeur as an apprentice with a surgeon whom he knew there, promising to bring him back to Marigny in a year and a half. At that time, Benoît assured him, "all of this will be nothing." Skeptical of promises and still fearful for his life, La Valeur tried to escape to Italy. He quickly ran out of money, however, and with nowhere else to turn, he appealed to the Giroux family for help. Of course the Giroux were in no position to deny La Valeur's request, since their former servant, if his account was to be believed, knew so much. In 1641 they placed him as a servant in the household of the Marquis de Venasque, a friend of the Giroux family who lived in Provence. There he remained until January 1646, when he emerged as a star witness in the murder trial mounted by Pierre Saumaise de Chasans against Baillet's widow—and Philippe Giroux's rumored lover—the reputedly beautiful Marie Fyot.

Such was La Valeur's account, and it points the finger of guilt directly at Giroux, Saint Denis, and Devilliers. But can we believe him? Is his story plausible? He describes a house normally teeming with bustling servants but now in the early evening empty and quiet. He describes noises so loud that Baillet's servant could hear them downstairs in the kitchen, yet no other witness called in the case heard them. He describes the blood-soaked room, yet no other witnesses could be found to confirm his account. The removal of the corpses from the house and the darkly humorous attempted burial were done so openly that one might expect someone to have witnessed them, yet judging by the depositions gathered by the court, no one did. And why did Giroux not simply kill La Valeur for what he supposedly saw? Simply because his help might have been needed in burying the bodies or cleaning up the mess? And if La Valeur was armed, why did he wait so long to draw his pistol? Most troubling of all, La Valeur's testimony was heard only on 6 January 1646, nearly three years after the trial for the murders of Baillet and Neugot had been concluded. Philippe Giroux was tried for the murders of his cousin and the valet, but the case against him and his supposed accomplices—and eventually there were thirty of them, including the fugitive La Valeur—was concluded on 8 May 1643. La Valeur's testimony had nothing to do with the sentence, but it might have had a great deal to do with his attempt to exonerate himself later when he was apprehended, in a desperate ploy to deny his suspected guilt.

So what actually happened? How can we know now, or how can the judges have known? Is this tale of two murders true? Was Philippe Giroux guilty of murdering his cousin Pierre Baillet and the servant Neugot? On what evidence was the final judicial decision based? As we will see, there is substantial evidence surviving from this case, and not all of it points the same way.

CHAPTER 2

Passion and the Beautiful Cousin

On the afternoon of 27 February 1628, Marie Fyot married the noble-man Pierre Baillet. It was a match, like all matches between noble fami-lies in seventeenth-century France, in which the material and political inter-ests of the families involved dwarfed considerations of sentiment. If Marie, nineteen years old, and Pierre, twenty-one, could come to like or even love one another, so much the better, but what mattered was the merging of family wealth and influence. The bride and groom in this particular arrange-ment, however, would never find happiness. Their life together lasted barely a decade, and ended abruptly with the disappearance of Pierre on 6 Septem-ber 1638.

Marie was from a distinguished, noble Burgundian family, daughter of François Fyot, lord of Barain, Vaugimois, Couches, and Boussernois. Marie's father was a busy man: between his duties as a lawyer, judge in and eventu-ally dean of Burgundy's Parlement, and member of king Louis XIII's select Conseil Privé, he sired sixteen children. Marie was his fourteenth child and the sixth of nine born to his second wife, Chrétienne Morin. With so many children to provide for at marriage, it is a testimony to the wealth and in-fluence of this Fyot family that Marie could bring a dowry to Pierre worth 20,000£, a substantial although far from staggering sum at the time.[1] More indicative of the importance of this match and of these families than the dowry are the names of the signatories to the marriage contract. It was cus-tomary for the families linked by a marriage to invite other family mem-

Bust of François Fyot de Vaugimois, lord of Barain
and father of Marie Fyot. Copyright and used by
permission of Musée des Beaux Arts de Dijon.

bers, friends, and most importantly patrons to give their "blessing and consent" to the marriage by witnessing and signing the contract. This document
ends with a veritable roll call of some of the most distinguished family
names among the nobility of the "robe" (that is, the office-holding class)
in the province—Fyot, Baillet, Le Goux de La Berchere, Brulart, Bouchu,
Desbarres, Valon, Jacquot, Millière, and, notably, Giroux.

When the marriage was arranged, the prospective groom did not have
good looks going for him (he was reputed to be quite ugly) but he did have a
name and a title that would make this match a distinguished one. Pierre was
already a *trésorier de France* (holder of a royal financial office worth 56,000£ at
the time of the marriage) and within five years would become a président at
the royal financial court in Dijon, the Chambre des Comptes, an only slightly
less august body than the Parlement. As a Baillet, Pierre carried a name of re-
nown, but it was more his uncles and cousins than his father Jacques, lord of
Crécey, who distinguished the line. Pierre's only sibling, Jean-Baptiste, died
in the year of Pierre's marriage, but two years before his death his father had

bequeathed his office of conseiller in the Parlement to him. Oddly, Pierre's marriage contract says nothing of a paternal inheritance at all, even though his father was dead (for no more than two years) and his mother Jeanne Burgat was an unmarried widow. It was Jeanne who provided the funds to Pierre for the purchase of the office of trésorier de France.

This marriage between Marie and Pierre may have been a match that made sense for reasons of family, but as far as the husband and wife were concerned, it was star-crossed from the beginning. No children issued, and soon Pierre began physically abusing his young wife. Divorce or separation in this Catholic kingdom was theoretically possible but it usually occurred for reasons of state or for property interests, not for the kind of marital dissatisfaction that plagued this couple. Pierre and Marie were forced to suffer each other's presence until death. Of course, extramarital relations could result from such unhappiness, and in seventeenth-century France they often did. Adultery technically was illegal for both husbands and wives (a capital offense, in fact), but in practice a double standard held sway, making dalliance outside marriage a significant risk only for women. Pierre's sexual attentions were directed elsewhere, likely to prostitutes, since he contracted "the pox" and then transmitted it to Marie.

Unhappy in marriage and suffering blows and sexual abuse from a boorish husband, Marie Fyot, according to some accounts, eventually found solace and affection from a young man who loved her passionately. No doubt Marie had known Philippe Giroux her entire life, for he was the scion of a family that was accruing power at a prodigious rate in the first three decades of the seventeenth century. Moreover, he was her husband's first cousin (Pierre Baillet's father Jacques was the brother of Philippe's mother, Madeleine). In the same year, 1633, that Philippe, then twenty-eight, assumed the office of président at the Parlement and so became one of the seven most important nobles of the robe in all of Burgundy, Marie stood next to him at the baptismal font in Notre Dame church in Dijon as one of the godparents of the son of a cobbler. The baby was given the name of his godfather, Philippe.

Whether a passion between Marie and Philippe flamed when the cobbler's baby was christened we will never know, but if it did, it was not enough to keep the house of Giroux from allying with another prestigious family through marriage, the Le Goux de La Berchere. Single at the baptism of

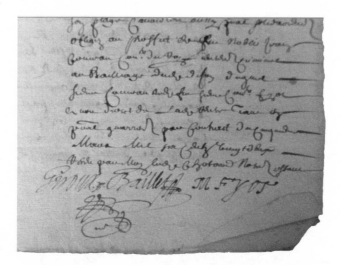

Signatures from left to right of Philippe Giroux, Pierre Baillet, and Marie Fyot. This is a contract of a personal loan made by Giroux to Baillet, witnessed by Fyot in 1633. Archives Départementales de la Côte d'Or, Notaires. Photograph by author.

the cobbler's boy, Philippe was married only nine months later to another Marie, this one the youngest of nine children born to the Parlement's first president. Marie's father, Jean-Baptiste Le Goux de La Berchere, held this highest office in the Parlement from 1627 until his death in 1631. His son and Marie's brother Pierre succeeded him, and so at the time of the wedding between Philippe and Marie Le Goux de La Berchere, the Giroux were allied by marriage to the family which counted in its ranks the most powerful royal judicial official in the entire province.

A child issued from this union in November and was given the name Henri, in honor of the godfather who held the baby in his arms as it was christened. The godfather was Henri II de Bourbon, the prince of Condé, prince of the blood, cousin of King Louis XIII, governor of Burgundy, and arguably the third-most powerful man in all of France, behind only the king and his prime minister the Cardinal de Richelieu. We will hear more about Condé and the power of the House of Giroux later, but clearly this was a family on the make and Condé was central to its success. Would Philippe

Funerary statue of Jean-Baptiste Le Goux de La
Berchere, Philippe Giroux's father-in-law, who died
in 1631. This statue graces his coffin, now empty but
prominently displayed in the Cathedral of St. Bénigne
of Dijon. Photograph by author.

jeopardize it all for the love of a woman, going so far as to murder his first cousin?

Many people in Dijon thought so, and many people from all levels of society seemed aware that Marie and Philippe were passionate about one another. This kind of love was considered deeply dangerous in the seventeenth century, a time when authoritarianism was gaining ground, and if any word were to encapsulate the mood of the age, a good candidate would be "discipline," or perhaps "self-discipline." During the sixteenth century French men and women had seen their kingdom rent by religious and civil war, and a profound sense of a loss of moorings—political, religious, intellectual, and moral—swept over them. The traditional sense of community and the system of moral order that secured it seemed to have been destroyed, and one pressing issue of the day and for the entire seventeenth century was how to restore an order of morality to a world that seemingly had lost it. The new order would be authoritarian, and within it sexuality would be construed as the epitome of disorder and subversion, a primal force to be controlled and regulated at all cost.

Nicolas Brulart, a man who would become first president of Burgundy's Parlement in 1657, summed up the connectedness between moral and social order, between authority imposed from above and imposed through self-control from within, that all men of his rank felt when he wrote about the grave problem of harnessing the passions, especially those of a sexual nature. Like all neostoic thinkers, Brulart held that the passions posed a very real threat to the individual and to society. "The passions," he declared, "seduce man with such force that the light [of reason] is often eclipsed . . . throwing him into disorder and confusion." [2] For Brulart as for every learned man and woman of the time, among the most dangerous passions was "concupiscent appetite." The preacher and Brulart's close contemporary Vincent Houdry spoke for a generation when he avowed that "passions are the cause of all our disorder because it is from them that comes our unfortunate penchant toward evil." [3] And Jacques-Bénigne Bossuet, the renowned bishop and tutor of the royal dauphin (and nephew of one of Philippe Giroux's closest friends), wrote a book—called The Treatise on Concupiscence—in which he gravely warned of the destructive consequences of lust, which was at the core of the passions. So when some people suspected Fyot and Giroux of being attracted to one another, they framed their opinions while supposing their passion to be destructive, all the more so because both Marie and Philippe were married. No wonder some people assumed that Philippe would go to any lengths to have Marie.

Philippe did not seem to help his case much either, doing little to hide his amorous intentions, if certain witnesses are to be believed. Michelle Clermont, the fifty-six-year-old widow of a tanner in Dijon, reported that one of her neighbors had once seen Philippe and Marie standing together in front of a window in Baillet's house and Philippe indiscreetly running his hands up under the sleeves of Marie's dress. In another incident, Bernard d'Ostun, the keeper of a garden near the Abbey of Saint Étienne in Dijon, claimed to have seen Philippe and Marie strolling there one evening from supper until midnight, and the next day to have found some of his flowers smashed from the weight of bodies lying upon them. He assumed that the bodies were Giroux's and Fyot's, the ruined flowers a telltale trace of an amorous tumble in the darkness.

On another occasion, after a militia squadron made its rounds as the night watch in the late winter of 1639, the captain reported that he caught a glimpse of a man and a woman on the steps of a merchant's shop. Since to be out after dark without a light violated curfew laws, the captain drew his sword and advanced, only to stop short when he recognized Giroux and Fyot. The captain was as unsure of what to do as Giroux was, but according to his account Giroux took no chances and attempted to defuse the situation by befriending him. The two knew each other on sight because they had rubbed shoulders at the gaming tables in Dijon, and Giroux seized this chance familiarity by telling the captain that if he needed money sometime he would gladly advance him some. The captain never said if the veiled bribe was ever paid, but in any event, perhaps to protect himself from a very powerful man caught in compromising circumstances, he sheathed his sword and nervously withdrew.

Anne Moisson, the widow of a président in the Chambre des Comptes, had her own story to tell about seeing Marie and Philippe shamelessly open in their affections. She recalled that one time after Baillet's disappearance she was attending Mass at the church of the Jacobins in the heart of Dijon. She heard loud footsteps in the tribune, and looking up, she observed that they came from Giroux's boots as he noisily followed Marie. When Giroux caught up with her, they sat down together on the benches used by the monks during their offices. Giroux's sister Barbe (wife of Jacques Sayve, another of the eight presidents in the Parlement by 1638) told Moisson that her brother Philippe was in love with Fyot, whom he called "his beautiful cousin and the most beautiful woman of her family line."

Many people seemed to know that Philippe was passionate about Marie. Hugues Mené, a secretary of Philippe Fyot who was yet another president in the Parlement and cousin of Marie, recounted that Giroux had told him that if his wife were to die he would remarry only Marie Fyot. Giroux also told Marie Vitier, this wife of the trésorier Jant recounted, that if Baillet were dead he would have no other wife but Fyot. Once while the two were chatting, Vitier had asked Giroux what his wishes were, and he replied candidly that he would like to sleep with Marie Fyot, adding that Baillet was a wicked man because he had given the pox to Marie. His desire for Marie he reportedly expressed more than once, to more than one person. To Denise Petit, with whom he shared a carriage, he added that he knew that Fyot was deeply unhappy with Baillet because he beat her, and that if he had such a wife he would take care of her and caress her. Anne Moisson, the friend of Giroux's sister Barbe, was convinced that Giroux's intention was to marry Fyot, an intention that Giroux himself alluded to in a letter he sent in April 1638 (four months before the disappearance of Baillet). He sent it to Pierre Bouvot de Lisle, Giroux's lawyer and close friend. Most ominously of all, given what Baillet's ultimate fate seemed to be, was something that Giroux allegedly said to Damoiselle Anne Blondeau in the summer of 1638. He confessed to her, she said, that he would take great pleasure in seeing someone take the life of Marie Fyot's husband.

Many believed that Philippe was doing more than caressing Marie, long before he might ever have made her his wife. Giroux's servants claimed to know that their master was often at Marie's residence and Marie often at Philippe's, at all hours. When Marie was at Philippe's, a servant testily recounted, she acted as though she were the mistress of the house. The servant Huguette Moussey reported that Marie and Philippe were passionate about each other and were together often, while another servant, Antoinette Carbolot, recounted that Marie had spent an entire night with Philippe, in the upstairs bedroom of Philippe's son, no less. Jeanne Bordereau, a servant of Bouvot, the Giroux family lawyer, stated that one of Fyot's servants had told her that her mistress had slept with Giroux, often. One of Philippe's foot-

Abraham Bosse (1602–76), "Les femmes à table en l'absence de
leurs maris." A gathering of aristocratic women in 1636. We have
no portrait of Marie Fyot or Marie Le Goux de La Berchere, but
they were from the same social class as the women depicted here
and probably dressed themselves in similar fashion.

men recounted how his master came home one night after a visit with Marie
and that the front of his breeches "were all wet with semen."

As one would expect, all this reportedly got back to the spouses of the
reputed lovers. Philippe's wife Marie Le Goux de La Berchere, several witnesses said, was deeply suspicious of her husband's wayward affections, and
Philippe did not help convince her otherwise by always referring to Marie
Fyot as "his beautiful cousin." Le Goux cared little if Philippe had sexual
relations with prostitutes, but that her husband's love was engaged elsewhere she could not stomach. She railed one time in front of the servants
that she cared not at all if her husband frequented all the whores in all the
neighborhoods of the city as long as he did not see Madame Baillet.

When Philippe was away from the house, and he frequently was, Le Goux suspected that he was with Fyot. Giroux reputedly made only lukewarm efforts to conceal his whereabouts, sometimes sending a servant to inform his wife that he was dining in one place when in fact he was with Fyot. At other times he would slip out of his house in disguise, furtively making his way to Fyot's back door. One could hardly be surprised that such careless disregard on the part of Giroux, if true, would inevitably lead to an explosive encounter, and it reportedly did. On a summer night in 1636 Giroux secretively paid a visit to Fyot, ordering his coachman René Poyrot to leave him and return home. The unfortunate coachman later recounted how he found Giroux's wife waiting for him and demanding to know where he had taken her husband. Well she knew the answer in any case, and after screaming "To hell with the whore!" she stormed over to Baillet's townhouse, entered unannounced, and on finding Pierre Baillet absent ran upstairs to Marie Fyot's bedchamber. There she found Philippe and Marie alone, and according to servants watching the whole scene a "tempest" ensued. Le Goux then wheeled and flew out of the room in a rage. Deeply hurt, she quitted Dijon for her country estate—as one witness put it, "loving and hating" her husband equally.

Giroux and Fyot were seemingly caught red-handed, and what they did next remains cloaked in obscurity. However, shortly after Marie Le Goux retired to the country, her husband followed her. She then mysteriously fell ill, and with her husband at her bedside, several witnesses later recounted, she was denied a visit from her personal physician, a man named Sineau. Instead Giroux's personal physician, Lazare Rhodot, from the Burgundian town of Avallon, was called in to attend to her. Le Goux worsened, and even so her husband prevented Marie's own mother, the distinguished Marguerite Brulart, from coming to her daughter's side in this time of crisis. Only when it was clear that Marie was about to die did her mother and Sineau gain entrance. Marie Le Goux de La Berchere, the wife of a president of the Parlement, the daughter of a former first president and the sister of the current one, died in October, and was buried in the church of the Cordeliers in Dijon on the 9th of that month.

Curiously, the physician Sineau followed her to the grave soon after, and rumors swirled around Dijon that both Le Goux and her physician had been poisoned by Giroux with the aid of Giroux's physician Rhodot and manservant Denis Cartaut, whom everyone knew as Saint Denis. Indeed, Cartaut's mother-in-law later told Elizabeth Mairet, a servant in the household of Giroux's neighbor DeGand, that at Giroux's bidding Saint Denis had put poison in a pot of veal stew intended for Giroux's wife. When Marie fell ill, her doctor Sineau reportedly had suspected poisoning and fed the stew to a dog, which then promptly died. If this testimony is credible, then Giroux seemed to have had good reason for keeping the suspicious Sineau away from his wife if his intention was to be rid of her, and good reason also for silencing the doctor. Mairet added that Saint Denis's mother-in-law had told her that Sineau met his fate by poison as well.

If Giroux wished to silence those who may have known too much about the death of Marie Le Goux, then Sineau was not the only target. Marie's mother Marguerite Brulart feared that she also was at risk: she had been denied entrance to her daughter's sickbed by her son-in-law Giroux, and as she later told the authorities, she openly wondered why her daughter's own physician was not permitted to treat the patient. So when it was rumored about town that there was a conspiracy to poison Brulart and that Saint Denis was involved, Giroux was assumed by Brulart and others to be behind it. Several people reported that around the time of Pentecost in 1638 Saint Denis had put poison in a bottle of wine that Madame Brulart would drink. Brulart took only a sip, and recognizing a foul taste, she sent it to her physician for examination. The doctor apparently left the bottle untended in his kitchen, and when his cook and a female servant helped themselves to a draught they both fell ill. Saint Denis's widow reported after the death of her husband in May 1639 (also by poisoning, it seems, but more on that mysterious death later) that on his deathbed Saint Denis had confessed having been ordered by his master Giroux to poison Madame Brulart, and he specifically charged his wife to beg for him the forgiveness of so distinguished a lady.

With Marie Le Goux de La Berchere in her grave, Pierre Baillet remained the only obstacle to a marriage between Giroux and Fyot. Given their open, some would say brazenly open, affections and the trail of purported poisonings since the death of Giroux's wife, a charged atmosphere enveloped Dijon in the summer of 1638. Giroux was not the only one suspected of plotting murder: Marie Fyot came in for her share of suspicion. In fact, given the tendency of people at the time to blame women for the lust that men felt, Marie was assumed by several people to be the instigator. Giroux's sister Barbe believed that her brother was led to his evil actions by Fyot, a view shared by Claudine Pechinot, the wife of a local baker.

A common rumor about town after Baillet's disappearance on the night of 6 September 1638 was that Giroux and his henchmen had done the deed, but many also believed that Fyot had had Baillet killed so that she could marry her lover Philippe. Why else would Fyot have paid Devilliers (as several witnesses reported) — one of the three men who reportedly killed Baillet in Giroux's chamber — shortly after the disappearance of her husband? And why else would Philippe have hastened to Marie's side late in the evening of 6 September — at a well-attended ball, no less — and reportedly have said within earshot of more than one person there, "It's done"? And did not Marie's rather sacrilegious reply — "Praise be to God!" — signify her complicity?

Whoever committed the murder or was behind it, many believed that the murder on that night was simply the crowning blow of a conspiracy to do away with Baillet that had been hatched some years before. One evening in the spring of 1637 Marie Fyot, much like the Marquise de Brinvilliers decades later, reportedly tried to poison her husband. One of Fyot's ladies-in-waiting, the Damoiselle de La Rente, told her husband, who later told the authorities, that Baillet had returned home from the Festival of the King in the Chambre des Comptes that evening and demanded some wine. When handed a goblet by Fyot, he grasped it and gulped down several large draughts. He suddenly jerked upright. Spewing wine from his mouth, he gasped, "I'm burning! I'm poisoned! Get a doctor!" He then plunged to the floor and became violently ill. Marie watched, and then while her husband was doubled up on the floor and retching, she coolly picked up the goblet and the bottle from which the tainted wine had been poured, strode to the window, and emptied their contents into the street. She then rinsed out the goblet and commanded de La Rente, who had been watching all of this, to fetch a new bottle from the cellar. Upon de La Rente's return, Fyot opened the fresh bottle, poured some of its contents into the goblet, placed both on the table, and calmly awaited the doctor's arrival. When the doctor arrived, of course he inspected the wine goblet and the bottle. And of course he found no trace of poison.

Another series of testimony told this story: shortly before Fyot's supposed attempted poisoning of her husband, fifteen days before Carnival in that same year of 1637, Giroux's most trusted servant Saint Denis traveled to the village of Lux, twenty miles northeast of Dijon, with money in his pockets and promises to pay several men who would lay an ambush "to kill a president." Saint Denis first approached the winegrower François Tabourot but was turned down. The weaver Guillaume Moullier would have no truck with the conspiracy either, even after Cartaut had offered him twenty écus and then upped the offer to six pistoles and a horse. Three others, however—the peasants Jean Peruchot, Claude Froul, and Prudent Roussotte—could not resist. No one said what Peruchot was to get, but Saint Denis reportedly paid Froul (who was also his brother-in-law) twenty-two pistoles up front, while Roussotte was to have his debts paid off and receive twenty écus in cash in the bargain. Once the conspirators were assembled they were told of the plan and of their target, Froul adding that the murder had been planned because Saint Denis's master had fallen in love with a great lady. Of course, the president to be ambushed was Pierre Baillet. The plan was to lie in wait for Baillet on the road that cut through the woods of the valley of the Suzon river, a few miles north of Dijon, as Baillet was on his way to his country estate of Crécey. The appointed day and hour arrived. The would-be murderers split up and hid in the brush, but just as Baillet rode right in front of Roussotte, he lost his nerve, froze, and let the quarry slip away. Saint Denis was furious. So was Froul, since Cartaut demanded that he pay back the twenty-two pistoles.

This ambush failed, but eventually Baillet was nonetheless done in. From what has been recounted so far, the evidence points to Marie Fyot and Philippe Giroux as the plotters of the murder of Fyot's husband. Anne d'Humbercourt, a friend of Marie, recalled a visit in the late spring of 1638 to Fyot's country estate. D'Humbercourt's husband had died recently, and his widow was still wearing mourning clothes. When Marie saw her veiled and dressed in black, she chortled and said, "I laugh to see you so afflicted for so long from the death of a husband!" Then, sensing that she had offended d'Humbercourt, she hastily added apologetically, "If you had a husband like mine you would not regret his death." She then recounted to d'Humbercourt how Baillet mistreated her. Often he would leave home for two to three days at a stretch, wallowing in debauchery the while. He would then come home drunk in the middle of the night, sleep until noon, and when awakened would rain crude rebukes upon Marie and occasionally strike her when she dared upbraid him for his behavior.

Marie and Philippe, it seemed to many, were so passionately in love that they would risk everything to marry and spend the rest of their lives together. The story told thus far is drawn from the testimony of scores of witnesses eventually called before the court in a trial against Philippe Giroux, but was their testimony truthful? After all, does it not test our credibility to accept so easily that Giroux would take such a risk? He and his family had shrewdly and successfully maneuvered through the tangled and dangerous thicket of political intrigue for forty years before Baillet's disappearance and had constructed a "House" that in short order vaulted to the center of the power structure in this province. Giroux appears to have been very close to Condé, increasingly important in the prince's patronage network in Burgundy through which Condé expected to rule the province. How could Giroux be so shrewd yet so careless, so openly foolish about affection when there was so much to lose? Could the passions truly be so destructive? Might there be another explanation for this story of love, conspiracy, and murder?

CHAPTER 3

The Trial Opens

Jean-Baptiste Lantin's Investigation, 1639–1640

Pierre Baillet and his valet Philibert Neugot were last seen alive during the evening of 6 September 1638. When they disappeared men and women from all walks of life at once began gossiping that a crime had been committed. Washerwomen, bakers' wives, and servants crowded around public fountains and shared what they thought they knew, or what they had heard. Shoemakers, tailors, and lackeys did the same in smoky, dark taverns over tankards of Burgundy wine, while notaries, lawyers, and merchants did so in paneled drawing rooms or libraries. Even nobles and their ladies, it seems, could talk of little else, for a crime of stupendous proportions seemed to have been committed in their very midst, one whose impact would reverberate all across France and seize the attention of the king himself.

Despite what everyone seemed to "know," official investigation into the disappearance of Baillet and Neugot only began six months later. Perhaps no judge at the Parlement, the court of law responsible for investigating the crime, could bring himself to haul before it the prime suspect, not just one of his fellow justices but one of the court's eight presidents. Philippe Giroux was among the most powerful men in the province, and as everyone knew, the powerful exerted influence in many ways. And anyway, the magnitude of the purported offense staggered the imagination and strained the credulity of Giroux's colleagues. To kill a president at the Chambres des Comptes, the suspected murderer's first cousin? Over a woman? Could these men believe that Giroux would do such a thing? To think that he would entailed great risk for these men, because Giroux was one of the prince of Condé's favored clients. To take on Giroux would mean taking on a political faction that wielded prodigious power and influence, and to lose could spell political and social ruin. The stakes, in short, were as daunting as the nature of the suspected crime.

Still, two men had disappeared, and six months had passed without a sign or word of them. The judges at the Parlement took their roles as guardians of justice seriously, and to simply ignore the disappearance of Baillet was as unthinkable as proceeding against Giroux. Yet it took a request for investigation from Baillet's mother, Jeanne Burgat, and his wife, Marie Fyot, to initiate proceedings. Why these women waited six months to move is an important question, one that can slowly be answered as we explore the circumstances surrounding this extraordinary case.

The investigation into the disappearance of Pierre Baillet began on 24 March 1639 as all investigations into suspected crimes did, with the gathering of people's reports about the day the alleged crime took place. The judge named to lead the investigation was Jean-Baptiste Lantin, one of sixty-five conseillers du roy advising the eight presidents who composed the full body of Parlement, the eighth having been added in 1638. Lantin set about calling in witnesses to give testimony. What these witnesses said was recorded by a court official, and scores of their statements have survived. The first order of business for Lantin, an experienced judge who had sat on the court of Parlement since 1608, was to determine that a crime had been committed within his jurisdiction. After all, it was possible that Baillet and Neugot had simply disappeared, and if they were dead, they might have perished at the hands of highwaymen or brigands who haunted the notoriously dangerous roads of early modern France. In the case of a murder this meant, according to legal procedure at the time, that evidence of the crime (called corpus delicti) in the form of the bodies of the victims had to be recovered and identified. Conviction also required two unimpeachable witnesses, preferably eyewitnesses, or a confession from the accused.

To begin to find anything out, Lantin needed first to determine where Baillet and Neugot had been on the night of 6 September. The first witness Lantin heard was Catherine Goy, a thirty-year-old who testified that on that night she had been sitting in front of the house of the notary Collot when she saw Baillet pass by. A man whom she could not identify followed close

This woodcut, from Jean de Milles de Souvigny, *Praxis Crimins* (Paris, 1541), depicts the deposition of witnesses before a judge and a recording scribe (in background). The process would have been similar in Giroux's day. Records like this one are invaluable sources for historical studies.

behind. Goy recalled that she first saw the two on her side of the street, and watched as they crossed over to the other side. That is, they were headed in the direction of Giroux's residence. She added that she knew one of the two was Baillet because even though it was after nightfall, she still got a good look at him, what with all the lighted torches attached to the dwellings on that and every other street in Dijon. She finished by saying that she did not see the men come back.

New witnesses said much the same thing. But then others testified that they saw Baillet out walking that night, but *away* from Giroux's house, and out of town. The possibility that Baillet might have left town and perhaps encountered misfortune on the road was not entirely implausible. Guillaume Galoche reported to Lantin that about a year earlier, when he and Baillet were target shooting with their crossbows at the range in Dijon called the Jeu de l'Arc, Baillet had said that if his wife Marie Fyot did not have a child within a year then he was going to leave permanently for Italy. Galoche was with Baillet and some others at the Jeu de l'Arc again on 6 September, the day when Baillet was last accounted for, and he noticed that when Baillet placed a bet, lost, and refused to pay the winner, named Bassan, it was not for lack of money. The entire company saw Baillet pull a pocketful of large-denomination coins out, and then heard him tell Bassan that the coins were not for him. Galoche left it to Lantin to surmise that the sizable amount of cash might have been for a voyage. Lantin's doubts may have been further supported by the testimony of Claude Petit, the receiver general of finances in Burgundy, who was with Baillet and Galoche at the Jeu de l'Arc on the 6th and, like Galoche, saw Baillet pull a lot of cash from his purse. Baillet told Petit that the money was for a voyage to the king's court in Paris.

Lantin continued to pursue his objective, tracking down witnesses that could help him determine Baillet's whereabouts on the evening of 6 September. He found Odo Brancio, who reported that while he was passing by Baillet's house around 6 on the night in question, Baillet spotted him and invited him in for supper. Brancio accepted, and told Lantin that the subject of their conversation turned toward Philippe Giroux. Brancio asked Baillet whether he knew if his cousin had left town yet (everyone seemed to know that Giroux was a litigant in a very important case being heard before the Parlement of Rennes in Brittany—a case, as we will see, that had a great deal to do with the unfolding of this one just beginning in Dijon). Baillet replied that his cousin had not left but would do so in the morning. Baillet added portentously that he was going to Giroux's house a bit later that day to bid him safe journey. This is something that Baillet had also told Petit earlier in the day while target shooting. Brancio and Baillet then sat down to a game of cards, playing until about 8, when Baillet called to his valet to follow him and the two left. Brancio noted that they took the street heading toward the Grande Rue Notre Dame and then passed by the back door of the Logis du Roy. That is, they headed toward Giroux's residence. And that was the last that Brancio saw of them.

In early May 1639, a dramatic development further charged the already tense atmosphere in Dijon. On 13 May Saint Denis died. He was Giroux's most trusted servant, and Giroux had provided well for him and his family. One of Saint Denis's sons had a Bossuet for a godfather (arranged by Giroux), and his second son had Philippe Giroux's own son Henri for one. The circumstances of Saint Denis's death made every other servant close to Giroux fear for their lives. Saint Denis was scarcely cold in his grave when rumors ran through town that he had been poisoned.

In the autumn of 1639 Lantin requested a *monitoire* concerning the disappearance of Baillet and Neugot. Monitoires were oral and written pronouncements by the church demanding that anyone knowing anything about the case in question come forward to the authorities and reveal in sworn testimony what he or she knew. To ensure compliance, monitoires doomed anyone withholding evidence to damnation. Soon new witnesses came forward. A twenty-two-year-old servant in the Giroux household named Claude Lucia, called Champagne after his home province, just north of Burgundy, gave Lantin leads that brought suspicion even closer to Giroux. Lucia reported that more than two years earlier he had come to Dijon looking for work as a domestic servant. He found employment here and there, and was eventually hired by Giroux on 7 September 1638, the day after Baillet's disappearance. On the very day of his appointment he accompanied his new master to Brittany, and so was away from Dijon until the following February. When he returned from Britanny he heard from Eleanore Cordier that another of Giroux's servants, Claude Bryot (La Valeur), was sporting on his hat a fancy cord that had belonged to Baillet. Later Cordier showed Lucia a piece of something, he could not say what, that she said when eaten could counter poison. She said she had been given the antidote by Giroux's late wife, Marie Le Goux de La Berchere. Marie had had many of these anti-dotes, since for some reason she was fearful for the life of her mother, Mar-guerite Brulart, the widow of the former first president, Jean-Baptiste, and the mother of the current one, Pierre.

Lucia went on. He reported that a valet of Philippe Giroux's father, Be-noît, claimed to have heard Cordier acknowledge having Baillet's hat. More-over, referring to Baillet as "the invisible man," she told the valet that Baillet had been killed in Giroux's bedchamber, with the assistance of La Valeur and Saint Denis, and that Baillet's valet had met his end in the cellar. Lan-tin heard this amazing story continue: as Lucia recounted, according to this unnamed valet of Benoît Giroux, Cordier had said that the bodies of Bail-let and Neugot had been burned by Benoît Giroux himself, a very respect-able man but, like any father, one who would do anything to save his son. Lucia rambled on before Lantin. After the murder Philippe Giroux, accord-ing to Cordier, went to a party and whispered in the ear of Marie Fyot, "It is done." For Saint Denis's part in the deed, Giroux was going to buy his henchman the office of huissier (a man at arms) in the Parlement. Cordier did not tell Lucia's source (that unnamed valet in Benoît Giroux's service) what La Valeur was to gain from his participation, but after the bloodbath he was put to cleaning up the mess.

If such explosive testimony were not enough for Lantin, Lucia had more. He began to talk about another servant who would figure largely in the en-suing investigation. Antoinette Carbolot, a domestic in the household of Giroux's attorney Pierre Bouvot de Lisle, had told Lucia that Cordier had made Carbolot carry a sword to the house of the tailor Godart. Lucia con-cluded his extraordinary testimony with this: he said that after ending his service with Giroux he was ordered by him to leave town, and offered money to do so. Giroux had followed this offer with a grave threat, saying that if Lucia did not get out of town he would take him to court alleging theft. Lucia knew that he could hang for this.

No sooner had Lucia finished his testimony than Jeanne Bordereau came forward. Like Carbolot a twenty-three-year-old servant of the lawyer Bou-vot de Lisle, she testified to hearing from Carbolot, who in turn had heard from Cordier, that La Valeur was wearing a cord on his hat that had be-longed to Baillet, and that on the night when Baillet vanished La Valeur had entertained Baillet's valet, the two drinking wine "like rats" in the cellar.

Much of this Lantin had already heard, but Bordereau then added something new. She told him that after Giroux had returned from Brittany she heard that Giroux's four-year-old son Henri was in the kitchen one day and, grabbing a knife from the table, had said to La Valeur, "I have to kill you!" When La Valeur laughed and replied, "Do you know how to kill someone?" the little boy said, "Yeah, yeah. Like you killed M. Baillet." As we will see, many ears seem to have heard this exchange, and we can imagine that La Valeur's laughter caught in his throat.

Bordereau continued nervously with rambling, disjointed observations. Eleanore Cordier had told her, she reported, of the widely held view that the clothes of Baillet were lost but that Saint Denis's wife, Françoise Pailley, was dressing quite well of late. The oblique implication was that Pailley had used the material from Baillet's clothing to fashion fine outfits for herself. Then Bordereau reported Cordier's comment to her that Giroux liked La Valeur and Saint Denis better than any other servants, because they would do things for him that no one else would do. She had also heard from Carbolot that on the Saturday before Giroux's voyage to Brittany (that is, two days before Baillet vanished), Marie Fyot had spent the entire night at Giroux's house. Jeanne Bordereau also reported hearing from Antoinette Carbolot, who had heard it from Eleanore Cordier, that Giroux had killed Baillet in order to sleep with his wife. The flurry of testimony continued, Bordereau now mentioning a servant named Marie Rousselotte and a declaration that she gave to the curé, or priest, of the parish church of Saint Nicolas in Dijon. Bordereau reported that Bouvot de Lisle's wife and Madame Anthide Regnault had gone to the curé's house and tried to retrieve it.

From just two witnesses, Lantin now had many fresh leads. Guilt was pointing toward La Valeur, Saint Denis (now dead), and Giroux, and evidently Antoinette Carbolot, Marie Rousselotte, and especially Eleanore Cordier knew a great deal about what had happened. Lantin was not prepared to make any arrests just yet, however, because the testimony so far was based on hearsay, second- or third-hand reports. Lantin's only option was to follow up on the leads and see where they might take him.

Rousselotte and Carbolot came next. Marie Rousselotte, a thirty-year-old servant also in the lawyer Bouvot de Lisle's household, confirmed that she had made a "revelation" to the curé of Saint Nicolas, Claude Marchand, who wrote it down in a book. This was entirely in line with accepted legal procedure, which allowed witnesses to offer their testimony to men of the church or even notaries as well as court officials. When Giroux found out that she had done this, she added, he had Bouvot withhold her wages and threatened to accuse her of stealing and see her hanged for it. She could save herself, however, by retrieving her declaration from Marchand. Giroux arranged for her to go with Bouvot's wife to a Jacobin priest named Maillet, who then counseled Rousselotte to do as Giroux asked and retrieve the declaration. It was invalid, anyway, Maillet told her, because it was based on hearsay. He then gravely warned the woman, she said, that if the declaration were not withdrawn the "house of Giroux would fall."

Unfortunately for Giroux, the curé Marchand refused to relinquish the declaration, protesting that "everyone knew about it" anyway. Rousselotte lamented to Lantin that she was getting conflicting advice on what to do. Shortly after Bouvot's wife and Maillet counseled her to retrieve the declaration, the Damoiselle Geliot took Rousselotte to a Jesuit father named Girardin who advised her against retrieving it. Then Giroux's family solicitor, Antoine Chuttin, told her that she must get the declaration, that Giroux would get it by force anyway. Then her employer Bouvot ordered her to deny that she had made any declaration at all. As if such conflicting advice were not distressing and confusing enough for the poor woman, later, in front of Chuttin, Giroux himself angrily informed Rousselotte that he had acquired the declaration and had burned it (which seems not to have been true), and that now for her disobedience she must leave town or he would make life miserable for her.

When Lantin received Chuttin's testimony, it largely confirmed what Rousselotte had said. Chuttin knew about Rousselotte's declaration, he reported, and added that Damoiselle de Lisle had warned Rousselotte not to speak against a man of the social rank of Philippe Giroux. When de Lisle told Rousselotte to retrieve the declaration, however, Chuttin said that he had prevented her from doing so. He did not tell Lantin why, but when Giroux heard of Chuttin's obstruction he summoned Chuttin to his house and commanded him to retrieve the declaration himself. So Chuttin dutifully trudged off to Marchand, only to discover that he had sent it to the dean of the parish church of Saint Jean in Dijon. Following the trail of the elusive declaration, Chuttin then went to the dean, who informed him that he would not give it to him, but would instead send it back to Marchand.

No one, it seems, wanted to be caught with the declaration, and so it can hardly be surprising that it never turned up.

Lantin would hear no more testimony about the elusive declaration, nor about its contents. There still remained Antoinette Carbolot, however, and the matter of a sword being taken to a local tailor's house. So in came Carbolot, who told Lantin that it was Eleanore Cordier who had told her about the death of Baillet, about bodies being buried in a cellar, about blood all over Giroux's bedchamber. She confirmed what others had said about La Valeur's foolishly trotting about with Baillet's cord on his hat, and reported everyone's warnings to him that such brazenness would get him hanged. She told of what Jeanne Bordereau had also mentioned: Cordier's statement that Baillet's clothes had been lost but that Saint Denis's wife was wearing some "handsome corsets." Then Carbolot began to talk of the latrines in Giroux's courtyard, how they were always locked and no one ever used them anymore. She concluded her testimony by reporting that she had heard La Valeur moan to Giroux's coachman René Poyrot, "There's no doubt that I'm damned." And then to the matter of the sword. She confessed that Cordier had sent her with a sword to Philipotte Godart, the daughter of the local tailor, with instructions to hide it.

Lantin heard further testimony on the sword, first from Philipotte Godart, who confirmed that Carbolot had given her a sword to hide in her father's house. Anne-Marie Randu, the sixteen-year-old servant of Godart, then completed the story. She said that her mistress had indeed received a sword from Carbolot and in turn given it to her to hide. It was too big to fit in any of the trunks in the house, however, and a subsequent witness, a thirteen-year-old servant in the same household, confirmed what Randu had reported but added that because the sword could not be concealed Cordier had taken it back. Three other servants or seamstresses in the household also knew all about the obviously indiscreet Carbolot, Cordier, the sword, and the trunk, and now so did Lantin.

Did Lantin now have enough evidence to make some arrests? Or would he gather more testimony? Evidently the latter, because no arrests were made. Instead, Lantin turned his attention to Saint Denis's death, and testimony began to be gathered on it. By now it was the fall of 1639, and the first witness to testify about Saint Denis's end was Jeanne Regnier. She told Lantin that about a month after the death of Saint Denis (that is, in June 1639), she had run into his widow, Françoise Pailley. Pailley told her that her husband had died suddenly after being poisoned. Pailley added that her confessor had told her not to speak of the matter until the prince of Condé came to town: then she should tell him everything.

Now came Catherine Voisine, who recounted how at the end of May 1639 she had come out of the Jesuit church in Dijon and stopped by the home of the widow of Saint Denis. There she too heard from Pailley that Saint Denis had been poisoned, and that on the evening before his death Philippe Giroux had been at Saint Denis's house. While standing at his manservant's bedside, Giroux had reportedly told Pailley to go downstairs, but she could still hear Giroux say to her suffering husband, "My son, do you have anything to tell me?" Saint Denis asked him to look after his wife. At 10 in the evening Giroux left, and at 2 in the morning Saint Denis died.

The third witness telling of the death of Saint Denis was Jeanne Lambert. She testified that she had heard the news from Saint Denis's sister Catherine, who had told her of the popular belief that he had been poisoned on a trip he had made to Chalons-sur-Saône with his master, Philippe Giroux. The clear implication was that Giroux had slipped poison into Saint Denis's food or drink. Finally, in November 1639 Lantin heard from the Damoiselle Jeanne Bouhin: about five months earlier, she testified, a woman named La Monniot had told her about hearing from Saint Denis's widow that those men who had performed the autopsy on Saint Denis demanded payment for it from Pailley. The autopsy report itself recorded that it had been ordered by Pailley, but she let it be known that she was not responsible for the request: she told Bouhin, as she had told La Monniot, that she had said to those men who asked her to pay for the autopsy to go collect from the man who had ordered it. Pailley never mentioned Giroux by name to Bouhin, but she clearly feared him. Bouhin reported that Pailley now examined everything she ate for traces of poison, and laughed at anyone who suggested (and some did) that Baillet was not dead, but rather alive and well in Paris.

By late autumn of 1639, Lantin's investigation had turned up reports about the whereabouts of Baillet and Neugot on the evening of 6 September 1638. He had also heard about a sword and a cord from a hat that may have belonged to Baillet, about a declaration now missing that recounted what might have happened on the night of 6 September, and about the death of Giroux's manservant Saint Denis. All of this cast suspicion on Philippe

Giroux. Lantin also heard quite a few witnesses speak of Marie Fyot's amorous relationship with Philippe Giroux. One witness observed that "Président Baillet was quite ugly" and his wife "a very beautiful woman . . . the reason my lord Giroux was the way he was."

So much for the testimony that Lantin heard. How much he actively collected and how much simply came to him as a result of a monitoire and guilty consciences we can never know. He continued to record testimony into February 1640, but no arrests were made under his commission. Perhaps he was being scrupulous to the letter of the law, and surely he must have felt that to arrest Philippe Giroux he had better have compelling evidence and good cause. He had turned up no concrete evidence of guilt—no confessions, no murder weapons, and above all no bodies, and though he had testimony from witnesses about Baillet's murder, none were eyewitnesses, and often what they reported was second- and third-hand information about a man's sword, a hat and a cord from it, and pieces of fine clothing that found their way into the corsets of Saint Denis's wife. In short, Lantin had little tangible proof that could dispel lingering doubt about whether Baillet was murdered or had simply disappeared. True, Giroux seemed to have a motive to murder Baillet, but being in love with another man's wife, or even having an affair with her, was far from proof that he had killed him. To take on a sitting president and one of the most powerful members of the Parlement, surely Jean-Baptiste Lantin would need more than what he had, no matter how suggestive.

Yet critics of the investigation (and as we will see, there were many) wondered why Lantin did not pursue more vigorously some leads that were laid plainly before him. They may have ascribed Lantin's timidity to his association with the house of Giroux, since Lantin had been a witness and signatory to the marriage contracts of both Philippe's sister Barbe (in 1623) and Philippe himself (in 1634). Moreover, the daughter of Philippe's other sister Madeleine married Lantin's son, making Philippe Giroux his uncle. The Lantin clan seems rather closely tied to that of the Giroux and its allies, and this may account for why Lantin never sought testimony from Saint Denis (who was alive during the first two months of his investigation) or, amazingly, from Giroux's servants Devilliers, La Valeur, and Eleanore Cordier. And neither Marie Fyot nor Philippe Giroux was asked to give testimony. Lantin heard from Antoinette Carbolot something about the locked latrines in Giroux's courtyard, but he never ordered a search of them, much less of Giroux's mansion. As critics may well have snorted, no wonder no bodies were found. No one had looked for them! Obviously Lantin was keeping clear of Giroux's family, his lover, his servants, and even his house.

Perhaps Lantin would eventually have called in for questioning Devilliers, La Valeur, Cordier, Giroux, and Fyot, or ordered a search of the premises, but before he could do so, other powers in Parlement moved first. In late February 1640 Jean-Baptiste Lantin was removed from the case and a new team of investigators was appointed. On 5 March Parlement named the conseiller du roy Antoine Jacquot to join the king's advocate general (avocat-général du roy) for the Burgundy Parlement, Pierre de Xaintonge, to investigate the disappearance of Pierre Baillet and Philibert Neugot. On 9 March at Jacquot's request a second commissioner was named, a conseiller named Michel Millière. With this abrupt turn of events La Valeur suddenly vanished, but Eleanore Cordier remained in town, and she was one of the first people whom Jacquot and Millière called in for questioning.

CHAPTER 4

A Hat, a Rapier, a Knife, and a Dagger

Jean-Baptiste Lantin's investigation ended in late February 1640 when he was removed from the case. The records do not indicate why. For some reason, Lantin did not aggressively pursue those who he had good reason to suspect were either involved in the possible crime he was charged to investigate or knew a great deal about the circumstances in the Giroux house on the night of 6 September when Baillet and Neugot vanished. Many witnesses pointed toward La Valeur, Philippe Giroux, and Marie Fyot as guilty parties, and many others reported that the governess of Giroux's child Henri, Eleanore Cordier, was the source of much of the information the witnesses had about that night. Perhaps the closeness of the Lantin clan with the Giroux held back Jean-Baptiste, or perhaps fear of taking on the great with only hearsay or circumstantial evidence gave Lantin pause about questioning Fyot, Giroux, and their most trusted servants, La Valeur and Cordier. The monitoire of November 1639 had flushed out several of Giroux's servants, perhaps fearful for their souls, but Cordier and La Valeur were not among them. Whether Lantin would have called them for questioning eventually we do not know.

On 5 March fourteen judges and a commissioner were sworn on the Gospels to investigate the disappearance of Pierre Baillet and his valet Philibert Neugot. As in any criminal case, a président was named and charged with overseeing the commissioner (the *rapporteur*), who along with the royal prosecutor general (procureur-général du roy) and royal advocate general organized the prosecution. Among the fourteen judges were two brought in from the Parlement of Metz in Lorraine, including the man who was to preside over the case, Jean de La Mothe. In a departure from custom, every one of the judges swore to keep the proceedings secret, to speak of them to absolutely no one. As a failsafe to confidentiality, the proceedings were to be recorded by a specially appointed court clerk (a *greffier*), Étienne Donet. Moreover, these proceedings were to be written down not in the customary register of the Grand'Chambre (the most important of the four chambers in the Parlement) but rather in a separate volume. Every entry, and every deliberation, was to be signed personally by the presiding judge and the commissioner.

Initially there was but one commissioner, but on the 9th that official, Antoine Jacquot, requested that a second one be appointed. The judges sworn to the case agreed, and by a plurality vote they named the conseiller du roy in the Parlement, Michel Millière, to join Jacquot. Jacquot and Millière were no newcomers to Parlement, both having joined the court as conseillers many years before, Jacquot in 1620 and Millière in 1618. For a few days, however, from 5 to 9 March, Jacquot worked alone, and as the sole commissioner, he had as his very first order of business to try apprehending the three people who besides Giroux and Fyot were likely to know the most about the disappearance of Baillet and Neugot: Eleanore Cordier, Antoinette Carbolot, and Claude Bryot, known by everyone as La Valeur. On the same day when Jacquot took the oath, following standard procedure, he requested approval from the royal prosecutor general to send a huissier to apprehend Cordier and bring her in for questioning. The next day he sent the huissier after Carbolot and La Valeur. Cordier and Carbolot were promptly collared and jailed, but La Valeur slipped away.

Jacquot discovered that Antoinette Carbolot would mostly tell him only what she had already told Lantin, and he knew this because during her hearing he held in his hands the written testimony she had signed the previous autumn. He also possessed all the other documents that Lantin's investigation had generated. Jacquot did hear a few new things from her, however, although not about Baillet or Neugot. Cordier had told her, Carbolot now revealed, that when Giroux's wife was sick in 1636 Saint Denis had sent his mistress some soup by way of a servant named Jeanne, and had warned the servant not to taste it or she would die. Carbolot also reported hearing from

Cordier that her master Giroux was an evil man with a "black soul," and that ever since Giroux and La Valeur had paid Cordier a visit in her room late one night, she was afraid to sleep alone. Carbolot had been thrown in jail with Cordier, and the two women had had time to talk briefly before being interrogated. When it was time to offer testimony, Jacquot found out from Carbolot that Cordier, fearful about what information Carbolot might reveal to the law, had warned her to watch what she said or she would get them both hanged.

Finally on 8 March, two days later, Jacquot was to hear firsthand from the source of so much hearsay evidence, Eleanore Cordier, the twenty-seven-year-old governess of the five-year-old boy Henri Giroux. Cordier protested that she knew nothing at all of the business about Baillet, other than what everyone else had heard through rumors. When asked about her whereabouts on 6 September 1638, she told Jacquot that she had spent the entire day and night in the upstairs bedroom of Henri, who was deathly ill, and held him in her arms. Indeed she claimed that she remained at the boy's bedside for fourteen straight days, never once coming down the stairs, much less leaving the Giroux dwelling. Given this, how could she have any idea who came and went in the household on the day in question? Perhaps to convince Jacquot that she had nothing to hide, she did mention that by Christmas of 1638 the rumors that Baillet had been killed in Dijon had spread to the prince of Condé, who ordered a full investigation. Beyond that, she knew nothing.

Jacquot was armed with information from other statements gathered during the Lantin investigation, and so he had reason to suspect that this woman might have known more than she was telling. He pressed her, and sure enough she did have more to say. The fancy clothing that the widow of Saint Denis had been sporting, she revealed, was given to her by Giroux. Then, responding to leading questions from Jacquot about the possibility that she might be hiding something in a trunk, she said that he could search her belongings if he wished, but that he would have to go to the town of Langres in Champagne—her home town—to do so because she had sent her trunk there. In a continuation of her testimony three days later, Cordier confirmed what she had said, defiantly arguing that anyone who contradicted her testimony could only have been bribed or forced to do so. As we will see, her allegations of corruption were not at all implausible.

The same day that Michel Millière was named to join Antoine Jacquot as commissioner, 9 March, the presiding judge in the case dispatched Étienne Donet, the special clerk assigned to the case, to Langres to search the trunk and inventory its contents. As Langres was in the province of Champagne and so beyond the jurisdiction of the Parlement of Burgundy, Donet was to conduct the search in the presence of the chief criminal officer there, the lieutenant general. If by chance he found any pieces of men's clothing or any other items used by a man, Donet had orders to seize them, bring them back to Dijon, and turn them at once over to the commissioners.

While Donet was in Langres, Cordier asked the commissioners to hear her again. She suspected that two witnesses had testified against her, and she wanted to set the record straight. The commissioners agreed, and this is what they heard on 16 March. On 7 September 1638—that is, the day after the disappearance of Baillet—Cordier said that she went down to the wine cellar in Giroux's house. There she found a round, black hat of fine wool that was missing its decorative cord. She picked it up, carried it inside, and stashed it in a closet near Giroux's bedchamber, but then later retrieved it and tucked it away in one of her trunks. Still unsure of what to do, she later offered it to Benoît Giroux, her master's father, who commented that it was a fine piece but declined to take it because he said he had no use for it. So back the hat went into the trunk, and off to Langres it was sent, en route to the home of her former employer there. Bundled into the trunk with the hat were also a small knife, a sword, and a dagger. These weapons Cordier had also found on the 7th along with the hat. She enriched her already fertile revelation by observing that she thought the dagger belonged to La Valeur.

Then she turned to her master. Philippe Giroux, Cordier went on, knew nothing of these items until just recently, because shortly after Carnival in 1640, apparently having heard that she was hiding something in her trunk, he came to her and asked her what she had packed away in it. When she told him, he was surprised, saying he could not imagine where the items had come from. She informed the commissioners that she then gave Giroux a letter addressed to her former mistress in Langres, asking her to return the trunk to her by way of the messenger bearing the letter.

The trunk duly arrived back in Dijon, and when it did it came into the hands of Giroux. He promptly summoned Cordier and asked her to identify the contents. She hesitated and said that she might be able to but could not be sure. Giroux, frustrated with his servant's dodge, retorted, "Don't give me suppositions! This is no child's game!" Frightened, Cordier then assured her master that they were indeed the same items—hat, sword, knife, dagger—that she had packed in her trunk and shipped off to Langres.

Cordier several times described the hat as having no decorative cord, which made the following story she told of particular interest to Millière and Jacquot. She recounted a quarrel between La Valeur and the servant Claude Lucia. Many fights among men in the seventeenth century began with verbal insults to honor and masculinity, but in this case the authorities were not interested in the slander or the fight but rather in what had been said by Lucia, who had set off this quarrel with La Valeur by sarcastically ridiculing his appearance: "You make a handsome warrior! Go to war in your hat with a cord and feather!" It was the cord that attracted Lucia, the authorities, and Cordier, for she overheard Lucia's words and, on wheeling around and seeing the cord holding the plume in place, admonished La Valeur for his foolishness, saying, "If that cord is Lord Baillet's, you could hang for it!" The commissioners must already have been impressed by Cordier's testimony, which had now run into a second day, but there was still more to come. She told them her version of how little Henri threatened La Valeur with a knife in the kitchen, but they already knew this. What must have surprised them, however, was her telling them how on 7 September—the day after Baillet's disappearance—she came into Giroux's chamber and saw ashes spread on the floor (although there was no sign of blood), and was put to cleaning them up with Marie Rousselotte.

The trail was leading ever closer to Philippe Giroux. During Jean-Baptiste Lantin's investigation, we heard nothing from Giroux—no testimony, no protestations of innocence, no outrage that witnesses were suggesting he was somehow involved in the murder of Baillet—but with the new proceedings under Jacquot and Millière now striking closer to him than anything Lantin had overseen, we hear Giroux's voice for the first time. On 13 March, with all the judges of Parlement in attendance, Giroux protested that his enemies were spreading a rumor about town concerning the "disappearance" of his first cousin Pierre Baillet. He was stunned that anyone could suspect him of having anything to do with it, but seeing that "evil designs" were afoot to frame him and that his domestics were being arrested under this pretext, he asked the Parlement, by way of a formal request tendered to the commissioner Millière, to declare publicly who was denouncing him.

After handing his written request to Millière, Giroux strode out of the hall. While he was out the first president of the Parlement, Jean Bouchu, called forward a conseiller, Pierre Saumaise, lord of Chasans, a man who detested Giroux as much as Giroux detested him. The reasons for this mutual enmity ran deep, and everyone in the Parlement knew what they were. So all the assembled judges, no matter their sympathies or sentiments, suspected that Saumaise was involved somehow in this whole affair. The first president Bouchu shared their suspicion and called Saumaise to the bar to be heard. With his colleagues looking on, Saumaise protested that he had no idea what Giroux was talking about when he accused his enemies of spreading rumors, but he insisted that when Giroux spoke clearly, he would respond to him with equal clarity.

Giroux then reentered the hall, was told by the first president what Saumaise had said, and then did indeed speak clearly. He had good reason to believe, he declared, that Saumaise was the *partie instigante* in the case that was inching toward Giroux as a guilty party. A partie instigante in French law at the time was a person, and not necessarily the one wronged in an alleged criminal action, who either openly or secretly joined the prosecution in a case and assumed many of its legal costs. For kings whose treasury was always empty because of the wars they were usually fighting, legitimating a system in which private parties paid the cost of public prosecution made great sense, and anyway a partie instigante joined a case ostensibly to see justice served. Of course, the system unofficially allowed these friends of the court to use public law for private vengeance, and this is precisely what Giroux suspected Saumaise was doing, masking vengeance with justice.

When Giroux leveled this accusation at Saumaise for all his colleagues to hear, Saumaise was again called forward by Bouchu, and he and Giroux confronted each other face to face. Saumaise explained what difficulties existed between them, but he quickly added (no doubt speciously) that he never suspected Giroux's guilt in the disappearance of Baillet, he did not spread any rumors to this effect, and he had no wish to be a partie instigante in the case. Both men then withdrew, followed out of the hall by a stream of judges, who as kin by marriage or blood to either man were now expected to recuse themselves from any further discussion of the case.

The judges who remained presumably had no conflict of interest and could remain impartial. It was to these judges—and there were only fourteen of the full complement of seventy-three—that the commissioner Michel Millière then read Giroux's request. Aside from listing his reasons for suspecting that Saumaise was denouncing him, Giroux demanded that Jacquot be removed as a commissioner from the case. Giroux alleged that Saumaise had provided Jacquot with the names of witnesses to summon and that the commissioner had already—and secretly—taken their depositions in Saumaise's house. The judges deliberated on Giroux's request, and decided first to consult with the royal advocate general Pierre de Xaintonge. This man had worked with Lantin in his investigation, and the court wanted to confirm whether Saumaise had been involved. Before hearing de Xaintonge's report, however, the judges ruled that Jacquot would remain in his charge as commissioner, the first reversal of many for Philippe Giroux.

The very next day, on 14 March, de Xaintonge confirmed what Saumaise had claimed, that he had not been a partie instigante in the case against Giroux and that Baillet's mother and widow, Jeanne Burgat and Marie Fyot, had openly requested the investigation. Nor did he know of any documents supposedly given to Jacquot by Saumaise suggesting the names of witnesses to call. The court then concluded its business for the day by ordering that another monitoire on the disappearance of Baillet and Neugot be published, in the hope that new witnesses with new facts would come forward.

As Millière and Jacquot began preparing the monitoire to submit to the bishop, who would then distribute it to be read from every pulpit in the diocese, they were shocked by two turns of events. First, Burgat and Fyot announced that they were no longer interested in pursuing the case, and officially removed themselves as parties instigantes. Burgat was probably acting on counsel she had received from an unnamed male relative that to pursue Giroux would just bring more hardship and tragedy to the family. The clan had already lost one son, Pierre Baillet. To continue to pursue Giroux, she was advised, would only end in the loss of another. The second shock to the commissioners came when for reasons never explained, they were given grounds to believe that during the Lantin investigation witnesses had been enticed, suborned, or intimidated into giving false testimony for and against Giroux. To prevent this from happening again, the new monitoire explicitly forbade such conduct, and provided that any witnesses who had testified falsely must now come forward to testify truthfully.

Prompted by the monitoire, for the next month a flurry of witnesses came to the commissioners. Some admitted that their lives had been threatened if they bore witness against Giroux. Others had additional information building upon what Lantin had already uncovered. Still others offered testimony that brought entirely new things to light. Many of these witnesses, especially the ones who claimed intimidation, had sought out the commissioners and asked to be placed under the protection of the king and court. The commissioners reported this to the judges of the case, who then ordered Millière and Jacquot to proceed "incessantly" with their investigations.

Meanwhile, the commissioners dispatched representatives of the court to Langres to interrogate witnesses there who might know something about Cordier's infamous trunk. On 19 March the Damoiselle Isabelle Gondrecourt, wife of the royal bailiff of Langres, Claude Humbelot, and former mistress of Eleanore Cordier, was the first to be heard. She reported that about three months earlier, that is, in December 1639, a messenger named Jayet had brought a trunk to her belonging to Cordier. The next day Jayet followed with a letter from Cordier asking Gondrecourt to keep the trunk for her. Then, around the time of Carnival (late February) in 1640, she got another letter from Cordier, this time with a key and instructions to open the trunk. Inside Gondrecourt found a small knife, a rapier, a dagger, and a hat. Then, a few days later, another messenger arrived, this one a servant of Benoît Giroux named Forest Netard. He carried yet another letter from Cordier, this one asking Gondrecourt to give the hat, rapier, knife, and dagger to Netard.

Gondrecourt did so, but she must have had quite a memory, since she was able to recount what the hat, rapier, knife, and dagger looked like in minute detail. When last we heard of these four items, they had been sent back to Dijon and somehow fallen into the hands of the authorities. The commissioners now held in evidence four items that they suspected not only were the ones Cordier had tried to hide but also belonged to Baillet, Neugot, or the assassins. The representatives of the court who traveled to Langres to question Gondrecourt must have carried the items with them, for they were presented to her. When asked if they were the same ones she had turned over to Netard, Gondrecourt unhesitatingly said yes. The hat in particular she recognized, unusual because it was missing its cord or band. Gondrecourt confirmed her certitude about the hat, rapier, knife, and dagger in further sworn testimony on 19 April, again giving detailed descriptions that squared with the items in the possession of the authorities. Gondrecourt's testimony favored the prosecution, but several loose ends still dangled. Where Gondrecourt was certain about the items, her daughter Anne was not: she did not believe, she testified, that the hat shown her by the authorities was the same one she had seen in the trunk. Gondrecourt's husband, Claude Humbelot, agreed with his daughter that the hat and the rapier shown to him were not the same ones he had seen earlier.

While Gondrecourt in Langres was giving useful testimony, back in Dijon on 24 March Eleanore Cordier was shown the hat. She confessed that she thought it was the same one she had sent to Langres in the trunk. Then, the same day, it was Giroux's turn. He denied knowing anything about a hat, although he did acknowledge having heard that Cordier had sent a sword in a trunk to Langres. Two days later Cordier was called again to confirm that the hat shown to her was the one she had sent to Langres. Her response must have been maddening to the commissioners, as she now wavered, saying that she could not be sure, and that the people in Langres would be a better judge.

Forest Netard was called in on 7 April, and he confirmed that he had been sent to Langres to retrieve the hat, rapier, knife, and dagger. He did so, but upon returning to Dijon he gave the rapier to Philippe Giroux. Without telling anyone, however, he hid the hat in a closet, but he did show the dagger to Cordier. When Netard was shown the hat and asked if it was the one he brought back from Langres and hid in the closet, he replied that he was certain it was the same.

While the affair of the hat, the rapier, the knife, and the dagger was unfolding, other witnesses were coming forward, a few giving Giroux favorable testimony. On 17 March Suzanne Odinelle, one of his servants, testified that on 6 September 1638 she was at Giroux's residence at 8 in the evening, but that she left around 9 and while in the street saw President Baillet walking down the Grande Rue Notre Dame, away from Giroux's house and toward his own. She knew it was he because of his gait, but he was followed by a man she did not know.

Some witnesses were frightened, and came forward seeking the protection of the king and the court. One of these was Marie Rousselotte. On 14 March she reported under oath that Giroux had threatened her shortly after he heard about the "revelation" she had given to the priest Marchand, and that Giroux continued to harass her. In fact she had recently been fired by Bouvot de Lisle, Giroux's attorney, and was finding that no one would hire her, as she put it, "because she had testified against Giroux." About a month later Rousselotte began a steady stream of sworn declarations to the commissioners. First, she told them that despite Giroux's pressure, she had never consented to withdraw her declaration. She added that she knew it had disappeared but did not know who was responsible. Then on 19 April, six days later, she reported being warned that Giroux was looking for her and had sent word that she had three days to get out of town. Friends cautioned her to watch what she ate. On the 24th she testified again, this time to the effect that Giroux had ordered her to stay at the house of his solicitor, Antoine Chuttin, and to avoid the commissioner Millière. It seems that Rousselotte had meanwhile found refuge with the wife of the gardener of the judge Jean Massol, and that Giroux had tracked her down. Or at least his father had, since according to Rousselotte, Benoît Giroux went to Massol's residence and demanded that Rousselotte be turned out. Benoît then told Claudine Pechinot, the wife of a local baker and a domestic servant of Massol, that 2,000£ would be provided to Rousselotte if she left town. He concluded by telling Pechinot that she would be wise to do as she was told, adding that this is what her confessor advised as well.

Pechinot herself then came forward with her informative if somewhat rambling account. She confirmed that "just after Easter" Benoît Giroux had indeed come by Massol's, just as Rousselotte had said, and asked him if he had spoken with Marie Rousselotte. Massol reportedly said no, to which Giroux replied, "My uncle" — the two were related by marriage — "you have a gardener who is doing everything she can against me, which is so much the worse for her." Pechinot added that Rousselotte herself claimed to be living in fear because Giroux's people were looking for her, and therefore when she went out she never went near the "tripot" on the rue de la Charbonnerie: the wet nurse of Giroux's son lived there, and Rousselotte was afraid that she would report her whereabouts to Giroux. Rousselotte also told Pechinot that she always watched what she ate, fearing poison.

Pechinot had more to talk about than Marie Rousselotte, however. When asked if she thought Baillet had simply left town and might return, she said he would return "only on judgment day." She rambled on, her scattered testimony jumping here and there, reflecting a nervousness before the commissioners. She cryptically admitted having said some things to Antoinette Carbolot that she wished she had not, and had done so only because she and Carbolot came from the same home town. She regretted her confidence, because she felt now that Carbolot had betrayed her (although she did not specify the nature of the betrayal, she probably assumed that she was tangled up in this dangerous affair of the great because of Carbolot). She then changed subjects, repeating accounts she had heard that Baillet's valet had been strangled with a rope, and that Baillet himself had had a blanket thrown across his face as his assailants tried to strangle him. A distinguished lady, she said, had told her that eight people were involved in the murder.

Then Pechinot turned to an incident supposedly witnessed by many people, the episode in which Giroux's son Henri threatened La Valeur with a knife. She told the commissioners that she heard this story from Michelle Poyen, who in turn heard it from the wife of the barrel maker Guillot. Henri, so the story went, was in the kitchen holding a knife and La Valeur said he ought not play with the knife because he might cut himself, to which little Henri impetuously retorted, "I'll do to you what my father did to my uncle Baillet!" And finally, Pechinot recounted the time when she was at Giroux's house with Eleanore Cordier and heard Philippe Giroux announce that forty écus' worth of silver plate was missing and that he would find the culprits "little by little."

Madame Anthide Regnault, at one time Rousselotte's mistress, had something to say about Rousselotte too, something that the commissioners had not yet heard. She recounted that she was at Mass with Rousselotte when the monitoire about Baillet was announced, and that upon hearing it Rousselotte had gone pale, turned to her terrified, and moaned, "I'm damned." It was right after this that Rousselotte went to the priest Marchand with her declaration. Regnault then recounted that Giroux had sent for her, justifying his summons by informing her, "You have a servant who is crazy and who has given a testimony against me. By God's death, if someone doesn't turn that revelation over to me, I'll see them hanged!"

More testimony poured in, offering what seemed to be ever more evidence, however circumstantial, of Giroux's guilt. Gillette Pourvoyeur reported a conversation with Carbolot, in which he told her that when Cordier gave him the sword and hat to take to the tailor Godart's house, Cordier had said, "Here are the sword and hat of the man in question." Then Bernarde Regnault recounted how she had asked Cordier why she no longer ate in the room of her charge, Henri Giroux, as was customary, to which Cordier replied that she ate with all the other servants because she was afraid Saint Denis would poison her. Cordier feared for her life, she told Regnault, living in the house of that evil man, her master, who had no conscience.

Others said much the same thing, one declaring to the commissioners that Cordier had told her she could no longer live in Giroux's house, that living there threatened her salvation because of the evil acts she had seen committed there. She may have wanted to leave, but she told many people that she could not. One was Claudine Sarasin, who testified that one time, in the middle of the street, a weeping Cordier had told her she could not change jobs because no one would hire her, and if she tried, Giroux would harm her, or worse. Then, Honoré Maire, seventeen years old, reported that Carbolot had spoken to him about the death of Baillet, and that Giroux's manservant was wearing the rapier that had belonged to Baillet. He repeated the story of little Henri threatening La Valeur, rounding it out by adding that after Henri had threatened to kill La Valeur as his father had killed his uncle, Cordier had rebuked Henri, saying, "Shut up or someone will sooner believe that *we* killed lord Baillet." Maire then offered testimony that seemed to run counter to what others had said about Cordier: he said that Cordier did not in fact fear Giroux, but rather, as she boasted to Maire, "held him by her finger, as she did the ladies Bossuet and de Lisle."

Dizzying testimony continued. Another witness came forward and reported hearing that whenever Odo Brancio encountered Giroux in the street, Giroux warned him, "If you talk, you're dead." Then the commissioners heard from the aunt of Giroux's servant Suzanne Odinelle, Michelle Arbelot. Odinelle had told her, she testified, that the widow of Saint Denis, Françoise Pailley, had said her husband had been poisoned. She added that Pailley said she knew well where Baillet's clothes were. On 30 March Pailley spoke for herself. She believed, she told the commissioners, that her husband had been poisoned in early May 1639, because he went to Chalons-sur-Saône with his master Giroux in good health, and deteriorated rapidly on his return. Her husband died in the middle of the night, she recounted, and the next morning Giroux ordered an autopsy. No report was ever drawn up about it, however, and Pailley suspected a cover-up. She complained loudly that she thought Saint Denis had been poisoned and that she wanted whoever had done it to him "to be hanged for it"; referring to the grisly custom of burning the corpses of hanged criminals, she also said "she would carry the wood to burn them." She had a great deal to say about the death of her husband, but not a word to share about Baillet's. The commissioners suspected that she knew more about this than she was telling.

La Valeur seems to have barely slipped through the net that Millière and Jacquot were spreading across the town, for as recently as Carnival (that is, in late February of that year, 1640) he had been spotted in Dijon. One witness said that while chatting with him she told him of rumors going around about the death of Baillet and of the belief that La Valeur had killed him. La Valeur replied that he had not even been at Giroux's house when the deed was supposedly done (as we have seen, he would change his story later), but that he had helped to gather some stones to wall up the latrines and had carried a great deal of sand to the cellar. He said that Giroux wanted to poison them all, as he had done to Saint Denis. Eleanore Cordier, this witness added, had told her that just after Carnival La Valeur, given to indiscreet comments, had been whisked away to the Giroux country estate of Marigny in the Charolais, beyond the jurisdictional reach of the Parlement of Burgundy and its inquiring commissioners.

Testimony being gathered suggested that Giroux seemed to have had good reason to silence Saint Denis, or anyone else who had information about the alleged murder. And we might speculate that Saint Denis told his wife Françoise Pailley a great deal about it, since much testimony suggests that she was well informed of her husband's activities. Shortly after the death of Saint Denis, one witness testified, his widow had told her sarcastically that he had been poisoned "for the good services he had rendered his master." Pailley reported that she had already told the same thing to twenty-two others. To one who asked her if it was true that Baillet was in fact alive and in Paris with the beautiful Madame de Reviremont, and if he would return, she answered again sarcastically while nodding her head, "Oh yeah, you'll see, you'll see." Pailley gravely added that she knew Giroux would kill her if he knew she was saying this.

More pieces of the puzzle creating a picture of Giroux's guilt were collected and assembled by the commissioners. One witness testified about hearing that Giroux had hired a mason to wall up the latrines in Giroux's courtyard, and that after the work was done someone had tried to poison him. The mason reputedly took an antidote and survived. And then, in this spring of 1640, the story broke about the conspiracy to kill Baillet on the road to his country estate. That plan involving Saint Denis, Claude Froul, and Prudent Roussotte purportedly failed with Roussotte's nerve, as we have seen, but it was becoming quite plausible to the commissioners that people very close to Giroux were responsible for the disappearance of Baillet and Neugot.

The spring of 1640 was a dark hour for Giroux, and on 11 May he met with still another reversal. This time he heard the court order his appearance in person before Michel Millière to respond to the growing intimations of his guilt in the death of Baillet. After this audience Giroux was to be confined to his house and not permitted to communicate with any witnesses under pain of conviction.

On 9 July, enough testimony having been gathered in the wake of the monitoire, the commissioners instructed all priests of all parishes within Parlement's jurisdiction who may have received additional statements to surrender them to the commissioners. This was the final preparation before moving in for the most thunderous action the court had yet taken: on 11 July 1640 Philippe Giroux, a sitting, presiding judge on the very same Parlement, was arrested and taken into custody for the murder of Pierre Baillet and Philibert Neugot. Following normal procedure, the royal advocate general Pierre de Xaintonge had just the day before presented his "conclusions" justifying the arrest to the court. Caught in the net with Giroux were Suzanne Odinelle (one of Giroux's domestic servants), Forest Netard (one of Benoît Giroux's valets), Bernard D'Ostun (a local gardener suspected of giving false testimony), his wife Denise Gentilhomme, Françoise Pailley, the widow of Saint Denis (also suspected of perjury), and Claude Marchand, the priest of Saint Nicolas church who had taken Marie Rousselotte's deposition during the Lantin investigation. As for La Valeur, the court ordered that all the belongings of this fugitive from justice be seized and inventoried.

CHAPTER 5

The House of Giroux

A Jacobin priest named Maillet had told Marie Rousselotte, the terrified young servant who offered a testimony to her parish priest about Philippe Giroux's supposed complicity in the murder of his cousin Pierre Baillet, that if she did not withdraw her declaration, "the house of Giroux would fall." The arrest for murder of someone from such a distinguished "house" as that of a president at the Parlement was a singular event in the history of Burgundy. It riveted the attention of everyone, high and low, living in Dijon at the time. The affairs of the great always attract the attention of ordinary people, all the more so when murder and sex are involved. This is what happened in Dijon after 1638, and the status and power of one of Burgundy's greatest "houses" hung in the balance.

In early May 1605 Philippe Giroux was born the youngest child and only surviving son of Benoît Giroux and Madeleine Baillet (in seventeenth-century France women kept their maiden names after marriage). Before him, his mother had given birth to at least five other children. Three of them, Robert and the twins Marie and Jeanne, died in infancy—sadly, the fate of about one in four French babies at the time. Two sisters who survived, Madeleine and Barbe, like their brother were born and baptized in Dijon. The accident of birth landed these three children in a family that in terms of social status had boldly emerged from the wreckage of the Wars of Religion, when battles between Protestants and Catholics ripped Burgundy and France apart over much of the second half of the sixteenth century. The

The Church of Notre Dame in Dijon in 1610, Philippe Giroux's
parish church and the place of his own baptism in 1605. Courtesy
Bibliothèque Nationale de France, Cabinet d'Estampes, U b 9.

Giroux family certainly was not the only one to climb the social ladder, but
it was among the most successful at it in the province. In 1597, when Benoît
Giroux fathered his first child, Madeleine, at twenty-eight, he had already
been a conseiller du roy in Burgundy's Parlement for two years.

Benoît made the move to Dijon and its royal court in 1595, the year when
Henri IV, the Protestant-turned-Catholic king, defeated the Duc de Mayenne
to effectively end the Wars of Religion. Henri routed the duke's forces in
the battle of Fontaine-Française, only half a day's ride from the walls of
Dijon. Before assuming his office and establishing his new residence in Burgundy's capital, the young Benoît had been a lawyer (an *avocat*) in the town
of Chalons-sur-Saône, fifty miles to the south of Dijon, a natural occupa-
tion for the son of the royal prosecutor in Chalons. Benoît's parents, Robert
Giroux and Barbe Ferret, provided well for their sons, and Benoît's brother

Jacques also was a lawyer in Chalons before becoming a judge himself in the Royal Presidial Court of Bourg-en-Bresse in 1601. Jacques would not rise to the social heights of his brother, but his was a privileged existence none-theless. He won the judgeship for the good services he had rendered to King Henri at war in the Savoy and Piedmont, loyalty which paved the way for him eventually to become the royal prosecutor in the bailiwick court of Chalons.

The brothers Benoît and Jacques were thus launched on careers of dis-tinction, but alongside public office, success in seventeenth-century France was spelled by landholdings. The Giroux were well positioned in this regard too. Robert Giroux, the grandfather whom Philippe Giroux probably never knew, had acquired the fiefdom of Vessey in 1575, a lordship that remained in the Giroux family until its extinction with the death of Philippe's son Henri in 1686. At some point Robert also acquired the lordship of Corcassey. Like Vessey, Corcassey straddled rolling, almost treeless hills in the Chalon-nais region, two days' ride southwest from Dijon. We know nothing of these lordships before the mid-seventeenth century (the records do not exist to tell us much about them or their worth), but if the inventories recorded in 1645 and 1666 are any indication, Vessey was the better of the two.

At Vessey, the lords Giroux could gaze from the small garden of their modest chateau (it had two chambers downstairs separated by a chapel, two rooms up, a stable, and a barn) across the deep moat that surrounded the dwelling. Their view encompassed fields of wheat, rye, and oats, and a few vineyards and orchards. All told in 1666, the land returned 1,100 *livres tour-nois* annually to the Giroux family (not the stuff of great fortunes, but over four times what a well-off master stonemason at the time might earn in a year). Corcassey likewise produced grains and some grapes, but being half a league in perimeter and thus smaller than Vessey at three-quarters, it was considerably poorer. It returned only 150 livres per year to the lords, and had no manor house at all.

Benoît and Jacques were well provided for by their father Robert. After Robert's death, their mother Barbe Ferret continued to take good care of her sons. She was widowed sometime in the early seventeenth century, and like about 20 percent of all French widows at the time she remarried. Her second husband was a wealthy man named Pierre de La Mare, the lord of Ruffey and Chevigny, the royal advocate at the bailiwick court of Beaune, and eventu-ally the mayor of that town. Between them they were able to provide Jacques and Benoît with even more means to scale the social ladder. In fact Jacques married a de La Mare too, his stepsister Barbe! From his mother Benoît inherited and then rented out several houses, stables, and barns in Beaune, as well as lucrative vineyards in the region of Beaune, Pommard, and Volnay. However, the best measure of the mother's wealth would be the price of the office that she helped her son to purchase in 1610, one of the seven presidencies at the prestigious court of Parlement. We do not know what Benoît and Barbe Ferret paid for it, but in 1615 Benoît's future son-in-law paid 54,000 livres for his presidency on the same court.

Openly buying a judgeship rings corrupt to modern ears, but in much of Europe at that time, and above all in France, nearly all public offices were purchased by private parties. Public offices like the presidency that Benoît bought were technically the property of the king. Although the monarch had the right to sell them, he also retained the right to repurchase them from the buyer if he so wished. Officially this royal prerogative would be exercised if the officeholder abused the office, or if he insufficiently dispensed its duties. In practice repurchase almost never happened, for the same reason that offices were sold in the first place: the king was always in need of money.

Venality of office (that is, the legal selling of public posts) began modestly in France in the late fifteenth century and increased dramatically in scale as the king's need for money escalated sharply in the sixteenth and seventeenth centuries. Royal budgets ballooned then, largely because the cost of warfare did. Rising public expenditures were one fallout of the "military revolution" that began in the fifteenth century. This revolution saw, among other developments, the widespread appearance and use of gunpowder, arquebuses (an early type of musket), and cannon. And it was not just the royal expenses that mushroomed, but the size of the king's armies as well. These musket-toting soldiers were mostly mercenaries, and so the costs of killing included not just powder and metal for the firearms but wages for the soldiers.

All of this placed a heavy burden on the king's budget. One way to meet the expenses was through taxation, and taxation did increase during these years. But in France (and nearly everywhere else at the time) the rural peasants and urban artisans and merchants bore the brunt of the tax load, the nobility being tax-exempt (theoretically nobles made their contribution to society as warriors or public servants rather than monetarily). When royal demands for revenue exceeded what taxes could bring in, venality seemed to European monarchs an expedient too convenient to pass up. Revenue would pour into the king's coffers, and an administrative, financial, and judicial bureaucracy of royal servants would be created in the bargain. Of course, since public office would be held in private hands, the risk of a rogue bureaucracy not responsible to the monarch was created, but more corrosive than this was the advent of a patrimonial system in which men used their public offices (women were barred from them) to promote the private interests of their families, friends, and political allies.

In other words, venality imported an irresolvable tension into public affairs, as became clear in the world of justice. On the one hand, judges like Benoît Giroux were bound by an oath of office: Benoît swore in 1610 as he ascended the presidency "not to have any other goal than to humbly perform service to his majesty." Yet on the other hand, families like the Giroux assiduously pursued public offices because they were favorable positions from which to amass landed fortunes; this was especially true of judgeships and presidencies. All of this—landed wealth and public office—delivered enormous prestige and power. High office and landed estates, quite simply, meant high social status. In this supremely status-conscious and hierarchical age, when no one thought of people as being equal (that revolutionary and subversive thought would only gain currency in the eighteenth century), improving the status of one's family was the fundamental desire of nearly everyone in society. This was as true for presidents at the Parlement as it was for the tailor who made the clothes for them or the blacksmith who shod their horses.

Public offices were essential for prestige, but they seldom brought riches in and of themselves. The salaries were invariably low, sometimes paltry, and often in arrears. Even though judges at Parlement garnered funds from court costs (called épices), they were not the stuff fortunes were made of. For example, in 1634 Benoît Giroux as a judge in the chamber of the Enquêtes at Parlement (where misdemeanors were judged) heard thirty-seven cases and received only about 1,700 livres in épices. A busier colleague in the Tournelle in the same year heard seventy-nine felony cases and earned just over 3,700 livres. These are not insignificant sums, to be sure, but when we consider that daughters had to be dowered and sons provided with public offices of their own, it is clear that the primary source of income—indeed the synonym for wealth in that age—was land.

Land was wealth, and this is why families who had the means feverishly acquired land every chance they got. In the sixteenth century and the first half of the seventeenth—that is, when the Giroux were on the rise—history was decidedly on their side. Everywhere in Europe during those war-torn years, population was growing. Population pressure combined with an influx into the money supply of gold and especially silver (from the mines of the newly discovered and conquered Americas) to generate inflation. The result was both increased impoverishment for Europe's unfortunates and enrichment for its privileged élite. As the tide of pauperization rose and engulfed more and more peasants, small family farms were forced onto the market, to be snapped up by families on the make like the Giroux. Benoît continued to be as active a property buyer as his father Robert had been, purchasing houses, vineyards, and even lordships whenever he could. Although we lack a complete inventory of his holdings, near the end of his life in 1650 he boasted the title of lord of Vessey, Corcassey, Marigny, Ocle, and Saint Vallier. Multiply the real estate acquisitions of the Giroux by the number of all of the other upwardly mobile office-holding families of that century and a half, and we see a massive land transfer from countryside to town. The result was that most of the lands of Burgundy by 1650 were owned by city dwellers, many of them residing in Dijon.

The backbone of power and wealth for families like the Giroux was thus public office and land. Men like Robert and Benoît Giroux did not amass wealth entirely or even primarily for themselves, but rather for their families and descendents. It was essential, therefore, that ways be found to keep one's patrimony intact in the family, and simultaneously to increase its dimensions at every possible turn. The institution of marriage was the key to these aspirations.

We must not underestimate the importance of marriage to these families. As with the monarchs who ruled over them, marriages were alliances between families with political stakes. Sealed by contract, marriage forged an almost unbreachable loyalty between the parties. So important was marriage that it was rare for a father, whether a king, judge, lawyer, or even master baker, to dare allow affection to enter into the choice of a mate for his

A townhouse, or "hôtel," in Dijon that was typical in appearance
of the homes of seventeenth-century judges like Giroux. Giroux's
townhouse no longer exists. The Préfecture de Police stands
on its site. Photograph by author.

daughter or son. Marriages were mergers between families, and the legal
and spiritual bond was reinforced by ties of friendship. Contracts were witnessed and signed by close friends, allies, and protectors of the two parties,
all signatories giving their *avis et consent*, or official blessing, to the match.
These participating families were thereby "allied." Blood and friendship
made a thick bond.

When a marriage between Benoît and his future bride was arranged by
the Giroux clan and that of the Baillet, an alliance between a rising family
and an established one was anticipated. By the mid-seventeenth century
the Baillet would be lords of nearly twenty seigneuries, several of which
returned substantial revenues (the lordships of Villeneuve and Saint Ger-
main du Plain paid nearly 5,000 livres each in 1666). Benoît was betrothed
to Madeleine Baillet, the daughter of Robert, a judge at the Parlement since

1571. At about the time of the marriage, Madeleine's brother Jacques—the father of the man reportedly murdered in 1638—assumed his father's seat at Parlement. Madeleine's uncle Philippe, the lord of Vaugrenant, had for several years been wielding a heroic sword for his king Henri IV in the Wars of Religion. Philippe had not always been a warrior, but in the late 1580s this judge and then president at the Parlement took up arms for the royalist cause, eventually resigning his presidency in 1595 for the sword. With royal victory, Philippe Baillet de Vaugrenant ascended to almost mythical status. The Baillet name was indeed an illustrious one, and any child born of the match between Benoît Giroux and Madeleine Baillet would benefit from its reputation.

Marriage was a blood bond. It was also a material one. When marriages between "great" families were arranged, the sums involved could be large. When it came time for Benoît to seek a spouse for Philippe Giroux's older sister Barbe in 1623 (Benoît's wife Madeleine Baillet died sometime before 1613, after which he remarried), considerations of power and prestige shared place with those of wealth. The resulting agreement—a match between Barbe and Jacques Sayve—was truly an affair of the great. Some of the most powerful and influential men in the province crowded into the room to witness, and give blessing to, the signing of the marriage contract. For the groom, for example, we count among others a baron, a canon, the bishop's vicar, and the first presidents at both the Chambre des Comptes and the Parlement. The groom had already been a president at the Parlement for eight years, and as part of the marital agreement his mother pledged 60,000 livres (surpassing the 54,000 that the office of President cost her son in 1615) and the lordship of Eschigey (in 1666 this had annual revenue of 1,200 livres). Benoît Giroux dowered his daughter with 75,000 livres. The newlyweds embarked on married life backed by substantial resources and a network of alliances that joined them with some of the province's most powerful families.

The marital agreement worked out by Benoît for Barbe's younger brother Philippe was even grander, signaling to everyone that the Giroux family was approaching the apex of power, prestige, and wealth in Burgundy. In 1629 Benoît, a president at the Parlement since 1610, began pursuing for his son the daughter of that court's first president (and therefore its most powerful member), already a judge on the same court. The first president, Jean-Baptiste Le Goux de La Berchere, resisted, no doubt hesitating to ally with a family of parvenus, no matter how wealthy. The Le Goux family possessed a barony, a marquisate, and a county, as well as over a score of ordinary lordships, so the Giroux wealth was not irresistible bait.

Undaunted, Benoît relentlessly directed his entreaties to Jean-Baptiste's widow after her husband died in 1631. The widow, Marguerite Brulart, was a woman of unrivaled stature in Dijon, being the widow of a first president, the daughter of another, the granddaughter of a third, and the mother of yet another (her son Pierre assumed the office in 1631 after the death of his father). Brulart finally gave in and signed a marriage contract with the Giroux on 2 January 1634. She dowered her daughter Marie with the huge sum of 150,000 livres. Philippe Giroux, for his part, came with the lordship of Vessey and 63,000 livres (covering the cost of his judgeship). He also received a pledge from his father of 117,000 livres, the sum it would take to cover the spiraling cost of the office of president that Philippe was soon to acquire after Benoît retired.

Witnessing the signing and thereby declaring a bond of friendship with the betrothed and their families were among others the bride's mother (Marguerite Brulart), her brother (the first president Pierre Le Goux), and her uncle (Denis Brulart, yet another president at the Parlement), but it was Giroux who brought in the really prestigious figures. Alongside Philippe's brother-in-law, the president Jacques Sayve, stood Jean Baillet, the dean of the most influential church in Dijon (the king's chapel, Sainte Chapelle). Most exalted of all, however, was his excellency Henri II de Bourbon, the prince of Condé, who signed the marriage contract after working behind the scenes to arrange the marriage for several years with Benoît Giroux. Almost certainly the Le Goux and Brulart families agreed to ally with the upstart Giroux because the prince had selected the Giroux as one of his most important clients. This was a marriage that made sense for political reasons. Of the seven sitting presidents on the Parlement in 1634, four (Giroux, Sayve, Brulart, and Le Goux) were now allied by marriage.

Alliances sealed by kinship and friendship were the bedrock of practical politics. True, a bureaucracy was forming, and coming into view were the outlines of what we have come to recognize as the modern state, in which authority is delegated through institutionalized chains of command, but real power was still personal and familial in the political world in which the Giroux moved. Gaining the favor of a patron was essential to success,

Funerary statue of Marguerite Brulart, Philippe
Giroux's mother-in-law. This statue graces her coffin,
now empty but prominently displayed in the Cathedral
of St. Bénigne of Dijon. Photograph by author.

and the more prestigious the patron, the more distinguished the client became. Patrons provided essential services to clients in exchange for loyalty—arranging advantageous marriages, obtaining clerical or military posts for sons, exerting influence in legal disputes—all of this and more worked within the system of patronage that deeply stamped the political process of the time. Political careers and social status hung upon gaining or losing the favor of a patron, and the most cherished patron of all in Burgundy was the king's cousin and, since 1631, its governor, the prince of Condé. It is a mark of the success of the Giroux that they were prize clients of the prince—at least for a while.

The keystone in the arch of the house of Giroux, therefore, was Condé. In 1626 he and Cardinal Richelieu became political allies. Richelieu was Louis XIII's prime minister and, one could justifiably say, the most powerful man in all of France. Condé himself was not far behind. For the remaining twenty years of his life, Condé amassed an enormous fortune and consolidated his power, notably in Burgundy where he became the royal governor in 1631. Condé then set about creating an extensive clientele to control the provincial estates (an elected body of men from the privileged ranks of society who convened every three years to deliberate on taxation matters for the province), municipal governments, and above all the Parlement. Richelieu, and after his death in 1642 the prime minister for the child-king Louis XIV, Cardinal Mazarin, distributed patronage directly in most of the provinces of France. They used networks of their own broker-clients to secure loyalty from provincial nobles and institutions and their support for royal policies and interests. In so doing, they bypassed the provincial governors who had enjoyed a near-monopoly on the brokering of royal patronage in the provinces of France in the sixteenth century.

Seventeenth-century Burgundy was a glaring exception to the prime minister's method of governance, however: there Richelieu and later Mazarin relied on Condé, leaving him to construct his own clientage system, and after his death on Christmas Day in 1646, they relied similarly on his son, who succeeded him. The princes Condé, father and son, operated their system with complete effectiveness. Marc-Antoine Millotet, one of the royal prosecutors general in Parlement in the 1630s and 1640s and a close observer of Burgundian politics, wrote that "no one obtained an office, whether in the Parlement or in other jurisdictions, other than through the mediation" of the Condés. "My Lords the Princes," he went on, "father and son, exercised all authority in governing Burgundy for more than twenty years."

The elder Condé built an interlocking network of clients that included many judges in the Parlement, and between 1627 and 1640 the Giroux family was an important cog in the prince's machine. The Giroux were newly rich, parvenus lacking in noble pedigree that for other families stretched back into the mists of the past, but this in fact well suited Condé's strategy. What better way to secure loyalty than to patronize a family that would owe its political power, even its social existence, to him? Indeed Condé's secrétaire Pierre Lénet said as much in his memoirs, where he wrote that the prince deliberately picked clients of young men from "new houses."[1]

Condé unquestionably anointed this family. Benoît Giroux was recruited into Condé's circle sometime in the 1620s. The first payoff for Benoît's loyalty was the acquisition of a judgeship for his twenty-two-year-old son Philippe in 1627. The double illegality of the underage Philippe serving on the same court as his presidential father (according to the letter of the law, conseillers du roy were required to be at least twenty-five years of age, and father and son could not serve at the same time on the bench) was swept aside by power politics, far from unusual in that age. Condé's influence again overrode the letter of the law a few years later, when Benoît resigned his presidency to Philippe in 1633. At twenty-eight, Philippe was still two years shy of the minimum age to hold that office. He was opposed by Pierre Saumaise de Chasans, who procedurally delayed Philippe's seating for three years, but the Giroux were finally vindicated when an exasperated Condé personally escorted Philippe into the Palais de Justice, the courthouse of Parlement, and seated his client in 1636. Philippe knew he was the prince's créature—literally, one created by a patron—even before this dramatic action. Recall that Condé arranged Philippe's marriage to the daughter of the former first president and the sister of the current one, Marie Le Goux de La Berchere, even personally signing the marriage contract. Then, less than a year later, the first child of the union between Philippe and Marie was born. The baby was given the name Henri, after the prince. Condé was thus his godfather, personally holding the boy at the baptismal font and so forging a bond of "spiritual kinship."

Godparents agreed to ease a child's path in life in any number of ways. Godparenthood was another ritualized form of institutionalizing trust and fidelity in a society where power rested upon personal relationships. The selection by a parent of a godparent for the child was therefore a serious business, and the bond created was yet another strand in the rope binding families together in the power relations that defined politics at the time.

All these forms of alliances—blood, marriage, friendship, patronage, godparenthood—wove the families of Burgundy together in networks through which they exerted political influence. The stakes were always high. Sometimes, as in the Giroux affair, in which the legal system was the table upon which cards of influence were played, a man's life was at stake. The law of France—and the judges who swore to administer it—in one respect existed to dispense justice, but one must wonder how effectively this objective could be carried out when the men who staffed the entire legal system were bound to one another and pledged to serve their own and their families' interests as well as the king's justice. What if these came into conflict? In the Giroux trial, would the power of the Giroux clan subvert justice if Philippe were guilty by getting him acquitted nonetheless? Or, if he were not guilty, would the influence of his enemies send him to the gallows anyway, a framed victim of superior power? Power hinged on political connections, on patronage and clientage, but what could be given could also be taken away.

Philippe Giroux certainly had his allies. On his side, it might appear, was the judge entrusted with the first investigation, Jean-Baptiste Lantin. Recall that his investigation, which lasted from the spring of 1639 to February 1640 and ended with no arrests, seemed tepid at best. The judge avoided contact with anyone closely associated with Giroux. It is certainly plausible that Lantin's timidity owed something to his association with the house of Giroux. After all, he was a witness and signatory to the marriage contracts of both Barbe in 1623 and Philippe Giroux in 1634. And the daughter of Philippe's other sister Madeleine married Jean-Baptiste Lantin's son, also named Philippe. That would mean that Philippe Giroux was Philippe Lantin's uncle. Moreover, Jean-Baptiste Lantin's first son's godfather was Philippe Giroux's father-in-law, the first president Jean-Baptiste Le Goux de La Berchere. The Lantin clan seems rather closely tied to that of the Giroux and its allies.

But Lantin was removed from the case, and after that it might appear that the tide was turning against Giroux. In fact, it looks as though one of the new investigators was in the opposite camp. This would be Michel Millière, who along with Antoine Jacquot was one of the two commissioners replacing Lantin. Consider that two of Millière's nephews had married into the Saumaise family, with their spouses Jeanne and Françoise both being daughters of Giroux's archenemy Pierre Saumaise de Chasans. And this man Michel Millière was entrusted to pursue a just investigation of Giroux?

Giroux had good reason to complain about Millière's lack of impartiality, but the commissioner was not the only one he had reason to be concerned about. What of Pierre Odebert, one of the supposedly impartial fourteen judges who were permitted to remain on the bench to hear the Giroux case because, officially, they had no conflict of interest? Yet Odebert's brother-in-law was the commissioner Michel Millière, and Odebert himself was godfather to one of the daughters of Millière's cousin of the same name (Michel). Both Millière and Odebert were also tied to Jean Bouchu, the Parlement's first president beginning in 1638. Bouchu was a close and faithful client of the prince of Condé, and so at first blush it may appear that this would have favored Giroux; but as we will see, the bond between Condé and Giroux was fraying at precisely this time. So when Millière stood as the godfather to Bouchu's daughter in March 1638, and Odebert did so for one of Bouchu's sons in January 1643, they were hooking up indirectly with Condé, and such an alliance was not necessarily friendly to the Giroux. Add to Giroux's woes the arrival of Pierre Lénet in the office of royal prosecutor general in 1641, the year after Giroux's fortunes took a turn for the worse. Lénet, like Bouchu, was a favored client of Condé (he was, as his father Claude had been, the prince's *secrétaire des commandements* beginning in 1638 and so held one of the highest offices in Condé's household).

What was happening in the constellation of patron-client relations that seemed to be shifting against the Giroux? Until 1637 Philippe Giroux had every reason to feel confident that Condé's patronage was secure. However, in that year cracks began appearing in this once solid alliance. The year before, the king, deeply mired in the Thirty Years' War against his historic enemy the Habsburgs, had imposed upon the Parlement of Dijon a levy of 10,000£. The assessment was to raise a corps of troops and pay for fortifications to defend Dijon against imminent invasion from Imperial Habsburg soldiers who were ranging far too closely to Dijon. Parlement refused (we do not know how the justices voted, or therefore where Giroux stood on this issue), and incurred the wrath of king, prime minister, and prince of the blood.

The judges further angered Condé, Richelieu, and Louis XIII by declining to register a royal edict calling for the creation and sale of new offices, including an eighth presidency in the Parlement. Members of Parlement protested that they had not been consulted as customary practice required. Richelieu, deeply engaged in war and unwilling to alienate powerful nobles in this frontier province and town, opted temporarily for conciliation. Condé agreed to go along with the cardinal's decision, but his counsel to Richelieu tells us a great deal about what kind of control he expected over the court. He wrote the following to the prime minister from Dijon on 18 September 1636: "I just received your orders on the Edicts; I will delay them as you wish. But you will please pardon me for saying that you are too good and that never will you see the authority of the king solidly established except by bringing the Parlements to heel, and bringing them into line as is their duty . . . When it pleases you I will push the business to its conclusion without danger of any resistance."

Condé was good to his word: in April 1637 he held a *lit de justice*—that is, he personally came to Parlement, and as a specified delegate of the king and speaking for him he constitutionally overrode the judges' objections— and registered the edicts. Many of the judges were promptly relieved of their duties, their suspensions only gradually lifted. The first president Pierre Le Goux de La Berchere, Philippe Giroux's brother-in-law, was blamed by Condé for having little control over the Parlement. As a result, he shouldered the greatest punishment of all. He was not only suspended from his office but exiled from Burgundy as well. He was replaced by the pliant Antoine Bretagne, an aged judge from the Parlement of Metz. Then, when Bretagne died a year later, Jean Bouchu became first president. Bouchu, recall, was a trusted client of Condé but no friend or ally of the Giroux. Condé was be- ginning to shift the patron-client constellation that would eventually isolate Giroux and, not accidentally, elevate his implacable enemy, Pierre Saumaise de Chasans.

In late 1638 Giroux was suspected of the murder of President Baillet, but only in 1640 did Giroux know decisively that his former patron had aban- doned him, for it was then that Condé refused an audience with him. Then the prince declined to receive his father Benoît in Paris, threatening to have him chased from the city if he did not leave immediately. Philippe Giroux was arrested in July 1640. It was beginning to look as though the forces ar- rayed against Giroux were emboldened to apprehend him because Condé was no longer Giroux's protector. Left isolated, what was now to become of this man?

CHAPTER 6

Prison

Philippe Giroux's prospects darkened as soon as the new commissioners
—Antoine Jacquot and Michel Millière—took over the investigation
into the murder of Pierre Baillet and Philibert Neugot in March 1640. First,
several of Giroux's household servants were apprehended, imprisoned, and
interrogated. Then he himself was called in for questioning, and after that
placed under house arrest. Then on 11 July the authorities made their boldest
move yet, calling for the imprisonment of a sitting president on the king's
sovereign court of Burgundy, the Parlement.

Drawing upon the findings of the commissioners, the royal advocate general Pierre de Xaintonge presented his *conclusions* (justifications for the arrest) to the fourteen judges in the Parlement who were charged with hearing
the case, and Giroux was quickly apprehended. Caught in the same net were
his supposed accomplices—the domestic servant Suzanne Odinelle, the
lackey Forest Netard, who worked for Benoît Giroux, the gardener Bernard
D'Ostun and his wife Denise Gentilhomme, and the widow of Saint Denis,
Françoise Pailley. Warrants for the arrest of Giroux's valet Pierre Borel,
called Devilliers, and Giroux's lackey Philippe LaQuille were also issued,
but these men had fled. Claude Marchand, the priest who first received
Marie Rousselotte's notorious but missing declaration, was also hauled in
for questioning. The jail was now crowded with Giroux and his supposed
accomplices: already imprisoned were the domestic servants Eleanore Cor-

dier and Antoinette Carbolot, the lackeys Claude Froul and Mathieu Clodon, and the coachman René Poyrot.

The first to be interrogated was D'Ostun. On 15 July he said he had been in Giroux's bedchamber the day after the supposed murder and had seen no evidence of the crime—no blood on the floor or the bedcovers or curtains. He did, however, recount the story about little Henri Giroux threatening La Valeur in the kitchen with a knife, recalling that the boy had said that if he did not get his way he would kill La Valeur just as his father had killed his uncle Baillet. D'Ostun was followed by his wife, who denied that she knew anything about the crime whatsoever.

The next day, to prevent the accused from concocting among themselves consistent stories about the murders of Baillet and Neugot, Odinelle, D'Ostun, Gentilhomme, and Pailley were placed in solitary confinement. Jacquot and Millière gave the jailer explicit orders to let no one whomsoever speak to the prisoners. For a time no such sanctions—and humiliation—were imposed on Giroux. However, so numerous were the people, and not just Giroux family members, milling in and out of the jailhouse visiting the imprisoned president that the court ordered the jailer to restrict visits only to close kin, and even then only in the presence of the jailer. To secure the order, the court posted an armed guard there.

On 17 July Pailley, Saint Denis's widow, was questioned. She said that her husband had never spoken to her about the disappearance of Baillet, and that on the night of the supposed murder Saint Denis had eaten dinner with her and, after going out for a while, been home with her by about 10 o'clock. She defiantly added that anyone who said otherwise was a liar. She said she had seen the room of the supposed murder, but like D'Ostun had seen no evidence of a bloody assassination. The commissioners must have been dismayed by the rest of what she had to say too, as she recanted all her earlier testimony that had incriminated Giroux. Saying that she loved the house of Giroux, she now denied that Philippe Giroux had anything to do with the death of her husband, or with the supposed irregular autopsy. Furthermore, she denied being reluctant to eat at Giroux's house for fear of being poisoned. She told the commissioners that she had said all these untruthful things in earlier testimony only out of anger. All of this must have troubled the interrogators trying to secure evidence for a conviction, but perhaps not as much as what Pailley said next: that Pierre Saumaise de

Chasans, Giroux's implacable enemy, had tried to bribe her into giving testimony against Giroux. The man who had approached her in Saumaise's name, with money in hand, backed up the enticement by telling her that Giroux had killed her husband as well as "seven or eight" others.

Next it was the priest Marchand's turn. He held no surprises for Jacquot and Millière, however, merely confirming what he had already said. Two days after the first monitoire about the disappearance of Baillet and Neugot was issued in November 1639, Marie Rousselotte had come to him and made a declaration about it. Since it was a "negative" one (unfortunately, we never do learn what the declaration actually said), he gave it to the dean of the parish church of Saint Jean rather than to the clerk of the court. The next day, he recalled, Madames de Lisle and Regnault appeared on his doorstep with the servant Eleanore Cordier asking for the declaration. The women said that it was all based on hearsay, and since Rousselotte was "a fool and an idiot," it was totally untrustworthy. The women must not have believed the priest when he said he no longer had the document, for shortly thereafter Pierre Bouvot de Lisle and Antoine Chuttin, Giroux's attorney and solicitor, came to Marchand demanding that he turn it over to them. Through all this testimony the priest offered no information to the commissioners about what was in the declaration, or what eventually became of it.

Before the commissioners heard Pailley and Marchand, they had asked for and received from the court an order limiting visitors to Giroux's cell only to close family members. By this the president was now denied access to his attorney, Pierre Bouvot de Lisle. Giroux protested the very next day that this order violated his rights to legal representation. Moreover, he complained that he distrusted the jailer, who he feared would eavesdrop on any conversations with his family and leak them to his enemies. Apparently, his protest was ignored.

Giroux himself, finally, was interrogated at length on 10 August. This is what he had to say. Armed with reams of depositions which Giroux had not seen, and by law was not permitted to see, the commissioners launched their questions. When asked the standard question, "Why are you a prisoner?," he responded that he had no idea, but could not be in prison for any crimes he might have committed, since he had committed none. He knew that the commissioners had alleged that he had, and had tried to assemble a case against him, but the crime he was falsely accused of was absurd, too horrible to contemplate. The interrogators then shifted promptly to the role that Marie Fyot, Pierre Baillet's widow, might have played in the bloody affair. Giroux defended her innocence too. He denied being in love with her. He never said, he protested, that if she were a widow he would marry her. True, he was concerned for her health, as a good cousin should be, and he noted that she had been in ill health since the night of her wedding. Presumably Giroux was referring to the venereal disease she had contracted from her husband: he told the commissioners that Baillet was an evil man for having given the pox to so beautiful a woman.

Now the questions came concerning the role of Saint Denis in the alleged murder. Giroux defended him too, asserting that it was simply inconceivable for someone with such a mild and loyal disposition to have committed such a violent and heinous crime. Before the commissioners could fire another volley of questions, however, Giroux counterattacked. He charged that Millière was intimidating witnesses, coercing them into giving false testimony against Giroux. The reason was that Millière was an ally of Giroux's archenemy, Pierre Saumaise de Chasans. Undaunted, the commissioners continued the interrogation, one that must have taken several hours, if not all day to complete, judging from the pages upon pages that it takes up in the records. They inquired about the night of 6 September 1638. Giroux retorted that he had seen Baillet that day around 10 or 11 in the morning, recalling that he was dressed in grayish white "field clothes." Giroux added pointedly that his cousin wore a hat with a silver or white ribbon, not a black cord. On the subject of the hat, the commissioners pressed him at length, but Giroux was more than ready to rebuff their allegations. When they described the hat that had been stowed away in the trunk in Langres, Giroux pointed out that it was twelve years out of fashion and so could not have belonged to his cousin, a man of proper taste who never wore anything but the latest style.

Baillet, Giroux also pointed out, was not the only person to come to Giroux's house that day, or that evening for that matter. Because it was the night before Giroux's departure for a lengthy voyage to Rennes, there was a great deal of bustle about the household. People were everywhere—servants preparing for the trip, friends, allies, and family coming by, as was traditionally done, wishing him well and bidding him adieu. How strange that the commissioners could find no witnesses to corroborate his claim that he was not, in fact could not have been, alone with Baillet that night. Giroux alleged that favorable witnesses had been avoided by the commissioners, or intimidated into silence by his enemies. Clearly Giroux was suggesting, with some plausibility, that he was being framed.

Giroux continued: If Baillet had been killed in Giroux's bedchamber the night of 6 September, why did no neighbors hear the victim cry out? And if the bodies had been burned, as one witness alleged, why were there no traces on the Giroux premises? Moreover, both Baillet and his valet Neugot were, as Giroux put it, "strong and vigorous men," so why were there no cuts, no bruises, no signs at all on the supposed assailants as there surely must be in an attack that allegedly left two men dead? Giroux further pressed his attack on the commissioners' investigation, making one wonder who was being interrogated. Why did the authorities not seriously pursue the information known by several people—including Giroux himself—that Baillet had been planning a long trip to Italy or possibly to the king's court, and had reportedly been seen in Paris after 6 September? Giroux said that Baillet's widow and mother knew of this and had encouraged Baillet to make the trip, presumably because it offered the opportunity for Baillet to come up with some needed money. Baillet, Giroux pointed out, was in debt (he had Italian creditors and a certain Rollin was threatening him, and he had better make the trip if he wanted to live another month).

Baillet's wife, Marie Fyot, may have wished him out of town to spare her the presence of a boorish husband, and his mother, Jeanne Burgat, may have recognized that her son's life was at risk as long as his debts remained unpaid. The mother likely was not that sentimental, however. Both she and Marie said that they would not pay a penny to look for Baillet after his disappearance. Burgat and her son had just quarreled over his inheritance, and perhaps it was in anger that the most Burgat would do was write a letter to Giroux in Rennes—which she did—asking if Baillet and his valet had accompanied him there. The two women obviously were in no hurry to track down the man's whereabouts or initiate legal inquiries into his disappearance.

Many of Giroux's responses in this interrogation aimed at undermining the validity of the prosecution's case against him. We have already heard from many witnesses pointing toward Giroux's guilt, but perhaps Giroux was right, that favorable witnesses had been avoided and incriminating ones

intimidated. Now he laid grounds for suspecting others of killing Baillet
—perhaps an unpaid creditor?—while deflecting suspicion from himself.
Moreover, he directly and indirectly attacked the integrity of the officials
entrusted with the prosecution, as well as of the proceedings themselves.
The commissioner Millière could not be trusted because he was in league
with the president's inveterate enemy Saumaise de Chasans, in fact related
to him. Could reliable witnesses, Giroux openly wondered, ever be found
who had not first been intimidated or suborned? Or even bought, for Giroux
alleged that someone—no doubt he meant Saumaise—had put up 10,000£
to find and buy witnesses who would incriminate Giroux. Indeed, several
times Giroux alleged that Saumaise de Chasans was pulling strings behind
the scenes, corrupting the law and manipulating the course of the trial.

When the subject of Saint Denis's death came up, and Giroux was interrogated about it, the president said that Saumaise had spread the rumor
about Saint Denis being poisoned, and that Saumaise had even told the commissioners the lie directly. Why, Giroux asked, would he poison so faithful a
servant? Saint Denis's wife was pregnant at the time of her husband's death,
and Giroux intended to arrange a suitable godparent for the baby just as he
had done for an earlier child of Saint Denis. In December 1638 Saint Denis's
son Jacques was held at the baptismal font by the lawyer and future conseiller
at Parlement Jacques Bossuet, while the baby born to Pailley and Saint Denis
in January 1640 had Philippe Giroux's own son Henri as his godfather. The
commissioners pressed Giroux on Saint Denis's death nonetheless, asking
whether he had ordered an autopsy. Giroux said that Saint Denis's wife had
ordered it, and to convince the commissioners of the integrity of the autopsy, he pointed out that one of the attending officials was the prince of
Condé's personal physician.

Repeatedly throughout this seemingly endless interrogation Giroux
stressed a particular theme. Could anyone seriously contemplate that a man
of Philippe Giroux's station would commit such a crime? Does it not stag-
ger the imagination to even think that a presiding judge at the Parlement, a
man at the very summit of respectable society and among a handful of the
most powerful figures in the entire province, would consign one of his close
kin to such a dishonorable sepulcher as a latrine? The family's honor rendered such a notion utterly imponderable. Giroux returned again and again
to the notion of honor during this interrogation. His honor and that of his

family were the most important possessions, more precious than life itself, and this fact precluded the thought that he could have committed such a crime. This supposed "abominable assassination was a horror to nature," Giroux said, "violating the laws of blood and hospitality." No, Giroux proclaimed, he was not guilty, and it would take more than "hearsay and common rumor," more than "emblems and hieroglyphics" to convict a president of the sovereign court of Parlement.

Philippe Giroux's counterattack seems to have thrown the prosecuting authorities back on their heels. What stung them most was Giroux's aggressive denunciation of their integrity; they went directly to the king's Conseil Privé for redress. And they got it. On 30 October 1640 the royal council issued an *arrêt* demanding that Giroux henceforth comport himself "modestly towards the commissioners, rendering to them the honor that is their due." Giroux was specifically prohibited from "using any threats, irreverences, or useless words that had nothing to do with his defense," nor was he "to slander or threaten the witnesses under pain of summary conviction." If Giroux continued his abuse of the commissioners, they were specifically empowered to use all force necessary to see justice take its course. The Conseil Privé's order contained another provision, and this one revealed the anxiety that the authorities felt about the security of this illustrious prisoner's incarceration. The council ordered that Giroux be moved from the Parlement's jailhouse (called the *conciergerie*) to the fortified castle that loomed over the town of Dijon and provided for its defense in time of war. On 14 November the royal order was received in Parlement and read to Giroux. He was moved to the castle, where he would remain for the duration of the trial.

While the commissioners were calling upon the king to back Giroux down, by November 1640, when they returned from the three-month leave that the court took every year, they had compiled a list of more witnesses to be heard. Some of them had not yet given testimony and several were from the pinnacle of Burgundian society. Despite injunctions leveled at Giroux against intimidating witnesses, men and women came forward alleging that he was doing just that, especially to socially inferior and thus more vulnerable folk. By 17 November the commissioners were told that Giroux had tried to intimidate a former servant, Claude Lucia, nicknamed Champagne, who had given explosive testimony to Lantin a year before. Word around the

A detail from Bredin's map showing the fortified castle where
Giroux was imprisoned. Note the bridge crossing the deep moat.
As Giroux crossed this bridge en route to the Palais de Justice
for sentencing on 2 May and again on 8 May 1643, a throng of
people gathered by the moat to watch.

Giroux house was that Lucia and Eleanore Cordier were sexually intimate,
and the commissioners assumed that Cordier had trusted Lucia with what
she knew about the fates of Baillet and Neugot. It mattered little to Jacquot
and Millière that her trust was betrayed by Lucia, if indeed she had told him
anything, since he had been the first witness to share the bloody particulars
of what happened in the Giroux mansion on the night of 6 September 1638.
Because his source was Cordier, the commissioners strongly suspected that
she knew a great deal more than she had as yet let on. In any case, Lucia
alleged that in retribution for testifying against him, Giroux had accused
Lucia of theft, a crime for which Lucia knew he would hang if convicted.

The commissioners suspected that Giroux's treatment of Lucia was a
chilling message sent to others who might yet be tempted to come forward
with testimony against him. They heard other testimony that seemed to

confirm their suspicions. One witness reported that Françoise Pailley, Saint Denis's widow, had told him of her fears that "if she spoke against those who were the cause of the death of her husband, they would see her hanged for it." Likewise, Aymée Labarre told the commissioners that one time when she was in Notre Dame church in Dijon a man named Rousseau (whom she knew to be an acquaintance of Giroux's lawyer Bouvot de Lisle) sidled up to her and said under his breath that if she testified against Giroux she would find herself in prison or thrown out of town, but in either case ending up with a broken neck.

Nonetheless, there was no shortage of witnesses testifying against Giroux. Theirs were not the only voices heard, as several witnesses now came forward in November 1640 speaking in defense of Giroux's innocence. Odette Caset reported hearing that Baillet was alive and well and in Paris. The Damoiselle Guillemette Massol, the eighteen-year-old sister of Giroux's godmother Madame de Marcilly, defended Giroux too, saying that she had never heard him say anything against Baillet, nor knew of anything illicit going on between Giroux and Baillet's wife, Marie Fyot.

For Philippe Giroux, probably the most influential friendly witness to date was Claude Lénet, like Baillet a président in the Chambre des Comptes. He reported that about a week after Eleanore Cordier had been imprisoned in March 1640 he had accompanied Giroux to her cell in the conciergerie. There he heard Giroux counsel her to speak freely to the commissioners and thereby "clear her conscience." Giroux implored her not to let the fear of torture lead her to charge an innocent man with a crime that he did not commit, and to always remember that God is just. Lénet recalled Cordier's reply that she would speak her conscience, and her advice to her master to be on guard in turn because forces were being mounted against him. Two oratorian priests, she informed him, had just recently been sent to her in prison "to suborn her" into giving false testimony against Giroux. It would have been difficult for the commissioners to discount what Lénet had told them: he was the son of the prince of Condé's *secrétaire des commandements*, one of the highest officials in the prince's personal household, and the brother of Pierre Lénet, another of Condé's men and soon to be named the royal prosecutor general in the Parlement.

No sooner was favorable testimony recorded for Giroux than two damning witnesses came in, as this topsy-turvy case rolled on. Both were men

nearly as socially reputable as Lénet. First was a Franciscan friar, who repeated the account of Jacques Valon, a judge at the Parlement who had told
him a few days after Baillet's disappearance that he had seen Baillet with his
valet knocking on the door of Giroux's residence the evening before Giroux
departed for Rennes (that is, the evening of the supposed murder, 6 September 1638). Valon told the friar that he could not recall whether it was
before or after supper when he saw the two, but he did note that both men
were carrying swords. Valon was promptly called in by the commissioners,
and he confirmed what the friar had said, although his testimony differed
in some details. Valon pointed out that Baillet's valet was also carrying a
large club, and where the friar had said that he had spoken with Valon at the
judge's home, Valon remembered that the men had had the conversation in
the street in front of the courthouse. Valon recounted how they had chatted
about this and that, and how the monk had asked Valon what many people
in town must have been asking everyone else: what news he may have had
of Baillet's whereabouts.

Conflicting testimony, from ostensibly reputable witnesses. What were
the commissioners to make of it all? If the testimonies against Giroux were
trustworthy, then they had good reason at least to keep Giroux in custody.
No right of *habeas corpus* was yet the law, and so men and women accused of
a crime could be held indefinitely if the judges believed there was probable
cause. As yet in November 1640, however, there still was no concrete evidence that a crime had even been committed. No bodies had been found, so
how could anyone be sure that anyone had been murdered? Without corpus
delicti no conviction for homicide was legally possible. The commissioners
and the royal advocate general decided to do the only thing they could do to
eventually gain conviction, and that was to keep Giroux right where he was,
in prison, and look for more witnesses who could give them clues to break
the case. So on 1 December 1640 the advocate general de Xaintonge asked
that yet another monitoire be published.

Recall that a monitoire was a religious as much as a judicial document
because it required anyone knowing anything about the matter stipulated
in the monitoire to come forward with testimony or suffer eternal damnation. Now, de Xaintonge could not simply request a monitoire every so often
for the same cause just to smoke out recalcitrant witnesses. Rather, the law
stated that new monitoires could be published only if new evidence had

been uncovered, so it was illegal in this case simply to announce that anyone knowing anything about Baillet's disappearance should come forward. Thus what de Xaintonge fastened upon in this monitoire was suspicion about a poisonous powder that had been made in the town of Avalon by Giroux's personal physician, Lazare Rhodot, which reputedly had been tried on a dog and had killed it.

The monitoire was announced, and in January 1641 we begin to hear witnesses with something to say about poison. The first was Huguette Jonchart, a seventeen-year-old domestic servant in the household of Philippe Giroux's mother-in-law, Marguerite Brulart. She came forward on 25 January and told of when, five or six days before Pentecost in the late spring of 1638, Giroux had left several of his servants in the charge of Brulart for a fortnight, a not unusual arrangement among family. One of these servants was Saint Denis. Jonchart recalled that one evening Brulart, the mother of the first president at Parlement, was dining and asked her lackey to serve her some wine from an open bottle on the nearby sideboard. He did, and no sooner did she taste it than she spat it out and railed at the lackey, "Rogue! You've poisoned me!" She then began retching, crying out that her stomach was burning. Loyal servants rushed in, and several tasted the wine as well. The first, Brulart's lady-in-waiting Jeanne Barbier, became sick almost immediately after swallowing a tainted sip. Others followed, all feeling ill and saying that their insides burned. Brulart, having recovered slightly, ordered that the whole stock of wine be taken to the family wine merchant for immediate testing. He reported that the wine was fine, not spoiled at all. Upon this news, suspicion of poisoning fell upon the guests in the Brulart household, and above all upon Saint Denis.

Jonchart testified that during the time Saint Denis had been in the Brulart residence, when he was not occupied with the debaucheries he was so fond of (more than one witness had spoken of Saint Denis's predilection for loose women and drink), he spent a great deal of time in the kitchen. Jonchart said that she and others suspected Saint Denis of adulterating various dishes. Some of the servants had become sick even before the attempt on Madame Brulart, the unfortunate Barbier from a pot of stew. So suspicious of Saint Denis was the staff that they tested everything coming out of the kitchen, and once had found a bowl of soup destined for Madame Brulart to be laced with poison. Another witness was the thirty-year-old cook in

Brulart's household, Claudine Virot. She confirmed Jonchart's story about the poisoned soup, saying that she too had vomited after tasting it. She also noted that Saint Denis hung about the kitchen in the mornings quite often, once asking which of the pots of food were destined for Madame Brulart's table.

Such suspicion was fueled by the animosity that the servants saw between Giroux and his mother-in-law. Shortly after the attempt on Brulart's life with the poisoned wine, she understandably banished Saint Denis from her home. Her son-in-law, offended, paid her a visit. He sarcastically inquired, "What, is this house haunted?" To which she coldly replied, "Yes, just like the wine someone gives me every day." Giroux retorted with an angry smirk, "Good God, Madame, do you take me for a wine servant?" Brulart said nothing to that, but ordered him from her house, forbidding him ever to return.

Madame Brulart's lackey and her lady-in-waiting rounded out the story. The lackey Gerard Sauvageot, another of those loyal servants who dutifully tasted the tainted wine, remembered how it burned his throat. Jeanne Barbier, the lady-in-waiting, spoke of tainted meat dishes, poisoned soup, and laced wine. She added that when Giroux visited Madame Brulart after she had expelled Saint Denis from her house, she heard him tell her that it pained him to visit her and that he only did so to "show society" that he was a good son-in-law. The encounter quickly went sour, and as Jonchart had already reported, he was ordered out of the house and forbidden ever to return.

After all the servants had been heard, the great lady herself came forward. On 6 February 1641 Marguerite Brulart declared that she never suspected anyone but Saint Denis of trying to poison her, but that upon his death she forgave him for it. Brulart was renowned for her piety, and so such a magnanimous gesture seemed credible to the commissioners. Given her stature in the community, they would have been disposed to believe her in any case, and probably found truthful what she told them about the unpleasant encounter with Giroux. Giroux had told her, she testified, that he was the reason why her son, Pierre Le Goux de La Berchere, had been relieved of his duties as first president. This is a puzzling revelation at first glance, although it does help to account for the simmering animosity between mother-in-law and son-in-law. Recall that in the fall of 1637 the prince of Condé had exiled the first president for having little control over the Parlement and specifically for being unable or unwilling to push through several edicts that Cardinal Richelieu and King Louis XIII wanted the Parlement to support. It is completely plausible that Giroux had counseled Condé to sack the first president, because Giroux was by then trying to distance himself from the Le Goux de La Berchere clan, once the darlings of Condé but now out of favor. Giroux's former wife, Marie Le Goux de La Berchere, was dead by the time of her brother's suspension and exile (she died in October 1636). By the spring of 1638, the time of the reputed attempts on Marguerite Brulart's life, the first president was in exile. Was his mother-in-law next, and was the visit to her after the failed attempt on her life by poisoned wine just what Giroux supposedly said it was, a cover for society, an instance of doing what a good son-in-law should? At any rate, Madame Brulart testified that she said the following to Giroux during the visit: "Since you hold such poison in your heart [for the Le Goux de La Berchere family], why do you come here?" His reply, she reported, was that it was only for show. To this she rejoined, "Come here no more."

On 10 March 1641 Giroux was called upon to respond to these statements. Predictably he denied everything, adding that such false testimony was orchestrated by his enemies. He did address specifically the charge by Madame Brulart that he had acknowledged being responsible for the dismissal of her son from the first presidency. He protested that he was still loyal to his in-laws, and even after Condé withdrew his support from the Le Goux clan, to the point of once denying Madame Brulart access to the prince's personal physician when she had fallen ill, it was Giroux who stood by her and provided her with the best possible medical attention.

While poison occupied the attention of some witnesses, the commissioners, following normal legal procedure, were also busy bringing Giroux into "confrontation" with the other prisoners, Eleanore Cordier, Forest Netard, Denise Gentilhomme, Bernard D'Ostun, Françoise Pailley, and Claude Froul. As in any criminal trial, each witness was asked to confirm what he or she had said, then Giroux was given the opportunity to comment on what he could only surmise was in the testimony, for he like any defendant had no legal right to read or hear the witness before the confrontation. Given the gravity of the crime and the status of the accused, the commissioners decided to depart from the normal procedure that kept the accused forever in the dark, electing instead to actually read the testimony to him, but only after the "confrontation." This took a great deal of time and indeed concentration on Giroux's part, when we consider that Cordier's testimony alone ran to more than twenty pages.

Even with the break from traditional procedure, Giroux still had to guess at what was in the testimony and respond before hearing it, and given such uncertainty Giroux stayed on safe ground. He challenged none of the witnesses, in hopes that their testimony would be favorable to him. Indeed it was, especially that of Pailley, the widow of Saint Denis, who reported that she herself had ordered and paid for the autopsy of her husband, not Giroux as the commissioners were inclined to believe. In fact, Pailley went on, Giroux's enemy Saumaise de Chasans had wanted her to insinuate to the commissioners that her "husband was opened by the order of Giroux," so that the president could cover up the cause of death. The commissioners then scrutinized an autopsy report that had been signed by the attending physicians and surgeon and discovered that it had indeed been ordered by Pailley. According to the report, an inflammation of the liver and "flux" of the stomach were caused by a continuous fever that after two weeks had eventually taken the life of Saint Denis. The report said nothing of poison, and nothing of Giroux.

Giroux, as we have seen before, seized upon every opportunity to attack the integrity of the judicial authorities, and on 10 February he did so again, boldly ignoring the orders from the king's Conseil Privé explicitly forbidding it. This time he lashed out at the advocate general Pierre de Xaintonge, saying that he was untrustworthy because he was a kinsman of Saumaise, that he was a man of evil conscience. He capped his diatribe with a shocking allegation, that de Xaintonge was a pimp for his wife. Giroux was sure that de Xaintonge wished him dead, and alleged that he was only involved in the present case for the money, just as he was in all the others that he pursued in his official capacity, including the notorious case against the Maréchal Louis de Marillac. The reference to Marillac implied that de Xaintonge was no stranger to rigged criminal trials: de Marillac had been convicted and beheaded in 1631, allegedly for embezzlement of funds from the army, but everyone knew that he was eliminated because he had become an enemy of Cardinal Richelieu. De Xaintonge was one of fourteen judges from the Parlement of Dijon called to Paris by the king to deliver Marillac to his fate.

Even with new testimony, the two commissioners and the fourteen judges at the "rump" Parlement did not have enough to gain a conviction, since they still had no bodies. So on 15 March 1641 they ordered the commissioners to make a thorough search of Giroux's premises—house, garden, the space beneath the walls, the latrines, the cellars, everywhere—and to draw up a detailed report. The report does not survive, but since the case against Giroux stalled at this point, it seems that nothing incriminating was found.

Eyes beyond Burgundy had been closely scrutinizing the unfolding of this case and now, perhaps frustrated by the impasse, they moved to action. On 2 May King Louis XIII intervened, demanding that all records of the case compiled so far be sent to him for review. The royal advocate general de Xaintonge was then ordered by a dutiful Parlement to gather it all together and send it forthwith to the king's chancellor.

Meanwhile in Dijon, even though there was no break in the case that would carry it toward conviction, the authorities still would not release the prisoner. Hopeful for that break, they piled up even more testimony, and it gives us cause to wonder about the fairness of the proceedings, as Giroux did, that they appear to have been interested only in hearing witnesses favorable to the prosecution. This simply confirmed for Giroux that the court had been captured by his enemies. He must have been deeply dismayed when on 5 July 1641 the court received but did nothing about Giroux's written request for release from prison. He was confident that the prosecution had no case, said so in his request, and demanded to be set free. Rather than release him, however, the court ruled the very same day not only that Giroux would remain in prison, but that it would not call any of the witnesses from a list of names Giroux had drawn up and submitted to the commissioners. One of these potential witnesses was Philippe Giroux's own father, Benoît.

Ostensibly the court was following the king's orders, that it must only hear testimony directly relating to the case and not be bothered by Giroux's bringing forward information that was "useless" or diverting. Giroux may have anticipated this, for in early August he submitted another list of witnesses whom he wished to have the commissioners hear, including such distinguished names that the court could hardly ignore the request. Giroux asked that the judges Claude Bossuet and his son Jacques be heard, along with the judges Dumay, Potet, de Maugey, Pouffier, Comeau, Bouhier, Le Goux, de Berbisey, and Catin. That Giroux expected such illustrious men to speak on his behalf may not resolve for us the question of his guilt or innocence, but it does suggest how divided the urban aristocracy was.

Curiously, no record survives of any testimony that these men may have given to the commissioners, even though on 9 August 1641 the court formally received Giroux's request. Did the commissioners simply not act upon it? Or have the records been lost or misplaced? It is impossible to say, but it does seem to modern eyes, from the proceedings in general, that to the prosecuting officials Giroux was obviously guilty and the trial was about amassing evidence to support a foregone conclusion. It is true that the judicial adage "innocent until proven guilty" undergirding modern, western systems of justice was foreign to Giroux's era, but the fact remains that within procedure at that time one could not just incarcerate a man and let him molder in jail forever. If conviction could not be gained in a "reasonable" amount of time, then release from custody was expected. The court could rule the case "out of court," which was tantamount to acquittal. This is, no doubt, what Giroux hoped for when he requested release from jail. If no conclusive case could be mustered but the judges still believed that the accused might be guilty, another option was to release the prisoner *jusqu'à rappel*, or sometimes *plus amplement informé*. That is, the accused would be released from prison but was subject to rearrest at any time if additional, sufficient evidence turned up. Giroux, as a judge trained in law and experienced on the court, certainly had every right to expect this option at the very least. He had seen his colleagues on the bench rule in precisely this way many times. Yet he remained in jail. What other conclusion could he draw than that justice was being corrupted by his enemies?

Giroux had a specific enemy in mind—Pierre Saumaise de Chasans, whom he had good reason to suspect for wishing him ill. Just as the prosecution's case seemed to be flagging, Saumaise actively entered the case. By July 1641 he had been a *partie instigante* for more than a year, but had done little to move the prosecution forward. Now, on the 8th of that month, three days after Giroux asked to be set free and on Marie Fyot's thirty-third birthday, Saumaise submitted a request to the commissioners. He demanded that Giroux answer to the charge that Saumaise had set aside money for buying witnesses.

In August the court adjourned for its annual leave of three months, and with no activity in the case now possible, Giroux could only gaze from the high windows of the castle across a town and a people over which only months before he had ruled. He could only yearn for his freedom now, and ponder how suddenly one could plunge from the summit of society to this, a prison where he faced charges for which, if proven, he would die. If this state of affairs were not bad enough for the president, in November two of Giroux's household servants for whose arrest warrants were outstanding were apprehended in Paris and brought under armed guard to Dijon, to stand trial as accomplices in the murders of Pierre Baillet and Philibert Neugot. Pierre Borel, twenty-nine, called Devilliers, was one of Giroux's personal valets, and Philippe LaQuille, fourteen, was one of his lackeys. From an interrogation of Devilliers in late November the authorities learned nothing—Devilliers was a hardened man with little fear of the law, as we will have ample opportunity to see later—but LaQuille gave them ever more reason to keep Giroux locked up in the castle.

LaQuille reported that he was at Giroux's house on the night of 6 September 1638. Although he himself never saw Baillet and his valet there, later a domestic servant of Giroux's named Philiberte told him that they had been. This Philiberte, whoever she was, had quite a tale to tell LaQuille. She said that Giroux had invited Baillet over to play a game of *piquet*, and while Baillet was seated at the gaming table, Saint Denis circled behind him, threw a rope around his neck, and strangled him. Baillet's valet rushed to his master's aid, and for the effort was killed as well. The bodies were then dumped in the privy. Giroux, according to this story, then hired a mason to brick it up—at night and without a torch. The mason suspected foul play, and when he glimpsed some human feet protruding upward from the bottom of the privy he refused to do the work. Giroux reportedly threatened to kill him on the spot, so the mason completed the job. The mason later told his wife that he continued to fear for his life, fully expecting Giroux to poison him somehow.

LaQuille's testimony, explicit as it was about the alleged murder, was still based on hearsay, so the commissioners were no closer to conviction. Leaving Giroux in prison, they shifted their attention to Lazare Rhodot, Giroux's personal physician, who was implicated in many of the attempts at poison that surfaced in more than one witness's testimony.

CHAPTER 7

Poison

Allegations of poisoning flew about this trial. So many fingers pointed toward Philippe Giroux as the instigator that at one point Giroux, with obvious exasperation, issued a sarcastic protest to the commissioners: a lot of people get sick and die in this town, but does that mean he poisoned all of them? Giroux's cries of innocence fell on deaf ears in any case, and the authorities, following the trail of poison, tightened their grip on Giroux by circling ever closer to him by way of his closest associates. In 1640 they zeroed in on Lazare Rhodot.

Rhodot was Philippe Giroux's personal physician, a trained and licensed medical doctor from the Burgundian town of Avallon, about a day's ride northwest from Dijon. Rhodot's ties to the Giroux clan were secure. Philippe's sister Barbe stood as godmother to the doctor's second-born son, Jacques, on 25 April 1636. The godfather, incidentally, was Jacques Fyot, conseiller at Parlement, the lord of Vaugimois—and Marie Fyot's blood brother. Almost exactly a year earlier, Rhodot's first son Henri also had a Giroux godparent, this time Philippe's own son Henri (never mind that he was only about five months old at the time). Moreover, Philippe Giroux's wife Marie Le Goux de La Berchere was baby Rhodot's godmother.

Ironically, what in 1635 or 1636 had to have been considered a spiritual alliance that locked Rhodot into a powerful network in the province by 1640 left him isolated and vulnerable. On 8 November 1640 the noose began to tighten around the doctor's neck. The advocate general Pierre de Xaintonge began formal proceedings against him on suspicion of complicity to murder with poison.

To suspect Rhodot of poisoning contravened a dominant cultural current of the time, for the crime of poisoning was usually associated with women. Ever since antiquity people had assumed an affinity between women and poison, because poison was almost always administered through food or drink, and the preparation of these was historically and culturally the responsibility of the woman. Moreover, poison as a murder weapon required no physical strength, only secrecy and duplicity, often thought of as feminine characteristics. It is no accident that the crime of poisoning was often linked to witchcraft (also often, though not exclusively, a feminine crime), and during Giroux's lifetime more women went to their deaths for witchcraft—by definition a crime of secrecy and duplicity—than at any other time in European history. Witches supposedly often killed by administering evil potions—poison. This was, after all, the age of a massive witch hunt in which upwards of 100,000 people were tried for witchcraft in the courts of law and at least 30,000 were executed in western and central Europe between 1560 and 1650. About 80 percent of those sent to the stake were women.

But suspect Rhodot they did. The first allegation against Rhodot came from Jeanne de La Place, a twenty-five-year-old lady-in-waiting who had served Philippe Giroux's wife Marie Le Goux de La Berchere from 1634 until her mistress's death two years later. She reported that Philippe Giroux's "doctor Rhodot" was about the house frequently, often meeting with Giroux secretly in the president's bedchamber. Once, she recalled, Rhodot came down into the kitchen, and with other servants including Saint Denis present said that he wanted a skillet in which to make a drug. After mixing up the concoction, de La Place told of how the doctor fed it to a little dog. The dog's eyes rolled back into its head, she vividly remembered, and three hours later it was dead. Another witness, Giroux's domestic servant Henriette Boudrot, confirmed what de La Place had said so far, adding that the dead dog had been unceremoniously pitched into the Suzon, the stream that flowed through Dijon and passed directly behind the Giroux residence.

In a rambling, lengthy testimony, de La Place also recounted how she overheard a quarrel between Philippe and his wife Marie shortly after their son Henri had been born in 1634. For no reason that de La Place could detect or was willing to reveal, Philippe had blasted his wife's family. He raged that he would poison her mother (Marguerite Brulart) and her brother (the first president Pierre Le Goux de La Berchere), even destroy her entire family line. Where de La Place went next in her testimony suggests that Marie herself was targeted, and that poison was the weapon. During his wife's illness before her death, Philippe Giroux had sent away her personal physician, a man named Sineau, and called in his own—Lazare Rhodot. De La Place told in 1640 of how a week or so before Marie died in October 1636 her mistress had told her that her doctors could not determine what her illness was, although she vomited a great deal. Vomiting, of course, was a telltale symptom of poisoning.

The trail on Rhodot seemed to cool right after de La Place's testimony in the spring, but come autumn it heated up again. On 8 November 1640 a dozen witnesses were heard, each having something to say about Lazare Rhodot and poison. The first to be heard in this round of testimony was Étienne Filsjean, a man from a well-respected family firmly entrenched in the robe nobility and a royal officer at the Chambre des Comptes. Filsjean promptly informed the authorities of having heard from Rhodot's assistant, a man named Hugues Reposeur, that Rhodot was a "great poisoner." Reposeur reportedly told Filsjean that Rhodot had once tried to poison a fellow medical doctor named Imbert, although he did not say why. Filsjean concluded by saying he had heard that Rhodot once killed a dog with poison.

Zachaire Imbaut, the next witness, apparently talked with Reposeur too: Reposeur had told him, he testified, that Rhodot had wanted to poison Reposeur himself (although Reposeur gave no indication why). Like Filsjean, Imbaut also said he had heard by common rumor that Rhodot had poisoned a dog, adding that it belonged to a peasant named Bodache. Impressive in their thoroughness, the authorities tracked down Nicolas Bodache, and sure enough he confirmed that his dog had died, violently. The word was that his dog had been poisoned, but, he added, he had no idea who had done it. He did say that Reposeur had told him not to inquire further about the matter, to leave well enough alone if he knew what was good for him. An apothecary from Avallon named Guillaume Curé then came forward with his own tale about this doctor Rhodot. In addition to having heard from his grandmother, he recounted, that Reposeur had described Rhodot as "worthless," Rhodot had several times come to his shop and purchased sublimé, a key ingredient in poisonous concoctions.

Many people seemed to know about Rhodot's penchant for whipping up poisons, and now Nicolas Ramonet, the next witness, had a similar story to relate. Again the key intermediary was Reposeur, the loose-lipped assistant to Rhodot, who told Ramonet that even though Ramonet and Rhodot had patched up some unspecified differences they had had, Ramonet had nonetheless best be on his guard with Rhodot. Reposeur warned him that Rhodot never forgave and never forgot, and had a poison that was foolproof in its deadliness. Moreover, unlike sublimé and arsenic, this one supposedly left no traces.

De Xaintonge believed that he had enough evidence of wrongdoing to issue a warrant for the arrest of Rhodot. On 16 November he did so, and while he was at it he ordered that Reposeur be picked up as well. By the 26th Reposeur was in custody, although Rhodot remained at large. Reposeur, who was thirty-three and called himself a surgeon, was promptly interrogated, and directly countering Filsjean's allegations, he denied that he had ever seen any poison on Rhodot's premises.

While de Xaintonge was looking for Rhodot, he discovered that the doctor had a trail of alleged criminal activities beyond poison. Rhodot, so some would say, was also a counterfeiter and a blasphemer. Two witnesses came forward in May 1641 with information about Rhodot's ties to a counterfeiting ring that was turning out bogus coins. Counterfeiting the king's currency was a capital offense (in the sixteenth century the convicted felon would be boiled in molten lead), so such an allegation was serious indeed. As de Xaintonge gathered testimony that linked Rhodot with poison and counterfeiting, he heard the lawyer Edme Borot bring up another crime in connection with the doctor, a crime that is perhaps not so severe as counterfeiting or homicide to modern eyes but was to some men and women of the seventeenth century—and certainly according to the law of the time. Borot recalled how he, Rhodot, and a man named Mailly were strolling along the ramparts of Dijon one evening when the conversation turned toward religion. Borot was stunned to hear Rhodot say that there were three charlatans in the world: Moses, Mohammed, and most shockingly Jesus Christ. Borot reported that he had been scandalized and upbraided Rhodot for such talk, that it was a "great impiety," but that Rhodot continued his blasphemy undaunted. Christian teaching, the doctor shamelessly proclaimed, had it that Jesus had performed miracles, but in fact each of those attributed to him could just as well have occurred naturally. Outraged, Borot promptly left the impious Rhodot and Mailly to themselves.

During the winter of 1640–41 de Xaintonge and the commissioners Jacquot and Millière scoured the province searching for Rhodot. On 14 April the Lord Jean Mortaine, the *controlleur ordinaire des guerres* for the king in Burgundy, reported to them that Rhodot had taken refuge with the count of Commarin in the count's castle scarcely twenty miles from Dijon, and that the count had refused to turn the doctor over to him. His whereabouts now uncovered, for the next month Rhodot was on the move. Then, on 20 May, the provost of the southwest Burgundian town of Autun informed the commissioners and de Xaintonge that he had nabbed the doctor in Bussière, a village in the forested region fifty miles west of Dijon called the Morvan. Rhodot had temporarily found refuge there in the home of the baron of Esguilly. We do not know much about either the count of Commarin or the baron of Esguilly, but it certainly would not be surprising to find that they were part of Giroux's extensive network of friends and allies. Whoever they were, they ultimately could not keep Rhodot from the clutches of the law, and on 20 May the doctor was taken into custody and brought to Dijon.

Five days later Lazare Rhodot was interrogated in Dijon. He apparently felt no compunction to explain why he was carrying a substantial amount of cash on him when he was apprehended (five Spanish *pistoles* and nine golden écus, in all more than a simple artisan might make in a year), but he became quite defensive about the poisonous drugs that were found on his person, protesting that he could explain the usage and the properties of these drugs. Vitriol and mercury, for example, he said were for treating venereal disease and for killing worms in babies. He noted that in any case it was not a crime for a doctor to have poisons, and that if he had purchased them from an apothecary, it was only to make medicinal cures. Of course, he denied that he was guilty of any wrongdoing.

De Xaintonge, not convinced of Rhodot's innocence, requested that other doctors and apothecaries be called in to examine the suspicious "powders" found in Rhodot's possession at the time of his arrest. While de Xaintonge was trying to confirm a case of poisoning against Rhodot, another crime in the doctor's wake attracted his attention just as much as poison and even more than the allegations of fake coins or sacrilegious musings about miracles. De Xaintonge discovered that Rhodot had been previously investigated for this crime, and tried for it a few years before. This crime was infanticide. On 17 June de Xaintonge obtained from the Parlement an order reopening the case, and with this accusation of infanticide he also brought formal charges of poisoning, counterfeiting, and impiety. Then de Xaintonge promptly began hearing more testimony, specifically about the crime of infanticide.

By reopening this case, de Xaintonge trod on thin legal ice, for the trial in which Rhodot was accused of the crime before had been dismissed, and to overturn an acquittal was of questionable legality, even before modern legal systems came to protect the accused from what came to be called double jeopardy. On 19 January 1634 the criminal chamber of the Parlement of Burgundy, called the Tournelle, had thrown a case of infanticide against Rhodot "out of court," effectively acquitting him. Had the judges at the time suspected that he might have been guilty but that insufficient evidence had been marshaled to prove it, they could have ruled the case temporarily closed, to be reopened if additional incriminating evidence were presented. They did not do this, suggesting that the judges were convinced that Rhodot was innocent. Perhaps so, but as we have seen, Rhodot was soon to be inserted in the Giroux entourage in 1634, and in that year both Benoît and Philippe Giroux sat as judges in Parlement. Let us not forget that the Giroux clan was at the height of its power and influence at that time, and power and influence, it would not be too difficult to imagine, may have had something to do with Rhodot's acquittal. Power and influence, or the lack of it, may also have had something to do with the reopening of the case in 1641, for now the house of Giroux was collapsing, and its allies like Rhodot could count on no help from it.

Perhaps this turn in the power constellation in Burgundy emboldened de Xaintonge to seek from Parlement annulment of the sentence of 1634. This opened the door to try Rhodot again for, among other crimes, infanticide. Testimony began in the summer of 1641. Claudine Disier, a neighbor of Rhodot in Avallon, remembered how on one night in May 1632 (her memory was faulty, for it was actually 1633) the doctor had come to her door with a small newborn in his arms. He told Disier that he needed her to breast-feed the baby. Disier recalled how little the infant was—no more than three pounds—that it had scratches on its head, and that its umbilical cord had not yet been tied. Rhodot told her nothing about the parents of the child, but the common rumor, she testified, was that the mother was a nun.

Josèphe Filsjean recalled in her testimony a comment by Rhodot that the baby was an unwanted product of an affair between a gentleman and a noblewoman and that it had been abandoned just after birth. Moreover, the baby had been clumsily delivered—hence the scratches and bruises on its head. Filsjean was skeptical of Rhodot's story about the baby's supposed parents, for she confirmed what Disier had said, that according to the rumor about town the mother was a nun. She added that everyone thought the father was Rhodot himself, who was said to have frequented the Ursuline convent of Saint Léonard in Avallon to see the nun, presumably to carry on the affair which eventually produced the baby.

On the trail of the nun and the convent now, the authorities found a servant who had worked at the convent. Sure enough, Françoise Chouart confirmed that Rhodot did indeed come to the convent often, and frequently even got the key to the stables from her. Although Chouart did not openly say so, the clear implication was that the doctor and his lover quite literally rolled in the hay more than once. She concluded her testimony by reporting the common rumor that a newborn had been left on the doorstep of the convent and then taken away. By whom she did not say.

When a person died a coroner's report was drawn up and the attending physician was called upon to determine the cause of death. On 1 June 1633, the day the infant in question died, such a report was produced. It stated matter-of-factly that the child who turned up on the preceding 21 May had been found dead in its cradle. A man named Imbaut (the Zachaire Imbaut who testified against Rhodot concerning poison?) and a midwife named Darion apparently discovered the corpse in the home of Disier. The midwife believed, she told the coroner, that the child had not been carried full term by the mother and that its premature birth had been induced. She could not say how, but she knew, as most women of the time did, that certain "medicines" could abort a fetus or induce a premature birth. This cast a suspicious shadow across Rhodot, a doctor who would have had easy access to such medicines. This child, she went on, was smaller than normal children who were birthed full term.

The coroner recorded all of this, and more. His report added that the child's head was misshapen, bearing open, infected wounds that oozed pus. The midwife said that the deep cuts on the head had probably been caused by the mother's pubic bone during delivery as the baby passed through the birth canal. She also told the coroner, noting what may or may not have been an indication of head trauma—which is what the coroner thought the cause of death was—that on the day before its death the baby had vomited a great deal.

Were the testimony and the coroner's report enough to prove murder? Evidently not. Tragically, many babies died shortly after birth in that time (between a quarter and a third of all babies born alive in seventeenth-century Europe died before their first birthday), and so to distinguish between natural death and murder was notoriously difficult in the seventeenth century. By definition, infanticide was likely to be committed in total secrecy, with no witnesses. An unmarried woman in desperate straits might conceal an accidental pregnancy, the better to hide the fate of an unwanted child and protect her own honor. A woman's honor was inseparably linked to her value in the marriage market, in which virginity was prized and fathers sought to advance the family's status by having their daughters marry men further up the social ladder.

Of course, taking the life of an unwanted infant was no easy step for a woman—no matter how desperate—and that some women did it shows how despairing women trapped in this tragic net must have felt. Still, infanticide did occur, of that we can be sure. The authorities were convinced that it occurred more often than was being prosecuted. In 1556 the king of France, Henri II, issued an edict that any unmarried woman who became pregnant must declare her pregnancy at once to the authorities or be accused of intent to commit infanticide if the concealed pregnancy were brought to light. In other words, concealed pregnancy was prima facie evidence of intent to kill one's child. This law was continually repeated by edict for the next century and a half.

Although the authorities clearly thought that infanticide was a common crime, because of its secretive nature historians cannot be so sure. Given the historical record that survives, all we can assume is that cases of infanticide were more numerous than the recorded criminal trials of those who got caught. Pity the few who did get caught, though, for their stories are heart-rending. Listen to the pathetic and bizarre story of Hélène Gillet, the daughter of the noble *châtelain* of the Burgundian town of Bourg-en-Bresse. Only eight years before the child linked to Rhodot and the nun died, Gillet found herself impregnated by a priest. Terrified of her father's reaction, she concealed the pregnancy and then reportedly suffocated the newborn. She was apprehended, tried, and ultimately condemned to death by Dijon's Parlement. Her execution was scheduled to take place in the square in Dijon, the Place du Morimont, where a permanent gallows stood. Gillet's noble blood spared her the indignity of hanging by the neck—she was to be honorably beheaded instead—but the executioner would bungle his job. As Gillet bared her frail neck, the executioner swung his broadsword—and missed, slashing Gillet's shoulder instead. When Gillet buckled under the misdirected blow the crowd, always present at an execution, stirred. The headsman's second blow missed high and gashed the back of Gillet's head, and the crowd exploded in sympathetic rage. Men and women in the crowd began pelting the headsman with stones. Rushing to her husband's aid, the executioner's wife tried to garrot Gillet, but prevented from finishing the prisoner off by a hail of stones now flung at her, she pulled out some scissors and tried to cut the poor girl's throat. Still Gillet did not die, and the crowd sensed that a miracle was occurring. They drove the headsman and his wife from the scaffold into the chapel beneath it (a grim place where the condemned heard their last rites), stormed the gallows, liberated the bloodied and dazed prisoner, and rushed her to a surgeon. Astonishingly, considering the extent of the wounds catalogued in the surgeon's report, Gillet survived. Parlement was prepared to see the execution carried out a few days later, and would have done so had not the king, Louis XIII, mercifully intervened with a pardon. Convinced that God had saved her life, Gillet dedicated the remainder of it to the Church by retiring to a convent in her native Bresse.

Gillet's case was notorious, and it must have given Rhodot pause if in fact he was guilty of infanticide. He may even have been present in the crowd that watched the executioner clumsily buffet Gillet. Still, he must have known that the crime was notoriously difficult to prove. Even if he had killed the baby that he and the nun had allegedly produced, he would no doubt have comforted himself had he known the improbability of being convicted of the crime. After all, between 1582 and 1726, only 3 percent of the caseload on the docket of the Parlement of Dijon involved charges of infanticide, and males were very rarely implicated and never punished as severely as the mother.

Before the case of infanticide leveled against Rhodot was dismissed in 1634, his story had been that an unnamed gentleman had asked him to take the baby because it was the product of an illicit affair with an unnamed marquise. Once the acquittal was handed down, however, Rhodot became more bold. Or so said some witnesses. Marie Minard, for example, recalled in 1641 how the doctor had made a big deal about the arrêt that acquitted him. Minard, like so many others, seemed to know better. She rebuked Rhodot, saying that the law might not be able to prove his guilt, but that God knew everything. (Given Rhodot's reported impiety, the warning may have had little effect.) Minard's sureness of Rhodot's culpability no doubt had everything to do with her knowledge of the trysts in the stable where doctor and nun supposedly met. Minard even knew the identity of the impregnated nun, Elisabeth de Saint Jean. Moreover, she recalled how Rhodot had told her in 1633 that he had tried to get the nun to take some "remedies" to abort the fetus.

Other witnesses also spoke confidently of Rhodot's paternity, if not his murder of the baby. Jean Minard reported hearing Rhodot confirm the rumors that the doctor was the father of the baby and that the mother was a nun. After the arrêt of acquittal was issued, Gabrielle Belot added, Rhodot had said openly at Madame de Marcilly's house in Dijon (recall that this woman was Giroux's godmother) that God was good and would pardon him, and that the infant was indeed a product of his sexual relations with an Ursuline nun. Olympe Massol confirmed this stark confession, adding that Rhodot had said he was unafraid to make it because he had a copy of the arrêt of acquittal in his possession.

Little did the doctor know at the time, but such cocky self-assurance would be held against him if witnesses reported it, and as we have now seen, they did. Ultimately, in May 1643 both Lazare Rhodot and Hugues Reposeur, after languishing in jail for two years, would hear their fate pronounced by Dijon's Parlement. On the 13th of that month, this is what the Parlement decreed:

> Seen by the court at the instigation and pursuit of [Jeanne] Burgat [mother of the deceased Pierre Baillet] . . . against . . . Lazare Rodot

[sic], doctor at Avalon [sic], prisoner . . . accused of impiety, of making poisons . . . , of having participated in poisonings . . . , of committing sacrilege, and also of making . . . false coinage; and [against] Hugues Reposeur . . . surgeon at Avalon, accused of having helped Rodot in the making of poisons . . . ; [also seen by the court is] testimony gathered in the town of Avalon by one of the commissioners as much on the composition of poisons sent to the town of Dijon as on the said poisonings, making . . . of false coinage, sacrilege, and infanticide. . . . Everything considered, THE COURT . . . sentences . . . Rhodot to life in chains in the king's galleys and 300£ fine payable to his majesty, . . . 500£ in damages to Burgat, and payment of court costs. The remainder of his goods will be confiscated. [The case against] Reposeur [is thrown] out of court.

It is likely that all the crimes of which Lazare Rhodot was accused — infanticide, poisoning, counterfeiting, and sacrilege — contributed to his conviction, although we cannot tell from the sentence which earned him the grim fate of pulling oars aboard the king's ships in the Mediterranean. It should be clear from the unfolding of the various legal proceedings to this point that judges had a great deal of latitude in disposing of criminal cases in seventeenth-century France. As we will see, there was a continual if unspoken tension between on the one hand royal legislation and articulated legal procedure and on the other hand the inclinations of a judge's "conscience," as it was put at that time, to pursue justice. This tension between absolutist kings gathering power to their person and judges intent on "legislating from the bench" and thereby sharing sovereignty with the Crown was a fundamental constitutional issue of the seventeenth century, and the trial of Philippe Giroux exposes it brilliantly. How the tension was resolved would also determine whether Philippe Giroux (or Lazare Rhodot, for that matter) would be judged guilty or not.

CHAPTER 8

Jailbreak

Philippe Giroux's personal physician Lazare Rhodot was jailed in the spring of 1641. His personal servants Devilliers and Philippe LaQuille soon joined him, caught six months later in Paris and brought to Dijon under arrest. By Christmas quite an array of the president's associates found themselves in custody, implicated in one of the greatest crimes of the century in Burgundy. The authorities had plenty of circumstantial evidence suggesting the guilt of Giroux and his people in the murder of Pierre Baillet and his valet Philibert Neugot. There were also many innuendos about the involvement of Saint Denis, Rhodot, and even Giroux in attempted—and perhaps success-ful—poisonings, most notably concerning Giroux's wife and his mother-in-law. Still, this was not necessarily enough proof to gain a conviction. First of all, much of the evidence was based on hearsay. Witnesses often couched their remarks in such phrases as "Common rumor had it. . . . ," "The word about town was . . . ," or "So and so told so and so who told me . . ." True, on occasion we get more direct testimony, as when Marie Minard and Gabrielle Belot reported hearing directly from Rhodot that he was the father of the child birthed by the Ursuline nun, effectively admitting to them that he had lied to the law about the child's parentage. He never did admit to infanticide, though, and that was the capital charge against him.

Even if the authorities believed that they had at least the two unimpeach-able witnesses required by law for conviction of a capital crime, witnesses who would testify to the guilt of Giroux—or any of the jailed accomplices—

they still needed tangible evidence that a crime had been committed. The charge was murder, after all, and how could anyone know for sure that Baillet and Neugot had been killed if their bodies had yet to be found? In other words, that other prerequisite of conviction—corpus delicti—had not been met. The authorities continued to look for the bodies, but so far, nothing.

Meanwhile, they believed that they had enough probable cause to keep everyone involved locked up. By the time they jailed Devilliers and LaQuille in the autumn of 1641, the authorities had evidently exhausted the potential list of witnesses willing or able to testify, for during most of 1642 there was very little movement in the case. Giroux and all the others spent this unhappy year languishing in prison. Giroux's alleged accomplices moldered in squalor in the jailhouse in town (the conciergerie), under the eye of a jailkeeper of lowly social condition. But men of the stature of Giroux were accorded more comfortable surroundings and personal jailkeepers of high social rank. Giroux was imprisoned in the castle, and his "jailkeeper" was the noble Antoine Comeau, lieutenant of the castle and therefore the highest-ranking officer on the premises. Comeau, like his father Jean before him, was also one of the prince of Condé's trusted men in Dijon, and both father and son bore the official title of Gentilhomme Ordinaire du Prince. Antoine Comeau, by the way, was also a first cousin of Françoise de Grand, the woman who married Pierre Lénet on 7 May 1641 (Comeau signed the marriage contract as a witness giving his consent to the match). Lénet, recall, became the royal prosecutor general in the Parlement in that year and was also one of Condé's most important and powerful clients in all of Burgundy. Comeau, in other words, was well connected and indisputably Condé's man.

Comeau, along with Giroux's other noble jailer, Antoine Remuet de Bussière (also a Gentilhomme Ordinaire du Prince), was entrusted with provisioning their illustrious prisoner, and judging from how much Giroux had to pay them for food (prisoners were responsible for their own board), there must have been quite a bit. Regardless of the quantity, however, Giroux complained bitterly that the food was horrible, and apparently balked at paying for it. By the end of March 1642 he was eight months in arrears, and when he was forced to settle up after the court intervened and ordered him to do so, Giroux handed over to de Bussière and Comeau a whopping 3,976£ for the costs of his own incarceration.

While Philippe Giroux languished in jail, his rumored lover Marie Fyot endured travails of her own. Suspected of complicity in the murder of her husband but never formally charged, she found the years from 1638 to 1642 trying indeed. With her husband missing she may have been relieved of a boorish mate, but she had lost precious income and had assumed his debts. About a week before Christmas in the year of Baillet's disappearance, she sued in court to collect a debt of over 3,000£ owed to her husband, and on the same day borrowed almost 200£. Over the next seven months she borrowed 2,000£ more. Marie fell so desperately ill in July 1641 that she feared she might die. On 21 July, at 7 in the evening in her home not far from the Palais de Justice in the parish of Saint Médard, her parish priest and her notary gathered by her bedside. A cobbler from the neighborhood stood off to the side waiting to sign her last will and testament as a witness. She dictated: "Being bedridden and ill but of sound mind, knowing that there is nothing more certain than death but nothing more uncertain than the hour it will call . . . praying [that] . . . the glorious Virgin Mary and all the saints of heaven will gather her soul among the blessed when it will be separated from her body . . ." and then bequeathed her earthly possessions. But Marie Fyot did not die, although given the psychological torment that awaited she might have wished that she had. In August of that year she plunged even more deeply into debt, borrowing nearly 10,000£ in that month alone. The year 1642 seemed little better, for she came borrowing yet again, this time for another 2,000£ from, interestingly, Pierre Odebert, one of the fourteen judges deliberating on the fate of Philippe Giroux.

Imprisonment, meanwhile, sat ill with Giroux, like the expensive but tasteless food he had to choke down. Always he protested his innocence, but the longer Giroux sat in his prison, the more convinced he became that his powerful former patron, the prince of Condé, had deserted him. Then in October 1642 he received the horrible news that drove him to the edge of despair. His father Benoît had just returned from Paris and paid his son a visit in the castle. He told Philippe that he had gone to Paris to entreat the prince to intercede on behalf of his son. For a father's efforts to save his son, what Benoît received instead was humiliation. Not only was his request for an audience with Condé turned down flat, he was also ordered to bother the prince no more, to leave town right away or suffer the dishonoring fate of being thrown into the Bastille, a formidable and shameful prison. When Benoît told his son of this turn of events, Philippe flew into a rage, and in desperation he reportedly hatched a plot to spring himself from his prison.

At least that is what two men said, Claude Godin and Jacques Simon DuMagny, called Le Gaucher. Who were these men, and could the authorities believe what stories they had to tell about Giroux's plan to break jail? The first to divulge the news to the commissioners Jacquot and Millière was Godin, a servant of one of Giroux's noble jailers, de Bussière. Godin had daily contact with the prisoner, and in early November 1642 he told the authorities of some compromising objects he found in his chamber and, even more alarming to the commissioners, some peculiar requests the prisoner had made to him.

First, Godin told them he had found two pairs of scissors in Giroux's cell, and when he recounted what Giroux had asked him, the presence of the contraband scissors began to make sense. Giroux, according to Godin, began asking about a fellow inmate, Jacques Simon DuMagny, a prisoner of war whom everyone knew by the nickname of Le Gaucher. In 1642 France was still locked in the Thirty Years' War against the Imperial Habsburg forces, and Burgundy was a frontier province bordering Franche-Comté, known as "the County," a French-speaking region which the Habsburgs held. The border between Burgundy and the County was barely twenty miles from Dijon. Before his capture Le Gaucher, who was from Besançon in Franche-Comté, had been a captain in the Imperial army.

Why was Giroux asking Godin about Le Gaucher, and what did he want to know? Godin reported that Giroux began inquiring at various times what Le Gaucher typically did during his day, and specifically what time he got up in the morning. Then one day, Godin saw Giroux cutting his fingernails into a point with the forbidden scissors. When Godin asked why he was doing that, Giroux replied angrily that he was going to bury them in Le Gaucher's face and tear his skin away. He did not care if Le Gaucher stabbed him with a dagger while he was doing it, so long as he got in four good jabs of his own. When Godin asked Giroux why he wanted to do this to Le Gaucher, Giroux responded evasively that he was paying him back for an earlier affront to his honor. This probably referred to Le Gaucher's refusal to meet Giroux in a duel, for Godin also reported that Giroux had given him a note to attach to Le Gaucher's night bonnet which bore these words: "Monsieur, do not fail tomorrow to go down into de Bussière's kitchen and obtain a knife; me, I will take one from the kitchen of Comeau. . . . You will find me behind the staircase [where] . . . we will settle our affair before the guards [have time to] descend upon us." Of course duels are designed to settle matters of honor, and the very fact that Giroux challenged Le Gaucher tells us that an earlier affront had occurred. What that was about we may plausibly guess from the subsequent testimony of Le Gaucher himself.

Returning first to Godin's story, however, we find him asking Giroux how he was going to carry out his plan. Giroux frankly told him that it would be best if somehow he could catch Le Gaucher alone in his chamber, preferably surprising him in his sleep. This was why Giroux wanted to have reports from Godin about what Le Gaucher typically did during the day, and above all when he arose in the morning. Giroux allegedly then told Godin that he needed his help to see these designs succeed, and that if Godin would leave the door to Le Gaucher's chamber open, Giroux would pay him ten écus (an enormous sum for a servant, who would not earn that much in a year). Giroux talked incessantly about this plan for days, Godin said, and once announced that he was going to make his move against Le Gaucher on a certain Saturday. He chose that date because the prince of Condé was arriving in Dijon on the following Sunday and Giroux feared that he would ransom Le Gaucher back to the Imperial army (this was often done with illustrious or valuable prisoners of war). In any case, the trap was set for Saturday, and this, according to Godin, is what Giroux planned to do. He asked the priest who held Mass in the prison chapel in the morning to hold it half an hour earlier than normal. Giroux's plan was to come to the chapel for Mass, stroll about, and then, in Godin's words, slip out of the chapel and "run like the devil" across the courtyard to Le Gaucher's chamber, hoping to find him unguarded and still asleep.

Godin's story was taken seriously by the authorities because Giroux's attack had actually taken place. Before Godin testified they had already heard of an attempt by Giroux to break into Le Gaucher's chamber, although they had few details on it as yet. They heard about it on the same day it occurred, 5 November, and then immediately launched an investigation into it. On that very day, the day before the prince was due in town, Godin came forward with his testimony. And he had even more to tell the commissioners than what we have heard already. He recounted how Giroux had told him the night before around 9 that the next day, Saturday, was the day to launch the plan because both de Bussière and Comeau would be away from the castle making preparations for the arrival of Condé. Giroux confessed to some anxiety about the attack, telling Godin that he feared some soldiers might be guarding Le Gaucher's chamber, or that his overzealous "ardor" to attack would cloud his judgment and jeopardize the whole venture. Godin tried to reassure Giroux, suggesting that perhaps there would be no soldiers about for the same reason that Comeau and de Bussière would be absent.

Whatever his apprehensions, when the bell rang for Mass Giroux descended from his chamber, entered the chapel, circled about as he had told Godin he would, and then sprinted headlong across the courtyard for Le Gaucher's chamber. He was spotted by some guards who sounded the alarm and chased after him. One of them, a man named Derey, reached Le Gaucher's door at the same moment as Giroux and tried to block him from gaining entry. Imagine what Le Gaucher must have thought when he saw Giroux halfway in his room, wedged between door jamb and door as he struggled with a soldier to get in so he could throw himself on the captain.

Not only had Giroux's plans been disrupted by the presence of soldiers, but he discovered that Le Gaucher was not asleep, nor even alone. As he looked into the captain's room he spied Simon Jonvelle, the sergeant major of the castle who Giroux hoped would be away from the castle with Comeau and de Bussière, preparing for Condé's entry into Dijon. Jonvelle was upon Giroux in a flash, and with the guard Derey he seized him and dragged him back into the courtyard by the chapel, where the two subdued and then frisked him. They hardly needed to search for hidden weapons: they found in one hand a pair of scissors and in the other a whip.

So much for Godin's account. Whatever we may doubt about its truthfulness, of one thing we can be sure, that Giroux did try to gain forceful entry into Le Gaucher's room. Other witnesses like the guards Nicolas Arot and Jean LeBoeuf and the priest who was saying Mass confirmed that Giroux had suddenly raced out of the chapel, streaked across the courtyard, and tried to force his way into Le Gaucher's chamber. Several pairs of eyes saw him stopped by a guard, frisked, and found carrying a pair of scissors and a whip. Arot added that Giroux shouted his intention of attacking Le Gaucher to get even with him. For what, no one seemed to know. Sergeant Major Jonvelle confirmed this, reporting that he was alerted by someone crying out "Murder!" and, bolting for Le Gaucher's chamber, arrived on the scene through a back door just as Giroux was trying to squeeze into the room from the front. He saw the president clutching a pair of scissors in one hand and a whip in the other, he said, and screaming that he was going to cut up Le Gaucher. For what reason, again, no one yet said, if anyone even knew. Nor did anyone come forward confirming the earlier part of Godin's testimony that dealt with the plan for the attack—no one, that is, except Giroux himself.

On 21 November Giroux was interrogated. The commissioners read him the statements of the priest, the sergeant major, and the guards, and Giroux confirmed that they all were true. He proudly confessed that his difference with Le Gaucher was an affair of honor, and he was not ashamed to admit that he had every intention of redressing an affront that the captain had made against him. He gave no details on this score, but he did say that he had no desire to kill Le Gaucher, only to cut him up. He even agreed that Godin's testimony was true, after a fashion. Giroux turned it around, however, trying to pin guilt on Godin by asserting that he was the one arguing that an assault on Le Gaucher was feasible. Giroux initially hesitated, he testified, saying that such a plan would be extremely difficult to execute, but he was ultimately persuaded by Godin that it could be carried off. Godin, according to Giroux, had even promised to help by springing Giroux from the castle, an offer that Giroux said he refused because he was innocent and wanted to walk out of the castle vindicated, his honor intact.

All that was left for the authorities to do was hear from Le Gaucher himself. Shortly after the interrogation of Giroux, Jacques Simon, the lord Du Magny and captured captain from the Imperial army, offered a very long testimony that oddly said nothing of the assault on his person by Giroux. What Le Gaucher said, however, was much more intriguing to the authorities, and fitted as another piece in the puzzle as they tried to figure out whether Giroux had anything to do with the deaths of Pierre Baillet and Philibert Neugot. Le Gaucher made it clear that he was offering his testimony for a price. He told de Bussière that he had some information of great importance for the prince of Condé and would divulge what he knew if the prince agreed to an exchange of prisoners with the Imperial army. In return for Le Gaucher the French would receive the Baron de Mausse—and the following testimony. Apparently the deal was made, for an extraordinary deposition has come down to us. This is what it says.

First, Le Gaucher told the authorities of Benoît Giroux's visit to Condé in Paris and his son's enraged response when he heard what shameful things his father had to tell. The captain said that he and Giroux had actually become quite friendly these past six months, and had talked a great deal. In late October, just after Benoît's visit, Le Gaucher entered Philippe's chamber, strolled over to the fireplace, and quite naturally asked Philippe, "What good news has your father brought from Paris?" Giroux, face purple with rage, told him of the denied audience with the prince, the order to leave town, and the humiliating threat of being thrown into the Bastille. Philippe's devastation at the news, Le Gaucher knew, was made worse by the dashed hopes that he and his father had suffered only a few weeks before. His father, Giroux had told Le Gaucher then, had reliable information that the king's prime minister, Cardinal Richelieu—closest of allies of Condé—was soon to be disgraced. With the cardinal's fall would inevitably come Condé's. Philippe Giroux imagined that Louis XIII's wife Anne of Austria, long an enemy of Richelieu and Condé and thus kept far from the reins of power, would stand again at the king's side, as would the king's brother, Gaston d'Orléans. Gaston had led a futile and in retrospect foolish rebellion against his brother Louis XIII and Richelieu in 1631. This event had brought the governorship of Burgundy to Condé in reward for his loyalty to the minister and king.

Giroux, his dreams in full gale now, supposedly told Le Gaucher that he expected the reinstated Gaston to arrive at the gates of Dijon bearing letters ordering the arrest of Condé, and would grant Giroux the honor of wielding a pistol and leading the party into the prince's chambers announcing the arrest. He could then watch firsthand the reaction of one of his most loathsome enemies, Condé, as he fell from power. With this turn of events, the Giroux were confident that the Président de La Mothe, who was overseeing the proceedings against Philippe concerning the murder of Baillet, would be replaced. According to Le Gaucher, they seemed equally sure that their ally de Thou would be named to take his place. All of this, in the Giroux scheme of things, would end in the acquittal of Philippe and the restoration of the family's honor and power.

Le Gaucher apparently passed this information along to the lord Comeau, Giroux's jailer and close client of the prince. Comeau, who had good reason to know, said that Benoît was ill informed. No such disgrace was imminent, although it was true that Richelieu was ill (he would die on 4 December 1642). Benoît soon discovered for himself that his information was false, and so went to Paris to control whatever political damage he could. These were desperate times for the Giroux. Benoît had sought an audience with the prince, an attempt, as we have seen, that ended in disaster. In Paris he now knew that the cardinal and Condé were fully in the king's good graces, and that the Giroux were not. To make matters worse, he discovered that the Giroux family friend de Thou had been arrested. Bearing such ill tidings back to his son, Le Gaucher concluded, triggered Philippe's thunderous explosion of rage.

If we can believe the imperial captain, such devastating news also planted the seed of a grandiose plan hatched in Philippe's fertile, perhaps even unhinged imagination. Recovering from his angry outburst, his voice now lowered, Giroux whispered to Le Gaucher that he knew how they could be freed from the castle and, in the bargain, allow it to be taken by imperial troops. Skeptical, Le Gaucher replied that the castle walls were too high to take by ladder and asked what Giroux had in mind. Giroux responded guardedly, saying that he would reveal what he knew if Le Gaucher would guarantee that he would free Giroux and take him with him to the town of Gray in nearby Franche-Comté. When Le Gaucher agreed, Giroux began to talk.

From what the president had to say, he obviously knew the castle well. He told Le Gaucher that its weak spot was the section facing the countryside to the north, between the Guillaume Tower and the half-moon fortification outworks called a *ravelin*. There one could find a wall about twelve feet in height, one that had previously been partially breached by cannon fire and had not yet been repaired. In its present condition it could easily be scaled from the outside by ladder. Moreover, this wall could not be seen by sentinels posted in either the Guillaume Tower or the Saint Martin Tower, and it was beyond earshot as well.

In Le Gaucher's account, Giroux clearly envisioned a secretive assault on the castle by a small expeditionary force. The commandos would secure the castle and then open its gates to a larger invading force. Le Gaucher and Giroux would then, of course, also gain their freedom. Once the commandos scaled the partially breached wall they would cross a small moat where, before it was filled with water, Comeau used to keep his rabbits. This would take them to the drawbridge attached to the main wall of the

castle. The door, Giroux assured Le Gaucher, could be breached by small ex-
plosives, which presumably the commandos would be carrying with them.
From there all that remained to penetrate before one could reach the castle
itself and the prisoners was a decrepit door on the other side of a small courtyard from the bridge. This could easily be broken down. As for the sentinels,
Giroux reassured Le Gaucher that he need not worry: they always remained
in the towers rather than patrol the walls, and they never bothered to look
in the direction of the drawbridge.

Le Gaucher must have listened to all of this with keen interest, since
he was able to recount all of it in close detail in testimony that must have
taken hours to give. At this point in Giroux's description of his plan, Le
Gaucher asked him how deep the water in the moat was. Giroux replied that
he thought it was shallow but could confirm this by getting a servant boy
in the castle whom he trusted, Jean Didier, to secretively sound its depth.
Right then he sent for Didier, who promptly did as Giroux bade, returning
the next day to tell the conspirators that it was only about knee-deep. Le
Gaucher also wanted to know how Giroux, a judge and not a military man,
was so well informed about the weaknesses of the castle's defenses. Giroux
replied that he had learned much from another prisoner in the castle, an
expert in fortifications named Boitrix. This man, who had been a gentleman in the royal household of Princess Anne before his arrest for unknown
reasons, had pointed out the castle's vulnerabilities while strolling on its
ramparts one day with Giroux. It was Boitrix who had shown Giroux the
spot between the ravelin and the Guillaume Tower where the wall was partly
breached. There, Boitrix said, was where an invading force could most easily
strike and take the castle by surprise. Giroux continued that if the castle fell
to imperial forces, the French army of Picardy would be forced to raise its
siege of Perpignan, a Habsburg-held city near the Spanish border, so that
it could come to Burgundy to retake the vital town of Dijon and its castle.

Grand plans for Giroux, but he had even more daring exploits to propose.
He told Le Gaucher that he knew of a way to bring about peace between
Habsburg and Bourbon, and in the bargain he could make the captain's
fortune. Giroux pulled him aside and whispered that he knew of a way to
capture the prince of Condé himself. Le Gaucher incredulously asked how
he proposed to do that. Giroux responded that he knew the prince's habits
well, and in the past when the prince departed Dijon he never failed to fol-

low the same pattern. First, he would hear Mass, then dine. He would then change his clothes in his residence in town for the journey back to Paris, then go to the castle to prepare his carriage and muster his cavalry escort. This escort, surprisingly, only numbered eight men, including the prince's secretary. A larger troop of cavalry followed at some distance. The prince always took the same route too, making his first stop after a day's ride north at a monastery in the town of Sainte Seine.

On the appointed day, Giroux and Le Gaucher, free now and safely situated in Gray, would be notified by one of Giroux's trusted spies of Condé's departure from Dijon. The two of them would then lead twenty horsemen — all gentlemen if possible — to ambush the prince and his entourage. So sure was Giroux of the venture's success and so set was he in his desire to avenge himself against the prince that he offered to leave his son Henri in Gray as a hostage. He could not believe, he told Le Gaucher, that his former patron Condé could abandon and humiliate him and his family as he had done, and this conspiracy to free himself from the castle, turn it over to France's enemies, and capture the prince himself was all driven by the thirst for revenge.

Giroux continued to lay his plans before Le Gaucher. To keep from being recognized and discovered by the prince's spies, Giroux said he would disguise himself and take the name of Gildart, an English lord who had the same coat of arms as Giroux. In Gray the conspirators would wait for the signal from Giroux's spy letting them know that Condé had departed Dijon and was on his way. Giroux, Le Gaucher, and the twenty horsemen would then position themselves in a wooded area in the hills outside Sainte Seine, waiting through the night. The next day the prince would ride into the ambush just after dusk, and under the cloak of darkness and surprise the trap would be sprung and the prince taken. He would then be spirited off to Gray before the soldiers riding behind would know what had happened. Once the king of France paid the ransom of 100,000£ (which, Giroux assured Le Gaucher, his majesty would surely do for his first cousin, governor of Burgundy, and second heir to the throne of the kingdom), Le Gaucher would be a fabulously rich man.

Le Gaucher now wanted to know more about the terrain where the ambush was to take place, and how far it was from Gray. He certainly expected a pursuit, and he seemed to hope that a quick dash across the border was all that was needed. Giroux was obviously well prepared for the question, Le

Gaucher recounted, since he pulled out a large atlas with a map of Burgundy, pointed triumphantly to Sainte Seine and then to Gray, and announced that there were only about ten leagues between them. Le Gaucher then cautiously asked what would happen if the plan failed and the men were retaken. Giroux boldly replied that he would put a pistol to the prince's head and pull the trigger, and then turn the firearm on himself, for he would rather die than be recaptured. On more than one occasion Philippe made it clear that he dreaded above all ending his life in dishonor. Blowing his brains out after he had done the same to the prince, or having the jailbreak end with Giroux dead in the attempt would be preferable to being executed "in a theater," in Giroux's words, referring to the ceremonial and ritualistic execution that Giroux would be forced to endure if he were convicted of the murder of Baillet. To die by his own hand or in battle would save the honor of his son, said Giroux.

So much for Le Gaucher's long testimony. Apparently he rebuffed all of Giroux's entreaties. This might explain why Giroux challenged him to a duel, and why he tried to break into his chamber and cut him up. When given the chance after Le Gaucher testified to counter his testimony, Giroux attacked it and discredited his person. How could anyone be so gullible as to believe an enemy of the state? And could anyone truly suspect that Giroux would turn against Condé, a man for whom he had said for years that he would lay down his life? Giroux never missed an opportunity to blast the commissioners either, and he did so now, always protesting his innocence, always alleging that his enemies had gained control of the wheels of justice and, as a result, the law was running over an innocent man.

Giroux may have been telling the truth, for nowhere in the testimony of Godin or Le Gaucher do we find implications that Giroux was guilty of the murder of Baillet and Neugot. He may have planned a jailbreak, but under the circumstances that is not an admission of guilt of murder. That extravagant and desperate plan may have been hatched out of fear that his enemies were winning the war over justice and successfully framing him. By Christmas of 1642 it was clear to all that he had lost Condé, and in those days to lose a powerful protector left one exposed, vulnerable, and maybe dead. Can we be terribly surprised that Giroux may have schemed to gain his freedom?

CHAPTER 9

A *"Minister of Vengeance"*

Pierre Saumaise de Chasans, a conseiller du roy in Dijon's Parlement and lord of ten fiefdoms, was at his new, stately home in the most desirable neighborhood in the provincial capital, only a five-minute walk from the Palace of Justice, when on 10 May 1636, living amid the prestigious and the great, he received most unwelcome visitors. A captain flanked by a company of twelve of the king's musketeers rapped on his door and demanded entry. With his wife Marie Virey and no doubt several of his seven children who had not yet reached the age of twelve huddled behind her and watching, Saumaise respectfully inquired after the business of the king's men. Well he knew that a visit from such a delegation — bedecked from head to toe in plumed hats, capes sporting the royal fleur de lys, and thigh-high leather boots — was far from commonplace.

The captain carried papers ordering the arrest of Saumaise, and was accompanied by the musketeers who would lead him away, by force if necessary. Saumaise had been delivered a *lettre de cachet*, a direct order from the king to arrest and imprison him without trial. Such a letter was deeply feared at the time, since it not only legally bypassed normal legal process but also signaled that the recipient had lost the political favor of the king and his ministers. So when Saumaise first saw the captain and the musketeers, he knew that the king had ordered his arrest. He also knew that his enemies had gained the king's ear and set in motion this most humiliating and dangerous turn of events. He was also certain that behind it all was Philippe Giroux.

This man, Saumaise and everyone else knew, had the favor of the great, and above all that of the governor of Burgundy, the prince of Condé. Saumaise had no choice but to follow the illustrious company into the street—a most disgraceful show in front of his neighbors—and be led away as a prisoner of his majesty. Three weeks later this journey toward dishonor ended in the Bastille in Paris, that fortress prison which held, among others, those miserable souls who had fallen out of favor with their king.

Saumaise protested then, and later in print, that he had been "falsely and calumniously" accused of wrongdoing, and that his enemy Philippe Giroux had corrupted the path of justice by steering the law against so faithful a servant of the king as Pierre Saumaise de Chasans. He was probably right that Giroux was behind his arrest, and this blow to Saumaise was not the first delivered by Giroux. By 1636 a blood feud had raged between the two men and their families for several years, and it showed no signs of abating. These men carried a smoldering hatred for one another, an enmity that more than once erupted before the eyes of their colleagues in Parlement, and even Condé and the king. If we want to know why in the spring of 1640 Saumaise joined the prosecution as a *partie instigante* in the case against Philippe Giroux concerning the alleged murder of Pierre Baillet and Philibert Neugot, we need to look into the vendetta that had consumed these men at least since 1627.

To hear Saumaise tell it, he became an enemy of the Giroux family, and Philippe in particular, because Saumaise was a trusted and loyal servant of the king. In 1636 he pleaded with his majesty that since 1632 he had "courageously opposed the oppressions . . . of the faction [in Parlement] of the Giroux [who] were invading" the king's court. This faction was corrupting the law by turning the court into an instrument of private, family interest, and he could not just sit back and allow this miscarriage of justice to happen to his king.

Saumaise first attracted the wrathful attention of the Giroux clan in 1627 when the sitting first president in the Parlement, Nicolas Brulart, died. Brulart had served in this office since 1610, having succeeded his father Denis Brulart. The office of first president was technically nonvenal—that is, unlike the other presidencies and the judgeships, the offices of conseiller du roy, it was not purchased openly by the officeholder. Incoming first presidents were first selected by the king, then received a *brevet de retenue* from the king which set the price that the new officer must pay to the outgoing one (or, if he had died in office, his estate). As the king's man, the first president was a very powerful member of the court. According to the records of the Parlement of Dijon, it was he who annually assigned his fellow judges (both conseillers and présidents) to the chambers in which they were to work. This mattered greatly to each judge and président because the amount of money a judge could earn from the cases he heard varied widely from one chamber to the next. Every judge was immersed in patronage networks and every judge knew that his chamber assignment depended on his relative favor with the first president. The most prestigious and financially rewarding chamber was the Grand'Chambre, in which civil cases were pleaded. This was especially remunerative because the cases there invariably involved property disputes, and thus litigants were from the propertied—and often wealthy—classes. Judges were paid wages, but they also received épices, and these supplementary payments, which were part of the court costs levied against the litigant who lost the case, were highest in the Grand'Chambre. The second chamber in the Parlement in terms of prestige and remuneration was the Tournelle, where felony and capital criminal cases were heard. Less desired by the judges were the chambers of Enquêtes (hearing misdemeanor criminal cases) and Requêtes (hearing small property disputes and requests from legally privileged prospective litigants for a hearing).

When Nicolas Brulart died in 1627, factions in Parlement lined up behind their favored candidates to replace him. Saumaise and Giroux stood on opposite sides of the fence, Saumaise supporting the eventual nominee, Jean-Baptiste Le Goux de La Berchere, and the Giroux clan opposing him. This may be surprising, for in 1633 Philippe Giroux not only received the office of one of the seven presidents in Parlement but was betrothed to the daughter of that first president, Le Goux de La Berchere, the man who six years earlier Philippe and his family had opposed for the office. As a supporter of Le Goux, Saumaise no doubt expected favor from him, and how galling it must have been to see the Giroux secure and eventually win it instead.

Condé, of course, was responsible. Philippe's father Benoît had been a president in the Parlement since 1610, his son Philippe a conseiller since 1627, and it is quite likely that they were recruited in the late 1620s by the prince to be among his *créatures*, men whose social and political existence was "created" by their patron. It is unlikely that Condé backed Le Goux for the first presidency in 1627, because the prince had not as yet consolidated his power in Burgundy. Roger de Bellegarde was the royal governor then, and Condé had to bide his time and busy himself with patronizing emerging families like the Giroux. Savvy in politics, the Giroux realized that the Le Goux family now wielded significant power, and the Giroux and Condé joined forces to penetrate and perhaps control its network.

When Bellegarde was deposed as governor in 1631 for his ill-advised support of the unsuccessful rebellion of the king's brother Gaston d'Orléans against Richelieu, the door flew open for Condé. As Richelieu's staunch ally, he was named governor of Burgundy in Bellegarde's place later that year. At once Philippe Giroux began wooing Marie Le Goux de La Berchere for marriage, a prospect initially opposed by the first president, her father Jean-Baptiste. However, Jean-Baptiste died in 1631, and was replaced by his son Pierre. Unquestionably now such a royal appointment could only go to one favored by Condé. More evidence of Condé's rising influence over the Le Goux clan came in January 1634, when Philippe Giroux and Marie Le Goux—sister of the current first president—joined hands in marriage. Among others witnessing and sanctioning the signing of the marriage contract was a man named Étienne Quarré. As knight of the Order of Saint John of Jerusalem, captain of the prince of Condé's guard, and gentleman of the prince's household, Quarré was one of Condé's most trusted clients. Marie quickly became pregnant, and if anyone needed further proof of Condé's favor of Philippe Giroux, the son born in the following November was named Henri, and the prince himself held the child at the baptismal font as his godfather and namesake.

Clearly, the Giroux were a good family for Condé to recruit and secure. Its connections in the parlementaire community in Dijon wove like a spider's web. Saumaise de Chasans, by contrast, could not boast such connections, or a similar ability to navigate the turbulent waters of mid-seventeenth-century power politics. It was not for want of trying, however. Indeed he had a good base from which to work, which makes his failure to gain the favor of Condé in the 1630s a sign of political clumsiness. In 1612, the year he became a conseiller in Parlement, Saumaise married Marie Virey, the daughter of Claude-Enoch, Condé's secrétaire des commandements and then his first Intendant in Burgundy. Saumaise's father-in-law, in other words, held posts in the prince's household from 1595 to 1616 that only those closest to and most trusted by the prince would occupy.

Such an advantageous marriage would seem to vault Saumaise into Condé's network of clients, and Saumaise continued to curry favor with the prince. In 1627 he wrote an obsequious paean to him entitled *Discours d'honneur sur les vertus . . . [du] Prince de Condé* and presented it to him in person; according to witnesses, the tract won gracious thanks from Condé. Still Saumaise was left on the outside, perhaps because he backed Jean-Baptiste Le Goux de La Berchere for the first presidency in 1627. Whatever the reason, Saumaise knew that he lacked Condé's favor. He acknowledged as much in 1637 when he pleaded for it in a printed document addressed to the prince. In it he referred to Condé's years of imprisonment (1616–19) after his rebellion against the king as "the bad season." Saumaise boasted his own "ardent passions . . . to serve him [then] in this Parlement amidst [the prince's] enemies." He recalls 1617 as "a time even more difficult" than 1616, "a time of tribulation when Saumaise had the courage and industry to see and speak to his highness" while Condé had fallen from favor and was imprisoned.

Despite these entreaties, nowhere before 1640 do we find him allied in any way with the central families in Condé's network, except his father-in-law who retired in 1629 and died in 1636. Most likely this was at least in part because Saumaise was tainted by the loyalties of two of his brothers, both of whom served prominently in the household of the king's brother, Gaston, the duc d'Orléans. By the late 1620s Gaston was Richelieu's and therefore Condé's main rival. One of Pierre Saumaise's brothers, Bénigne, was *secrétaire des commandements* for Gaston and another, François, was one of the king's brother's *maîtres d'hôtel*. In Condé's eyes, Saumaise was just too close to the prince's enemies to be fully trusted. If having brothers in the enemy's camp were not enough, Pierre himself did not help his cause with the prince by attempting to curry favor with Roger de Bellegarde, the governor of Burgundy until 1631, who would join Gaston in rebellion. One could hardly blame Saumaise for dedicating a tract he had written to Bellegarde in 1621—after all, this was how the patronage game was played. When the *Discours de consolation à Monseigneur le Duc de Bellegarde* went to press, Saumaise could not have foreseen that the governor would end up in disgrace ten years later and lose his governorship to Condé. All of this contributed to Condé's suspicion of Pierre Saumaise, a suspicion that must have grown during the 1630s, as Saumaise took on the Giroux clan precisely when Condé was becoming its protector.

Like everyone else in Dijon, Saumaise knew that the Giroux had won Condé's favor, and so to take on the Giroux meant taking on the prince. Saumaise also knew, however, that the favor of the great was mercurial, that patron-client ties were not for life, could be fragile, even broken. So even as he attacked the Giroux, he looked for opportunities to win the prince's favor. By elbowing his way into the prince's entourage he might even supplant the Giroux as a star in this privileged constellation.

Saumaise made his first bold move against the Giroux clan in 1633, when he challenged the seating of Philippe Giroux as a president in the Parlement. For three years he unleashed a torrent of petitions to the Parlement seeking to block the promotion on procedural grounds. In this way he tangled and delayed the promotion in legalisms that judges, sworn to uphold the letter of the law, were bound to respect. Thus we find Parlement, against the wishes of the Giroux faction and no doubt to the delight of its enemies, issuing a series of interlocutory *arrêts*, or injunctions, postponing Giroux's ascendancy. It was on 16 April 1633 that Benoît Giroux officially made arrangements to transfer his presidency to his son, but it was not until over three years later, on 26 April 1636, that Philippe officially took his seat. In the meantime, Saumaise may have frustrated the house of Giroux, but his strategy was fraught with danger. He incurred the everlasting hatred of the Giroux and he deeply angered Condé. In the short run, he brought down upon his head the retribution that came from a failed tactic.

If Saumaise's complaints can be taken at face value, the Giroux were so frustrated with his attempts to block Philippe's promotion that they resolved to eliminate him. Saumaise complained to the king in writing that attempts had been made on his life, and he knew that the Giroux were responsible for them. In May, June, and July 1635, Saumaise alleged, someone tried to kill him, first in a church, then in the courthouse, and yet again in the parlement's own chapel. Then, in September of that year, someone tried to kill him at his country home, and on 28 December 1635 came another attempt on the king's highway. Tireless if singularly inept, his enemies tried to kill him again and again, allegedly in the courthouse again on New Year's Day, and yet again on 11 January 1636. If Saumaise were to be believed, it must have seemed incredible after all of these supposed assaults upon his life that he was still alive.

Saumaise's claims about attempted assassination must have called his trustworthiness into question. The judges may also have questioned his allegation that Philippe Giroux had written printed libels defaming Saumaise's character while the Giroux were trying to be rid of Saumaise by all those covert and violent means. That allegation is supported by the registers of the Parlement, however. Offensive words were hardly idle or considered harmless, since when hurled in public with defamatory intent they attacked a person's honor. Honor in seventeenth-century France was the coin of reputation, and upon reputation everything rested—wealth, social status, political power. The possession of honor was the mark of esteem and of one's place in the social and political world. Honor no less than the formal system of law was a fundamental prop to social and political order, and during the sixteenth and seventeenth centuries both honor and law became crucially important in the lives of French men and women. As one jurist put it, "Of all the benefits of society, the most precious, without question, is honor; it is the very soul and principle of social existence." [1] To lose one's honor, and if onlookers believed the slander or libel this is just what one would do, was worse than death.

It was during these two transitional centuries, the sixteenth and the seventeenth, that the values of French society were gradually but fundamentally shifting. During the Middle Ages the social values of the French aristocracy had been rooted in the soil of chivalry and family lineage. These values—especially concerning family—remained strong during the sixteenth and seventeenth centuries, of course, but they were gradually being challenged. Nobles of the sword like the Viscount Turenne were still held up as ideal models of the gentleman, but within the class of judges and magistrates like Giroux and his peers, the nobility of the robe, another model was being fashioned. Among them the humanistic virtues of individual self-control and social discipline inspired by the social philosophy of neostoicism, and the godliness inspired by the Catholic Reformation, came to the fore.

Thus by the seventeenth century there were two ideal roles for a gentleman—the Christian knight and the godly magistrate, and for the magistrate the notion of honor in public office was thrown into bold relief. As royal magistrates like Giroux and Saumaise rose more and more to the top of the social hierarchy, they brought with them a justification for their privileged social status, one that rested upon their role as dispensers of justice. They came to see this task as a God-given privilege and charge. Their honor, in other words, was increasingly bound to their part in administering the law, and their view of honor and the law as socially indispensable became the foundation of their jurisprudence as well as the justification for their claim to high social rank.

To a Giroux or a Saumaise, honor was thus worth more than life itself. When in 1635 Saumaise lashed Giroux "with offensive words" in the Chamber of the Enquêtes in the Parlement before their gathered peers, everyone knew that Giroux must parry the blow with every bit of power he could muster. Perhaps, as Saumaise claimed, behind the scenes Giroux had sent and would send waves of assassins to simply kill him. The first alleged attack, recall, came in the same month that Saumaise hurled the offensive slanders in the Enquêtes. We know, however, that Giroux attacked in another way, and that was through the law. On 20 May 1635 he filed suit in Parlement against Saumaise for slander. Saumaise countered the same day, and both knew that the loser in the case would be forced to pay a monetary fine and, much worse, dishonor himself before his peers by being forced to pay the dreaded *amende honorable*: according to this judicial ritual, the accuser, having wronged "God, king, and justice," was required to get on his knees with hat in hand and beg the forgiveness of his gloating enemy, whom he would pronounce "worthy and honorable."

It is not hard to imagine that Giroux wanted to be rid of Saumaise, a man whose distasteful, arrogant personality must have rendered him insufferable to more than the Giroux. Fellow judges seemingly found little in Saumaise to like, and from all that he did during the decades in which he tenaciously struts across the historical record, we glimpse a personality of unrelentingly pious self-righteousness blending seamlessly into base self-interest. A quarrelsome man constantly at odds with fellow judges, Saumaise was involved in twenty-two quarrels with other judges in Parlement, was reprimanded eleven times as the culprit, and was censored seven times. During the seventeenth century the Parlement as a whole was drifting toward lenience in criminal sentences, but Saumaise swam against this current. For example, in 1633 Saumaise was assigned as a *rapporteur* to ten cases appealed to Parlement from lower courts across Burgundy. In only one of those cases did Saumaise seek to lessen the punishment imposed by the lower court. And in that one case the sentence at Parlement "mercifully" reduced the punishment from hanging by the neck to life imprisonment rowing in the king's galleys. More often, in cases where Saumaise was involved and unlike those in which he was not, the punishment was made more severe. In a case appealed in 1631, Saumaise gave a hint of how severe he could be and was going to be. When the domestic servant Perrenette Mugnier was convicted of stealing from her master and sentenced by the lower court to be banished for three years and to pay a fine of 5£, the judgment was altered in Parlement, with Saumaise leading the prosecution. Mugnier was now forced to suffer the pain of a public flogging before being banished not for three years but for five. Her fine was also doubled.

Another gruesome example of Saumaise's severity. In 1633, for conviction of a murder, the grapegrower Bazille Bordé was broken on the wheel (more often murderers were hanged or beheaded). As Saumaise watched, the executioner shattered Bordé's arm and leg bones with a metal rod, and then pitched him onto a raised wheel, face up, to die slowly and in agony. His accomplice merely had his head chopped off, after which Saumaise and the presiding judge split the *épices* of sixty-six écus (more than the victims combined would have earned in years).

Most disturbing of all of the examples of Saumaise's stern, unmerciful jurisprudence is the series of cases for witchcraft that Saumaise prosecuted in March 1633. In other parts of France and Europe a witch hunt swept widely during the early seventeenth century, but with the exception of a few flare-ups, Burgundy was largely spared. Saumaise oversaw one of those flare-ups. For a bloody week in the middle of March, Saumaise signed his name as a rapporteur to seven sentences which capped the trials of twenty-five accused witches. Lower courts had ordered banishment, but under appeal at Parlement (required by law for all capital offenses tried in lower courts) Saumaise and the presiding judge demonstrated their belief that firmer punishment was needed. Saumaise saw to it that several of the victims were tortured, and three were eventually burned at the stake. Saumaise and the president assigned to these cases, by the way, pocketed for their efforts 400 écus (that is, 1,200£, or more than a journeyman artisan—or any of the victims—might earn in fifteen years). In all, in 1633 alone Saumaise shared with his presidents about 700 écus in addition to his regular wages. Fellow judges, including Philippe Giroux, were deeply troubled by the severity of Saumaise as a judge. By Giroux's count, Saumaise submitted fifty-six people accused of crimes to be tortured, broken on the wheel, or beheaded, prompting Giroux to conclude in disgust that Saumaise was "a crow who is most content among dead bodies."

Saumaise never tired of posing as a champion of the king's and God's justice, boldly announcing that his unrelenting pursuit of Philippe Giroux was rooted in a conviction that justice is "public vengeance, not private." It is apparent that however much Saumaise may have been committed to justice, he also was using this vendetta and eventually Philippe's trial for the murder of Baillet and Neugot to bring down the house of Giroux and insert himself in its place. He was a self-appointed and self-proclaimed "minister of vengeance," but we remain unsure about whether it was the king, God, or Saumaise who was being avenged.

Saumaise's first salvo against the house of Giroux was the attempt to block Philippe's promotion to a presidency in 1633. He used the letter of the law for momentary effect, since at twenty-eight years of age Philippe was by law two years shy of the minimum age to serve in that office. Just as surely, Saumaise understood an accession of Philippe to a presidency for what it was, a near-domination of Parlement by the Giroux and their allies. And Saumaise was not one of them. He struggled to keep Philippe from his seat, but he had Condé to contend with. On 28 April 1636 Saumaise clumsily sent a request to Condé asking him to remove himself from any involvement in the ongoing criminal proceedings between Saumaise and Giroux concerning slander that had begun about a year before. To this request Condé tersely replied that he did not wish to know anything about Saumaise's affairs.

That same day, perhaps piqued to anger by Saumaise's effrontery, the prince of Condé had had enough, and the political fortunes of Saumaise seemed never bleaker. The prince personally escorted Philippe Giroux to the Palais de Justice, demanded that his man be seated as a president, and under his insistent eye saw the Parlement comply. Eight days later, at the instigation of Condé, the captain of that company of musketeers delivered to Saumaise the lettre de cachet, the sealed order from the king that summoned him before the king's Conseil Privé to account for his "conduct contrary to the will of the king and the interest of the state," and that by the end of May delivered him to the Bastille. That bleak symbol of the power of the great and the misfortune of the disgraced was a place that Saumaise wished above all to avoid: he fired off a last-ditch plea to the king's chancellor begging for his "necessary protection" to spare him the fate that Condé and the king were about to dole out to him, but the request was unavailing.

Saumaise was imprisoned in the Bastille for only a day. Evidently Condé, Richelieu, and the king wished to make their point simply by sending him there. It did not work: Saumaise continued to wield an angry pen. Already embroiled in a defamation suit with Giroux launched in May 1635, he now further inflamed the vendetta with the Giroux clan. First, on 24 November 1636 he addressed a twenty-eight-page complaint "to the person of the king on the oppression of Lord Saumaise de Chasans." In it he wrote of the "terror" that Philippe Giroux, "the evil angel of [this] province," and his allies visited upon Parlement. He intoned piously that they corrupted "sacred justice and the public interest [which are] inseparable from your majesty." He wailed in this "very just complaint" that he, a conseiller who had served faithfully in the king's "Parlement of Burgundy [for] . . . twenty five years with honor and without reproach," must now brace himself against the "cruelest persecution" that "barbarians and atheists" have ever thrown against "a Christian man." Giroux, a "demon" "inspired by a diabolical spirit," sent "masked and armed" assassins against him at night on many occasions—in his country home, his home in town, and even— what sacrilege!—in the chapel of the Palais de Justice.

Pulling out all the stops to bring the Giroux low, he brought to the king's attention a dark and still obscure chapter in the history of the family. To hear Saumaise tell it, Philippe's father Benoît had stabbed and killed a Jesuit priest named Carré in a nighttime fight next to the priest's church some years before. The case was heard in the Parlement of Paris in 1609, and Benoît was "released but not absolved" (jusqu'à rappel), meaning that the authorities could reopen the case at any time if sufficient evidence turned up to warrant doing so. Benoît had to live daily with this humiliating prospect hanging over his head, and he surely could not have welcomed having it brought to the king's attention by this intrepid enemy of the house of Giroux. Throughout the complaint, Saumaise styled himself as the king's true champion and the Giroux as overmighty subjects who "tyrannized" the king's court and were wanting in loyalty and devotion to their majesty. What a shock, he informed his king in his complaint, when the king's own musketeers arrested and hustled him off to the Bastille!

Saumaise was desperate to counter the juggernaut of power that was bowling him over in 1636. First, he wrote the complaint in which he tried to bring to the king's attention the alleged dangers of the Giroux. Then, in the autumn of that year, he alleged that Philippe Giroux was the author of some anti-Condé broadsheets that had been publicly posted about Dijon. These ridiculed the prince for his bungled siege of Dôle and for his handling of the defense of Burgundy in the face of an Imperial invasion. One might well ask whether it is credible that Giroux would do such a thing to the man who had made him; it seems at least as likely that Saumaise wrote the broadsheets, and then pointed an accusing finger at Giroux. This, at any rate, is what Giroux countered, and what Condé believed. Condé doubted that Philippe would be so foolish, and stood by his man. With the memory of the Bastille still fresh in his mind, on 20 January 1637 Saumaise was delivered an arrêt from the king's council. He was suspended from his judgeship in the Parlement, and exiled to his country estate near Beaune.

Saumaise's travails were far from over. Giroux now brought another charge of defamation of character against him, this time referring to some libelous broadsheets that Saumaise had allegedly spread not only in Dijon but "everywhere in Paris." Giroux petitioned the king to force Saumaise to pay him monetary reparations and to perform the amende honorable. Saumaise countered by pleading with the king in December to have the case evoked to another Parlement, pointing to the domination of Burgundy's Parlement by Giroux and "his kin" and hoping to escape the "oppression" that he suffered in his own province. On 16 March 1637 the king's council issued an arrêt granting Saumaise's request for an evocation, but it took care to point out to Saumaise that "Monsieur le Prince [de Condé] is said to be offended" by the "six writings against Messieur Giroux" which were the basis of the case.

The king then remanded the case to the Parlement of Rennes in Brittany. The very next day Saumaise made one last attempt to gain the ear of Condé, pleading with "the first prince of the first house of the world" to heed the signs that the house of Giroux was becoming too powerful. Saumaise made it clear that this clan and its kin dominated the Parlement and suggested that their loyalty to Condé was less than complete. He had warned the king of the danger of overmighty subjects just a few months before, and now he was warning Condé. Trust not the Giroux. Trust instead those devoted servants of the prince like Saumaise, a man who had served "his highness" selflessly and faithfully for over twenty years, even during the prince's darkest hours in 1616 and 1617.

Condé ignored him, and on 5 January 1639 Saumaise lost the case. Ordered by the Parlement of Rennes to pay court costs and to Giroux 3,000£ in compensatory damages, Saumaise bitterly lamented that the whole case had cost him 24,000£ and as a result that Giroux had "plundered" him. The sentence also suspended Saumaise yet again from his judgeship in Parlement, just four months after his first suspension had been lifted. And finally, what men like Saumaise dreaded above all, the sentence ordered him "to declare before the assembled chambers of the said court that he held . . . Philippe Giroux to be an honorable and worthy man." The humiliation could hardly have been more complete, and Saumaise could only gaze helplessly from the lowliness of his current state at his archenemy Philippe Giroux, sitting confidently and powerfully at the pinnacle of society.

As Giroux looked down upon his foe in early 1639, we can picture his eyes flashing hatred, now thinking that the moment had come to finish him off. This time, however, he overreached, and in a bizarre court case that would involve the alleged rape of a prepubescent girl, Pierre Saumaise de Chasans slowly began to exact his vengeance.

CHAPTER 10

Rape?

Just over a year after Pierre Baillet and Philibert Neugot vanished, on 14 November 1639 Philippe Giroux filed a request to the Parlement to be received as a *partie* (a co-prosecutor joining the king's officers) in a trial against Pierre Saumaise de Chasans "for a violent and bloody rape." The alleged victim was a twelve-year-old girl named Hilaire Moreau. A final, preposterous charge by Giroux intended to eliminate his enemy, once and for all, by hanging a capital crime around his neck? This was certainly what Saumaise assumed, and he countered with an accusation of a conspiracy against him.

However unlikely the charge may have seemed, the Parlement was required to take it seriously, and on 21 November it summoned Hilaire Moreau to appear. The next day it opened a case which saw Giroux and Saumaise squaring off once again as litigants, simultaneously both plaintiffs and defendants. Conseillers Girard Sayve and Michel Millière were named commissioners to investigate the case and lead the prosecution with the king's officials, the royal prosecutor general and the advocate general. Millière—the same man who six months later with Antoine Jacquot would be entrusted with investigating the murder of Baillet—was, as we have seen, allied by marriage to Saumaise and no friend of Giroux. Giroux could not have been very pleased with his appointment.

Whatever Giroux's apprehensions or misgivings, on 28 November 1639 Hilaire Moreau told the commissioners in person a most interesting story. She announced to them that she was a twelve-and-a-half-year-old orphan who had been raped by Pierre Saumaise de Chasans. The woman with whom she lived, the wife of a grape grower named Michelle Guyennot, had told her just two days previously that she should go to an inn in the village of Nuits called Saint Laurent where she would meet a monk with important information concerning the assault. She did so, and the monk informed her that a case against Saumaise had been filed in court on her behalf and that she would therefore be called to give testimony. The mysterious monk warned her to tell the truth and never renounce the accusation once it was given, for that would bring upon her the wrath of God and eternal torment in hell.

So here she was, telling her story. She recounted how Saumaise had first tried to seduce her in the upstairs room in the home of Guyennot, "kissing her with his tongue in her mouth." That first time he did not force himself upon her and "did not know her [sexually]." Perhaps hoping that she would relent next time, he gave her twenty sous. A second encounter followed. This time Saumaise told her frankly that he wanted to have sex with her, again in the same room in the home of Guyennot. Again he kissed her, but when he "wanted to put it in," Moreau recounted, he was unable to get an erection. Before anything more could happen, Guyennot arrived on the scene and Saumaise hurriedly left. It was the third time, in the woods near Nuits, that he forcefully violated her. This was a serious accusation, since rape was a capital crime at the time. Saumaise knew well that a convicted rapist would hang or, if he was of noble blood, have his head hacked off by the high executioner. Before a conviction could be reached, however, first the judges had to decide whether Moreau's word could be trusted. In any case, a conviction required not just an accusation but testimony. It was forthcoming soon enough, and soon the clouds darkened further for Saumaise.

On 4 December the court received a deposition signed by a man from Beaune named Marc-Antoine de La Tour that supported the accusation of rape. This document attested that the rape had occurred in the woods outside the village of Nuits, a settlement about twenty miles south of Dijon, halfway on the king's highway to Beaune. De La Tour did not claim to be an eyewitness, saying simply that he had heard of the assault. The next day, 5 December, two more depositions came to the court, bearing the signatures of two women from Beaune who claimed to be midwives. They attested that Moreau had been violated, that shortly after the rape they had taken her to the widow of an apothecary named Françoise Cornuelle, who still ran the shop and treated the girl with some unspecified medication. Normally in rape cases the Parlement would order a court-appointed midwife to examine the victim and determine if a rape had occurred. A broken hymen was indication of sexual activity, although not necessarily rape, and this would have been the first sign the midwife would have looked for. There is no record that Parlement ordered such an examination, or that one took place; we can only presume that the court accepted the validity of the depositions from the midwives from Beaune.

Then the judge read depositions from two more witnesses, Jacques Pierre and Jean Philibert de La Violette, who spelled real trouble for Saumaise because they claimed to be eyewitnesses to the rape. According to their depositions they had seen the assault by Saumaise in the woods near Nuits, and after Saumaise had left Moreau bloody and dazed, they had brought the girl to the midwives for help. Thus by the end of the first week in December, all the pieces for a capital conviction against Saumaise were in place: corpus delicti (the raped girl, her experience confirmed by testimony from midwives) and two eyewitnesses. Now the judges had to decide whether these witnesses were telling the truth or instead were pawns in the blood feud between Giroux and Saumaise.

Saumaise, predictably, challenged the credibility of these witnesses, asking where the depositions came from and who had given them. With the exception of Moreau's, the depositions had not been given in person before officials of the Parlement but rather given elsewhere and then submitted to the court, an entirely legal procedure. Witnesses wishing to offer testimony in a criminal case had several options. They could testify directly to the officials of the court: *rapporteurs*, commissioners, even court clerks called *greffiers* could legally record them. Witnesses could also legally give testimony to officials of the church—most often parish priests—who were expected to turn the depositions over to the civil authorities. Third, notaries could receive depositions, and though this more rarely happened, some of the testimony incriminating Saumaise was indeed from a notary who was also a priest, a man named Pierre Ravinet who worked and lived in Beaune. The other depositions in the Moreau case were taken by a priest in Nuits named Hector Méricault.

Saumaise suspected that Giroux was behind all of this. He even suspected that Giroux had drafted bogus depositions, had them signed by fellow conspirators trying to frame Saumaise, and then had them given to Ravinet and Méricault, who could then legitimately submit them to the Parlement. It may seem that Saumaise was guilty of a feverish imagination as well as rape, so blinded by his hatred of Giroux and desire for vengeance that he was given to dreaming up the most outlandish schemes. But perhaps his suspicions were not so far-fetched after all: as he began investigating the handwriting of the depositions, he discovered that they appeared to be in the hand of Philippe Giroux.

Saumaise submitted to the court his allegations that Giroux had drawn up the bogus testimony. The judges then brought in experts in the identification of handwriting, and called upon Giroux to submit eight samples of his own hand by signing his name several times with a thick-pointed quill and a fine-pointed one. The experts examined the signatures, compared them to the hand of the depositions, and concluded that the depositions did seem to conform to the hand of Giroux. Now the tide turned swiftly against Giroux as the authorities stepped up the pace investigating the witnesses and the alleged conspirators.

At just this time, the fall of 1639 and the winter of 1640, the first investigation led by Jean-Baptiste Lantin into the murders of Baillet and Neugot was winding down. The second one—much less friendly to Giroux—would not commence until March 1640. Giroux may have felt that the winds were blowing favorably in his direction, that the time was right for a bold move against Saumaise. He could not have been more wrong. He later admitted that vengeance drove him to become a *partie instigante* in the accusation of rape against Saumaise. He felt that although he might have been declared the victor by the sentence handed down by the Parlement of Rennes on 5 January 1639 against Saumaise, the punishment was not severe enough because it did not fully repair the injury to Giroux's honor that Saumaise had inflicted. It was not enough that Saumaise was forced to perform the shameful amende honorable, nor that Saumaise was required to pay to Giroux 3,000£ in damages, nor even that Saumaise was suspended from his judgeship a second time and exiled to his home in Beaune. Giroux wanted to be rid of him for good, and a conviction of rape would accomplish the task.

The unfolding of this case, which coincided with the murder trial, turned sharply against Giroux almost as soon as the depositions that spoke against Saumaise were delivered. In mid-December Michelle Guyennot, in whose

home Moreau alleged that Saumaise had twice tried to seduce her, testified
to hearing from Françoise Cornuelle that Moreau had accused Saumaise of
raping her. In fact, Guyennot reported that she had hastened over to Cornuelle's apothecary shop when Moreau had been brought there after the
alleged sexual assault and discovered no signs of a rape on the girl, but
only marks on her body suggesting a beating. The case, as far as Giroux
was concerned, unraveled further in January 1640 with the testimony of
Claude Poyet, the innkeeper of the hostelry in Nuits called Saint Laurent
where Moreau had met with the unidentified monk. Poyet recalled that in
late November a monk had indeed stayed at his inn. Because he was always
hooded his face remained obscured, and he never identified himself. Poyet
added, however, that he had since heard from a law clerk named Antoine
Thevenin who lived in Nuits that the monk was Philippe Giroux in disguise.
Thevenin had good reason to be able to identify Giroux had he seen him
that day, for Thevenin had worked for Giroux for two years, one year while
Philippe was a law student at the prestigious University of Bourges and another year while he was a judge on Dijon's Parlement.

Investigation continued to swing in Saumaise's favor. On 1 February an
order for the arrest of Mathieu Clodon was issued by Parlement. Clodon was
a lackey in the service of Giroux, and he was suspected of involvement in the
case because he had been no more effective in disguising himself than his
master had been in parading as a monk. On 12 March Clodon told the authorities that he had delivered some "letters" to the notary Ravinet in Beaune
and to the priest Méricault in Nuits. Were these the fake depositions Giroux
had supposedly drafted and had false witnesses sign? At this stage we cannot be sure, but Clodon did tell the authorities that to hide his identity and
so avoid implicating his master in this curious mission, he had dressed like
a grape grower and dyed his red hair black. He did all of this, he added, at
the behest of his master Giroux.

If cracks in the dam were opening in the winter of 1640, by the spring it
broke against Giroux completely. Testimony flooded in, and in nearly every
instance it favored Saumaise. The first witness to turn against Giroux was
Marc-Antoine de La Tour. On 23 April he confessed that he had given false
testimony on 4 December 1639 concerning Saumaise's supposed rape of
Hilaire Moreau. Furthermore, he admitted that Giroux and Catherine Rhodier, a peasant woman who was born a serf tied to the lands of Saumaise,

had concocted the scheme to frame Saumaise and persuaded de La Tour to testify against him. On 11 May, about the time when Dijon's jail was filling up with Giroux associates accused of being involved in the murders of Baillet and Neugot, the court suspected that more witnesses might have given false testimony. It therefore ordered the arrest of Françoise Cornuelle (the widow of the apothecary), Michelle Guyennot, de La Tour, Antoine Thevenin (Giroux's former law clerk), the notary Ravinet, and the priest Méricault. They also took into custody the Dijonnais lawyer Louis Gascon and a lawyer from Nuits named Jacques de La Barre. Counting Catherine Rhodier and Mathieu Clodon, who were already jailed, and the host of suspected accomplices to Giroux in the supposed murder of Baillet and Neugot who were also arrested that spring, the local jailhouse was now overflowing with servants and associates of Philippe Giroux.

The notary Ravinet was heard first. On 14 May he was asked by the judges at Parlement where the depositions that he had tendered to the court incriminating Saumaise for rape had come from. Ravinet broke down and begged forgiveness of the court and of Saumaise. He confessed that he had received the depositions, innocently, from Giroux and had the witnesses sign them because his religious superior, Dean Morelet of the Church of Notre Dame in Beaune, had told him to do so. Ravinet concluded his testimony by adding that Morelet was a cousin of Giroux, and that Giroux had promised Ravinet to protect him from any harm that might come his way as a result of the depositions. The other man to receive and then submit false testimony to the court was the priest from Nuits, Hector Méricault. He, like Ravinet, threw himself at the mercy of the court, while also trying to deflect blame elsewhere. He pleaded that he had taken the testimony only under duress, that a lawyer from Nuits named Jacques de La Barre had told him to do so because it was Philippe Giroux's wish. The hapless priest also told the judges that de La Barre had carried with him letters from Giroux expressly declaring his orders.

During the next week the law clerk Thevenin, Giroux's lackey Claude Lucia, and the Dijonnais lawyer Louis Gascon were heard. Thevenin confirmed that he had recognized Giroux disguised as a monk at the inn in Nuits, while Lucia said he had overheard de La Tour, among others, talking with Giroux about giving false testimony. Gascon confessed to knowing that Giroux had written letters and sent them to "some priests in Beaune" (probably Dean Morelet, Ravinet, and perhaps Méricault), asking them to take down the depositions. Gascon added that Giroux told the priests to do this because the commissioners handling the case—Sayve and Millière—were incompetent. Giroux ordered him to make copies of the letters sent to the priests.

On 30 May the judges called Hilaire Moreau before them again, and what she said was extremely damaging to Giroux. She reversed her earlier testimony and now denied that Saumaise had had sexual intercourse with her. She announced now "that the Lord de Chasans had never been in her and that she was [still] a virgin." She admitted that Saumaise had visited her at Guyennot's house, but that Saumaise had only kissed her "without force." True, he "kissed her with his tongue in her mouth and caressed her body, but didn't come to the act itself." She said that it was Guyennot's husband Patriarche who told her "four times that she had to say that Saumaise had raped her," and that Françoise Cornuelle told her to say that she was pregnant by Saumaise. She finished this confession by begging the forgiveness of the court and of Saumaise.

Now the job for the judges was to close in on all the guilty parties and move toward conviction. We have no evidence that they ordered an examination of Moreau to determine whether she was a virgin or not, but given the confessions that ensued perhaps there was no need. What Mathieu Clodon (Giroux's lackey with the dyed black hair), Marc-Antoine de La Tour, Catherine Rhodier, Michelle Guyennot, and Françoise Cornuelle had to say now sealed the case against Giroux. First, Clodon. He confessed that he delivered some letters to some priests in Beaune, and to dyeing his naturally red hair black in the hopes of escaping identification, but he did everything on orders from Giroux his master, who would have beaten him had he disobeyed. He denied that he had ever been in Nuits, however, and so hoped to deflect suspicion that he might have been one of the supposed eyewitnesses to the alleged rape.

De La Tour came next, and he too pointed his finger directly at Giroux. Right off he owned up that whatever he had done to Saumaise had been at the bidding of Giroux. He did so, he said, because Giroux had promised him that in exchange for his help in this case he would see to it that a civil case then in progress between Saumaise and de La Tour would be resolved in de La Tour's favor. With such a powerful incentive, de La Tour confessed, he hunted for other "witnesses" who would agree to testify falsely and frame Saumaise in the rape case. This witness also implicated Catherine Rhodier, saying that she too was sent looking for agreeable "witnesses." In fact, he blubbered, it was Rhodier who hatched the whole scheme with Giroux in the first place.

Naturally the judges wanted to hear what Rhodier had to say about all of this, so she too was hauled before them. The first thing she said was that she, like de La Tour, was involved in a civil dispute with Saumaise about a contested inheritance. It seems that she had had several bastard children by Saumaise's recently deceased uncle, and she was suing in court to have some of the property settled upon them. The case revolved around a contested last will and testament, or rather two, for in one the bastards were to receive an inheritance, while in the other Saumaise was declared the sole and universal heir. Rhodier was thus looking out for the welfare of her children against Saumaise, a man she held to be mean-spirited and greedy. It may have appeared that Rhodier had good reason to approach Giroux with a conspiracy to frame Saumaise for rape, but she resolutely denied having done so. She knew of Giroux's ongoing "difficulties" with Saumaise—as everyone did— but she did not use this as an opening to hatch a plot against Saumaise for her own benefit. Nor did she advise Moreau to become involved, and contrary to de La Tour's allegations, she did not seek witnesses favorable to Giroux who would perjure themselves and frame Saumaise. In fact, she had never even heard of the whole affair until it blew up in court before the Parlement.

Like Catherine Rhodier, Michelle Guyennot assumed a defensive mode in her interrogation, denying any wrongdoing whatsoever. She said that whatever had been reported against her was "invented" by her enemies, that she had only seen Saumaise twice before, once in her house when he dropped in unexpectedly to warm himself up on a cold winter night, and that she had never seen Saumaise do anything of a "lascivious" nature with Moreau. Finally, she said that the marks on Moreau's body allegedly resulting from the rape were in fact the result of a beating from Guyennot and her husband administered as punishment to Moreau, their servant, for sneaking into their cellar and drinking some wine. The third principal woman accused in the case was Françoise Cornuelle, the apothecary's widow. Like the other two she denied everything, although like them she admitted that she was involved in civil disputes with Saumaise and his mother and that she "hated"

Saumaise de Chasans, but her only involvement in the rape case was when she was told by Giroux and Morelet to lead some witnesses to the notary Ravinet. She did not know what for, and she said that the order frankly "surprised" her. That was all.

Giroux's plight looked grave. There were still some loose ends, of course. The eyewitnesses had never been located, but that hardly mattered when the supposed victim herself came forward and said that no rape had ever occurred. With that testimony, Giroux's case against Saumaise collapsed, and all that was left was to decide on the merits of Saumaise's suit that the case was about the defamation of his character and perjury. After all the depositions and interrogations were completed, in June 1640 Philippe Giroux was given the opportunity to offer his side of the story. The reason why these witnesses had altered or even reversed their stories, he plausibly said, was that Saumaise had got to them and somehow forced them to do so. After all, if Giroux could reasonably be accused of such tactics, why not Saumaise? When confronted with the letters and depositions that he had supposedly sent to Beaune, Giroux did not deny that some were in his hand, but he said that several key words had been altered which changed the entire meaning of the documents. He accused Saumaise of doing this, just as he had got a monk from the monastery of Cîteaux to go to that inn in Nuits and then later convinced witnesses that the monk was Giroux in disguise. At every turn, just as Saumaise had assumed about Giroux, Giroux alleged that Saumaise was pulling strings to derail the course of the law, corrupt justice, and destroy him.

One can hardly blame Giroux for feeling desperate. In March 1640 a second investigation into the deaths of Baillet and Neugot had begun, and was being led by two commissioners—Antoine Jacquot and Michel Millière—who were not friendly to Giroux. During the months of March and April supposed accomplices to that crime were being arrested, and they were all close to Giroux in some way—as servants, associates, friends. Then in May, with incriminating testimony in the Baillet murder trial piling up against Giroux and testimonies in the rape case against Saumaise being reversed, Saumaise officially joined the prosecution in the murder trial as a partie instigante. This was a terrifying spring for Philippe Giroux, and desperate measures must have seemed called for.

On 22 April a sergent général, or police officer, from Dijon, Roche Provin, came to the authorities with a most interesting story. On the advice of his father confessor, Provin began, he now believed that he must "reveal to justice a conspiracy that [Philippe] Giroux planned against one of the sons of [Pierre Saumaise de] Chasans." About six weeks earlier, Provin reported, a friend of Provin's named Mathieu Bailly, a professional soldier, came to his mother's house and joined her and Provin for dinner. While they supped, the conversation turned to a most troubling topic for Provin: Bailly told him that the next day Philippe Giroux wanted Provin to come to Giroux's house. It seemed that Giroux had a very enticing offer to make to him. The next day Provin went, and sure enough Giroux promised him a purse full of coins, a position as a *huissier* at the Parlement or as a captain commanding forty men at his family's country estate of Marigny, and an additional 10,000£ if only he would agree to do what Giroux was about to ask.

This is what he wanted, according to Provin. Giroux knew that Provin and Saumaise's son Marc-Antoine (not to be confused with Marc-Antoine de La Tour) were good friends. Giroux therefore thought it would be relatively easy for Provin to induce Marc-Antoine to purchase a pistol, and then make sure that he had it on him a few days later when Provin was to lead Marc-Antoine on a walk by Giroux's house. At a specified hour, Giroux planned to be mingling with some of his servants and lackeys, who would be casually hanging around the front gate to the Giroux townhouse. When Marc-Antoine and Provin reached them, Giroux would lurch suddenly from the crowd, fall into Marc-Antoine's path, and jostle him. This would simulate, Giroux schemed, an assault by Marc-Antoine against Giroux. In the ensuing fracas, when Giroux's servants would converge on Giroux and Marc-Antoine, Giroux would dislodge the pistol from Marc-Antoine's possession and drop it to the ground. At that point, some unspecified people in the gathering crowd would seize the pistol, shoot it, and, Giroux hoped, kill Marc-Antoine Saumaise. The way all this was orchestrated, it would look to everyone like self-defense. Marc-Antoine would be armed, would seem to attack Giroux, and would be killed with his own pistol.

Such was the plan. It failed, or maybe it never got off the ground. Sometime after Provin spilled his story Bailly was called in (his deposition is undated, but it had to be after 22 April and before 1 June, as we will see). As might be expected, Bailly denied knowing anything about a planned assassination of Saumaise's son, nor did he know about anyone giving money

to see it carried out or about the purchase of any pistol. In short, he denied knowledge of everything. About the same time, Marc-Antoine's father
Pierre Saumaise heard of the plot. The hatred that Saumaise and Giroux felt
for each other was limitless, and their conflict was hurtling toward a resolution that would see one of them, and even family members, dead. We can
only imagine the scene when Saumaise heard about the plot, or Giroux's reaction to its failure. We do know that on 1 June Pierre filed a request with Parlement for an inquiry into this attempted assassination. He told the authorities that twenty-eight witnesses could be called, beginning with Mathieu
Bailly. Too bad for Saumaise and for the prosecution that he turned up dead.

An autopsy was performed on Bailly on 13 June, and Saumaise for one
was convinced that Bailly had been poisoned by Giroux's henchmen. The
autopsy was inconclusive, however, simply listing the cause of death as "inflammation of the liver." Interestingly, this was also the cause of death of
Giroux's manservant Saint Denis about a year earlier, and many suspected
then that Saint Denis had been poisoned by Giroux to silence what might
have been a very damaging witness. Whatever the cause of Bailly's death, he
certainly could not testify now, and the prosecution stalled before it got off
the ground.

At this point, in June 1640, the prosecution of Giroux for the murder of
Baillet and Neugot was advancing, and the authorities decided to combine
the Moreau rape case with it, "the two criminal cases to be joined in order to
be judged together," as the records put it. As a result, the final judgment in
the Moreau case had to await the conclusion of the Baillet and Neugot case,
and the sentence for that one was not handed down until 8 May 1643. So between June 1640 and the early spring of 1643, we hear nothing about Moreau
and the rest. In the spring of 1643, however, as the Baillet and Neugot murder trial was nearing its resolution, we again come across documents about
the alleged rape. First is a printed factum, or legal brief, that clearly presents
Saumaise's side of the story. It is undated, but judging from dated references within it to specific events it was probably written on 25 March 1643.
Almost immediately came another one presenting Giroux's side, probably
written within a couple of days of the first one. The latter factum methodically rebuts the allegations presented in the previous one, probably on the
assumption that the reader would have had both factums in his possession.
The factum favorable to Saumaise, which he himself wrote, succinctly sums

up the case for the prosecution, and there is no need to recount its contents here. Giroux had been given little opportunity to rebut the charges back in 1640, but now in 1643 he fired off a lengthy factum of his own that took on Saumaise's account point by point.

First, Giroux made it clear that he considered the whole matter an attempt by Saumaise to capture the law to his private interest and thereby corrupt justice. In lobbing this accusation at the outset, Giroux intended to explode any preconceived notions that the official legal record was reliable, and to insinuate instead that it was a tarnished, untruthful product of the blood feud between him and Saumaise. It was distorted by influence, and Saumaise, for the reasons that Giroux would now lay before his readers, had perverted the law to rid himself of a personal enemy. Nothing written in this case or the one concerning the murder of Baillet and Neugot, in other words, was free of the sordid tangles of power politics and family interests, and so nothing written was above suspicion. Above all, Saumaise was trying to discredit, destroy, and eliminate Giroux so that he himself could win the favor and fill the opening in the entourage of His Highness the Prince of Condé.

To prove his case, Giroux wrote two factums, of over fifty and of one hundred pages, that discredited Saumaise's account. He pointed out that Saumaise's tactics to pervert the law for private interest had already been proven in the slander case concluded with a sentence from the Parlement of Rennes in January 1639, which ruled in Giroux's favor, and that therefore there was no reason to believe him now. Giroux also noted that the officers handling the Moreau case were kin of Saumaise and so were biased in his favor. The advocate general, de Xaintonge, was close to Saumaise by marriage (he was Saumaise's uncle), as was one of the commissioners, Michel Millière. Giroux also alleged that Saumaise had produced six false witnesses in the Moreau case. For instance, two of Giroux's former servants who reversed their testimony in favor of Saumaise did so because, according to Giroux, Saumaise had become their protector. Giroux alleged that these two men had stolen some silver plate from his home and had fled and found sanctuary in Saumaise's household. In return for the protection from Saumaise, they agreed to alter their testimony.

As a result of kin and friendship, other testimony was said to be equally tarnished. Giroux noted that Roche Provin, the police officer who claimed that Mathieu Bailly had come to him bearing a message from Giroux trying to hire him to kill the son of Saumaise, was a friend of Saumaise, something that Provin admitted during the heat of interrogation. Why, Giroux asked, would he be so foolish as to ask a friend of Saumaise to kill Saumaise's son? The whole of Saumaise's allegations, Giroux alleged, were fundamentally irrational. It was implausible that Giroux should have risked his reputation by falsely accusing Saumaise of the rape, after he had devoted his entire life to building and protecting his honor. Were it not for honor he would be inclined to simply ignore Saumaise's illogical allegations as unworthy of his attention. He writes this factum, he tells his readers, precisely because honor does not allow him to let them go by without a riposte.

Giroux continued his defense. Saumaise had accused him of suborning witnesses and forcing them to lie to the authorities. Using Moreau herself as an example, Giroux countered by pointing out that hers was hardly a credible allegation, since during her grueling first testimony, which lasted ten hours, the authorities did everything they could to trip her up by catching her in inconsistencies or contradictions. That Moreau remained consistent to the smallest detail in her story, under all that duress, proves that she was telling the truth about the rape the first time. The only explanation for the about-face in her testimony several months later is that Saumaise got to her and forced her to reverse her story. This, Giroux alleged, was obviously what happened to all the witnesses who changed their story. Giroux finished his attack by asserting that Saumaise was, as preposterous and pitiful as it may seem, in love with the little girl, a pretty street urchin, but that his affection was unrequited. This perverse passion had begun in 1636, when Saumaise had spotted her begging by the gates of a monastery in Beaune. He swooped upon her, placed her in the household of a grape grower who tended some of Saumaise's mother's vineyards, and paid for her upkeep and clothing. There was a price to pay for this generosity, however: Saumaise twice tried to have sex with her in the home of the grape grower but was rebuffed. Angered and feeling betrayed by this ungrateful child, he bided his time, and then raped her in the woods near the village of Nuits. How pathetic and criminal, lamented Giroux. A "little, aged man" with a "deformed body" who "snatched a child still thinking of nothing but her wet nurse," a senseless man who abandoned "all his serious occupations to amuse himself with a doll, imagining himself to be yet in his youth."

And so Giroux presented his case. Still, the Moreau trial, as important as it was, was a sideshow to the main event, the Baillet and Neugot murder case. Late March 1643 was the eve of a break in the case that would throw Giroux into the most desperate straits yet. Saumaise and Giroux, implacable enemies locked in a blood feud, would wage one last battle.

CHAPTER 11

Attack, Counterattack

Philippe Giroux's prospects began to dim in the spring of 1640. The timing of the reversals in testimony by the witnesses in the Moreau case could hardly have been worse. Just when this was happening Giroux's misery was compounded when the investigation into the Baillet and Neugot murders cut ever closer to him. What a devastating blow it was to see his nemesis Pierre Saumaise de Chasans not only elude the law in the supposed rape but at the same time join the prosecution as a partie instigante in the murder trial. It was not long before Giroux was arrested, and from July 1640 he remained in jail, first in the local jailhouse and then in the more secure castle that rose above the walls of Dijon.

From the summer of 1640 to the autumn of 1642, the case against Giroux and his suspected accomplices in the assassination of Baillet and his valet moved very slowly. First and foremost, no bodies had yet been found, and so a conviction for murder could not legally be reached. The authorities spent their energies searching for clues that might point them toward the earthly remains of these men. Meanwhile, the commissioners Antoine Jacquot and Michel Millière continued to pile up testimony and heard scores of witnesses — some more than once — who would provide them with enough circumstantial evidence to gain conviction if the condition of corpus delicti were met. During these two and a half years, Giroux must have flashed from guarded hopefulness to despair. He knew that the prosecution had not yet met the requirements for a conviction, and yet there he sat, a prisoner in the castle, day after day. Then, in the autumn of 1642, another blow was dealt him when his father returned from Paris with the unhappy news that political intervention from the Giroux family's former protector and patron, the prince of Condé, now seemed out of the question. Philippe may then have plotted the jailbreak with Le Gaucher, the captain of the Imperial cavalry who was a prisoner of war in the castle. We have only Le Gaucher's testimony saying that he did, and whether he was lying we cannot know. We could hardly blame Giroux for considering such a drastic plan, in any case. He must have felt that the tide was continuing to run away from him in this case, and without a protector he was dangerously isolated and frighteningly vulnerable.

In early 1643 Philippe Giroux, trained in the law and experienced as a judge, used what he knew best in a concerted attempt to swing the case back in his favor. He used the law. And he used "public opinion." He wrote, printed, and circulated several factums that presented his side of the entire matter and methodically and painstakingly punched holes in the prosecution's case. Factums like these circulated widely and were the common stock of every major court case, scores and sometimes hundreds of these pamphlets spewing forth from a single printing press run. Although a factum would be highly technical in parts, anyone who could read (and even a majority of craftsmen and merchants could read by the mid-seventeenth century) could easily grasp the author's central position. People from all walks of life must have been gripped by the ebb and flow of this celebrated case. No doubt some copies of Giroux's factums found their way into the hands of a shoemaker or a servant here, a merchant or doctor there. They must have been read and then discussed in groups, over the din of toiling craftsmen in workshops, over meals consumed by servants in hot kitchens, over tankards of wine quaffed by men in dark, smoky taverns.

This popular audience of craftsmen, merchants, and servants was not the one that Giroux cared the most about. He was set more on influencing members of his own social rank, men and even women who he hoped could exert pressure on the judges trying the case and sway them to his cause. Above all, Giroux's factums were addressed, explicitly, to "His Highness" himself, the prince of Condé. Two surviving factums presenting Giroux's case bear no dates, but because of the events he refers to within them we can be sure that they were written sometime after the supposed jailbreak in late November 1642 and before 9 April 1643. Both factums charge irregularities in legal procedure so great that a fair trial is out of the question. And so egregious have been these violations of procedure, Giroux thundered, that for the commissioners and judges to knowingly perpetrate them and to continue with the trial against him can only be evidence of the most heinous corruption of His Majesty's—and God's—justice. Quite simply, Giroux raged, he was being framed by his enemies.

The first factum, with the simple title "Factum of the Criminal Trial against President Giroux," wastes no time in accusing the prosecution of corruption, and the target is Pierre Saumaise de Chasans. Here is how it starts: "Pierre Saumaise . . . de Chasans, is a former . . . judge in the Parlement of Dijon. Philippe Giroux, aged 37, is . . . a President in the same Parlement. In the year 1635, the said Saumaise was summoned before the Grand'Chambre of the Parlement from [the Chamber] of the Enquêtes where he had insulted the said President Giroux." Giroux makes it clear from the start that this whole matter began as and continues to be a dispute between two men about honor, and that Saumaise is in the wrong. Giroux goes on to describe his adversary Saumaise as a man of overweening pride and insufferable, self-righteous conceit. When Saumaise was ordered by the Parlement "to live fraternally and without contention" with Giroux, Saumaise was dissatisfied and responded with a flurry of "factums and defamatory libels [against Giroux] that he spread everywhere in Paris." Even the most casual and ill-informed reader would know before finishing the first page of Giroux's factum that Saumaise and Giroux were locked in a blood feud, which had raged for at least eight years now and was all Saumaise's fault.

Giroux laid the blame for everything at the feet of Saumaise. The only reason why Pierre Baillet's mother Jeanne Burgat and his widow Marie Fyot were parties to the case was that Saumaise, working behind the scenes, had somehow convinced them that Giroux was the murderer. Moreover, Saumaise was behind the removal of Jean-Baptiste Lantin from the first investigation. Lantin, Giroux reminded his readers, was one of the best-respected and longest-serving judges on the court, but he was removed from the case because he was not "agreeable" to Saumaise, Burgat, and Fyot. Instead, Saumaise working "secretly" and the women openly and formally wanted the prosecution in the hands of their family and friends, and so demanded that a new investigation begin. This happened in the spring of 1640.

Then, just after the president of the Tournelle, Pierre Desbarres (a cousin of both Fyot and Saumaise), appointed Antoine Jacquot as commissioner to head the investigation, Saumaise came into the open and joined the prosecution as a partie instigante. How could Jacquot accept such a commission, given that he was a relative of Saumaise? In another criminal case involving Saumaise, Jacquot had removed himself because of conflict of interest, yet in this much more grave Baillet and Neugot murder case, Jacquot did not choose to step down and was not forced to do so. Compounding the corruption of justice by a perversion of accepted procedure, yet another kinsman of Fyot, Michel Millière, was quickly named to the prosecution as a second commissioner.

As if it were not enough for Burgat, Fyot, and Saumaise to have family driving the prosecution, Giroux pointed out that seven of the fourteen judges who were not asked to step down from the case for reasons of conflict of interest were nonetheless also related to either Fyot or Saumaise. In contrast, all of the judges tied to Giroux in any way were forced to recuse themselves. Giroux had sound legal ground to stand on, since royal legislation had long ago decreed that judges related to litigants within five degrees of kinship must by law be removed from the case. Yet for some reason, this law was not enforced in the Baillet and Neugot murder case.

Was more evidence needed, Giroux asked his readers, to prove the animosity that the judges held against him? Giroux claimed that even though scores of witnesses were heard by the authorities, those who could have testified on his behalf were never even called. And when Giroux tried to force the court to hear them, his petition to that effect was simply ignored, in yet another violation of accepted legal procedure. One witness in particular who could have badly dented the prosecution's case was Giroux's neighbor, one he never names but refers to as "a lady of honor." Giroux had entrusted his house to her care while he was in Rennes, and since he had departed for there on 7 September 1638, the day after the supposed murder, surely this woman would have seen signs of the bloody assault and assassination that allegedly occurred the night before. In fact, Giroux pointed out, she had been in his home the very evening of 6 September from just after supper until 10 p.m. This woman, better than any other, would know what went on in Giroux's home that night, yet she was never called upon to testify. Not even in September 1640 when she fell ill and Giroux, a prisoner by then and fearing that she might die, pointedly asked the commissioners to receive her deposition. Jacquot and Millière, against all accepted legal procedure, did nothing. They neither agreed to nor refused Giroux's formal request, instead just sitting on their hands until the woman did die, much to their relief.

Witnesses kind to Giroux were not given voice, Giroux alleged in his factum, yet many others who were hostile to him were. To balance the record, Giroux told his readers what these unfriendly witnesses had to say, and pointed out how unreliable was their testimony. Giroux devoted the remaining twenty pages of his factum to spelling out, deposition by deposition, why these accounts were inadmissible in court. He took the reader through the testimony of fifty witnesses, in every case showing how the testimony was either contradictory to known facts or other testimony, irrelevant to the charge, or, above all, based on hearsay. Twenty-five of the depositions were based on hearsay, and many of those witnesses claimed that they heard about the crime and Giroux's guilt from Eleanore Cordier, the governess of Giroux's son Henri who allegedly knew so much about the murder.

Much therefore hinged on Cordier's story. Giroux reported in his factum that the transcript of her testimony included these crucial words: "That all the hearsay attributed to her was false." She added that "it was as possible for Monsieur Baillet to have been killed in Monsieur Giroux's house that evening the 6th of September as taking the moon into your teeth." And then the clincher. "She believed that all of the false rumors came from people interposed by Monsieur [Saumaise de] Chasans, who had even tried four times to suborn her." Once, according to Cordier, Saumaise had sent a Jesuit priest named Gondrecour to do just that, the first time fully a fortnight before the depositions against Giroux were even heard. Then, after Cordier and the other "accomplices" were arrested in March 1640, it was another Jesuit, a father Dagonelle, who preached to all the accused in prison and singled out Cordier by name as he urged her to give testimony against her former master Giroux. Yet another time "four masked ladies" visited her in jail and told her that "she was doomed and that [the judges] might take pity on her if she spoke against Monsieur Giroux." If Cordier said this, Giroux wanted his readers to think, then one could hardly believe testimony incriminating Giroux that was based on something different from what Cordier herself had testified.

Cordier was certainly key to the prosecution, but it had other testimony damning to Giroux, which he also had to counter in his factum. First, Claude Lucia. This lackey of Giroux testified that Baillet had been killed by Giroux and others in his house the night of 6 September 1638. He said he heard this from Eleanore Cordier. Obviously, then, he was lying, since Cordier herself said she had said no such thing, and as late as the winter of early 1643, when Giroux was circulating his factum, she still had not. The only explanation for why Lucia would say such a thing was that Saumaise had suborned Lucia to testify falsely. As for Marie Rousselotte, the servant of Giroux who gave a deposition incriminating Giroux to a parish priest, Giroux admonished his readers that her word was totally untrustworthy because of her immoral character (she was a "public whore," Giroux wrote, who had birthed "two or three children without having been married"). Her testimony was just as false as Lucia's and for the same reason: it was based on hearsay from Cordier. This was also true of the testimony of Antoinette Carbolot, the other servant who seemed to point a finger at Giroux, and of Claudine Pechinot. Pechinot had claimed that on the night of the supposed murder someone had cried out in the home of Giroux, "Help! Someone is killing my poor master!" Pechinot's information, however, was fourth-hand. She said she had heard this from the wife of the huissier Moisson, who heard it from a woman named Morel, who heard it from "a woman or a girl who lived on the rue de la Boissière." This woman or girl was reportedly cleaning some dishes in Giroux's kitchen when she heard the cry.

In this factum Giroux poses as an incredulous victim of corruption, and he caps his attack on the prosecution (and Saumaise) with an argument intended to demonstrate that for him to murder his cousin Baillet would have been counter to common sense. He had already tried to put to rest suggestions that he was ridding Marie Fyot of a spouse so that he could marry the woman he loved, noting that if the two were in love she surely would not join the prosecution to see him tortured, beheaded, or hanged. Now Giroux urged his readers to conclude that there was no motive at all. Consider, he asked, that "President Baillet was his first cousin and his good friend." Four or five years earlier, Giroux pointed out, in 1636 or 1637, the two men had made a journey together and along the way Baillet had fallen deathly ill. Giroux took him to the nearby town of Melun, where Giroux knew a woman who could tend him. She administered some medicines to Baillet and rendered him such good care that he regained his health. Baillet realized that he was indebted to the kindness of Giroux for saving his life. It was implausible that Giroux would have done this for a man he wanted dead. Shortly after Giroux saved his cousin's life in 1636 or 1637, he recalled, Baillet incurred some debts that he could not pay off. Once again Giroux came to his aid, ceding some annuities to his cousin to help him out. Again, a man who wanted someone dead would not come to his aid like this in time of need.

Giroux then closed his factum as he had opened it, reminding the reader that the prosecution's case was but a piece of a vendetta that Saumaise waged against him. Saumaise had been dishonored, he wanted revenge, and he would corrupt the king's justice to get it. But the case trumped up by Saumaise and his accomplices was impossible for anyone with any sense to believe, so full was it of contradictions, lies, and outright nonsense. Most absurd of all, there was not even evidence that a crime had been committed, since there were no bodies. To convict Giroux of the murder of Pierre Baillet and Philibert Neugot, Giroux argued, would be as absurd as convicting someone of arson without evidence of a fire.

About the same time, Giroux wrote and distributed another factum with much the same intent. In this brief Giroux took greater pains to point out that there was testimony favorable to him in the trial record, and that it came from very reputable sources. He called attention to the deposition of Claude Lénet, a president at the Chambre des Comptes who in April 1641 told the court that he had advised Eleanore Cordier to hold strong to the truth and not bend to "the intimidations, subornations, threats, promises . . . or artifices of the enemies of . . . Giroux." He reported that Giroux had "always sworn and constantly protested to him that this was a horrible calumny to which God would never abandon him." Finally, Lénet knew that Giroux "had always lived as . . . a man of honor." Other witnesses were equally inclined to praise Giroux's "civility and honor," one lady testifying that according to what she had seen, Giroux's behavior toward Marie Fyot could cast no suspicion of love between them, much less of an affair. The Lady Jeanne de La Place confirmed Philippe's propriety, saying that he and his wife had always lived together in friendship and without quarrel. Henriette Boudrot, a servant of a Dijonnais lawyer, said exactly the same thing at about the same time, toward the end of July 1641.

In October of that year any suspicion that Giroux had murdered Baillet for his wife Marie Fyot was further undermined when Madame Marie Vitier, the wife of a royal financial officer, testified that Giroux had no such plans. When someone had reportedly said to Giroux that with Baillet gone he could now marry his widow, Giroux had retorted in the presence of Vitier that no honorable man would do that. After all, "he had more money than her and less pox." Once the questions of character and motive had been dispensed with, Giroux turned to logic, pointing out contradictions in the prosecution's case. For example, supposedly Giroux had masterminded an ambush of Baillet in the spring of 1637 as he was en route to his country estate of Crécey. The ambush, so the prosecution contended, only failed because one of the conspirators lost his nerve and allowed Baillet to pass unscathed. An odd story, Giroux countered in this factum, for Baillet did not go to Crécey that spring: he had not been there for over a year because of the open warfare raging in the area between French and Imperial troops. The roads were simply not safe. Anyway, on the date when Baillet supposedly galloped freely by his timid would-be assassins, 7 May 1637, Giroux could prove that Baillet was elsewhere. In truth, he was working as a president in the financial court, the Chambres des Comptes. To make his point, Giroux reproduced in his factum an "extract from the Daily Register of Messieurs des Comptes." There, in a record of the officers working in the court that day, was Baillet's name. Unless Baillet could be in two places at once, or unless the registers of the Chambres des Comptes were false, the whole story about the ambush was a lie.

Giroux used the same method to undercut the prosecution's case about his alleged plot to break out of the castle, turn it and the town of Dijon over to France's enemy, and ambush and capture the prince of Condé. First, Giroux asked his readers why they should believe the testimony of an enemy of the state who had committed shuddering atrocities. Le Gaucher, Giroux said, had made drums out of the skin of French prisoners whom he had first burned alive. Even if the man's character were not enough to discredit his word, what he reported was frankly absurd. It was ludicrous to suggest that a judge like Giroux, who was not a military man and thus knew nothing about castle defenses and their weaknesses, would have advised an imperial captain on how a commando raid could breach the defenses of a castle that was one of the most important fortresses along the border between Imperial and French territory. And Le Gaucher's story that Giroux thought Condé could be captured easily was equally unlikely. The road and the place that Giroux, according to Le Gaucher's account, suggested for the ambush could not even be located on a map, and Le Gaucher told the authorities lamely that he had inexplicably burned the map that Giroux had used to point out the place. Moreover, no sane person would suggest an ambush of Condé between the towns of Sainte Seine and Gray in January: first of all, as everyone knows, the four streams cutting across that road are too high to ford at that time of year; second, it was inconceivable that Condé, the first prince of the blood and thus second in line for the throne of France, would trot down a road as lightly guarded as Giroux supposedly alleged. That road was on the frontier between two warring kingdoms, and French garrisons were consequently posted strategically all along the way. French soldiers, in other words, would have been everywhere. No, Le Gaucher was hardly a credible witness. He simply fabricated this tale because of a quarrel that he and Giroux had had while they were fellow inmates in the castle.

Giroux then returned to a charge he had made repeatedly before, that the prosecution was breaking the law in its zeal to convict him. Most witnesses who could help his cause were ruled suspect and untrustworthy by the prosecution because of their connection or favorable opinion of him, while the accusers' witnesses were heard and believed even though they were just as closely connected to the accusers. Giroux was certain that he was being framed, and that his enemies, above all Saumaise de Chasans, had captured the law and the court. Giroux was certain that Saumaise was behind it all, and he never tired of telling his readers so. To take one example of many about how Saumaise had corrupted the ministrations of justice, Giroux reported that Saumaise had promised Philiberte Monyot, the wife of an honorable merchant in town, to help her cause in a different court case if she would testify against Giroux in the Baillet and Neugot murder trial. Monyot was locked in a lengthy civil court case involving "considerable sums," and Saumaise had promised her that he would intervene on her behalf by influencing the attorney who was handling the case for the opposing party. All Monyot had to do was testify to having heard from Suzanne Odinelle, Giroux's household servant, that Baillet had indeed come to Giroux's house around 8 p.m. on 6 September 1638. Monyot, much to Saumaise's disappointment, refused to do so.

In these factums Giroux hoped to mount an attack against the case that the prosecution had assembled for almost three years. Factums were not printed on a large scale, but there were enough copies floating around Dijon, Burgundy, and even Paris that anyone interested in the case could surely have got his hands on one. And Giroux and his lawyers made sure that the briefs reached the audience that mattered: the power élite (including judges in Parlement). Whether Giroux's account of the affair was convincing enough to derail the prosecution and gain Giroux his liberty would be determined sooner than Giroux might have imagined. In the meantime, however, Saumaise de Chasans launched an immediate counterattack on Giroux's position, and in his factum he recapitulated the case against him.

On 25 March 1643 a factum entitled "The Accusations and Permanent Facts Concerning the Assassination of the late Monsieur le Président Baillet and of Philibert Baudot his manservant" rumbled off an unknown printing press in Dijon, the capital of Burgundy, and quickly circulated up and down its streets. "Baudot" was the nickname of Neugot. A subtitle told the reader that this factum was intended to counter the ones Giroux had just distributed, and that the "Sieur de Chasans" was its author. As Giroux had done on the first page of his own factums, Saumaise announced that it was in his "interest" to set the record straight, and he set out to explain how Giroux in his factums had twisted the evidence. Saumaise never told the reader just what his interest in this case was, although it must have been obvious to all that it was about vengeance.

Saumaise sensed that Giroux's factums might well turn the case in the accused's favor, so he counterattacked, refuting the factums point by point. First, he told the reader that Baillet's mother and widow were only nominally interested in gaining Giroux's conviction. The mother, Jeanne Burgat, was Philippe Giroux's aunt, and the widow, Saumaise reminded everyone, was his lover. Obviously these women could not be expected to pursue Giroux's conviction and death, and there was nothing surprising about their failure to do anything to bring about the conviction: no requests to the court, no petitions, no recommendations of useful witnesses, nothing for nearly four years. In fact, Saumaise alleged, these women colluded with Giroux against the prosecution. With this point Saumaise hoped to undercut Giroux's allegations of procedural impropriety and conflict of interest. Giroux had railed that the whole process had been corrupted because many of the officials leading the prosecution were related to Marie Fyot—in particular one of the two commissioners, Michel Millière. Saumaise here turned the whole issue

on its head, saying that such kinship would, if anything, render these officials more sympathetic to Giroux than hostile. Moreover, Saumaise pointed
out that Millière could hardly be considered friendly toward him because the
two men ten years previously had become adversaries in a civil lawsuit "with
considerable stakes" that had not yet been resolved. If anyone had cause to
see Millière recused from the Baillet and Neugot case, Saumaise implied, it
was he, not Giroux.

Giroux had repeatedly pointed out the possibility that Baillet was not
even dead, and the considerable evidence that he was planning a voyage.
Saumaise agreed that Baillet was planning a trip, but insisted that he never
made it. On that night of 6 September 1638 when Baillet disappeared,
Saumaise stated that Baillet had paid a visit to Giroux to discuss the trip
because it concerned the two of them and indeed the whole Giroux and Baillet clan. Saumaise reminded his readers of an embarrassing episode in the
past that concerned Benoît Giroux and, according to Saumaise, Jacques Baillet. These men, the fathers of Philippe Giroux and Pierre Baillet, had been
tried inconclusively in the Parlement of Paris in 1609 for the murder of a
Jesuit priest named Carré. They had not been acquitted but rather sentenced
jusqu'à rappel. This trial therefore hung like a dagger over the heads of the
men and their families, and Philippe Giroux and Pierre Baillet were making
plans to get it resolved in their favor as quickly as possible. Baillet, Saumaise
alleged, had arranged an audience with the dauphin, King Louis XIII's child
(more likely with his advisors, since the dauphin was a newborn at the time),
precisely to wipe this trial from the record. It was for this trip that Baillet
had all the cash in his possession that the witnesses had referred to.

Baillet never made the trip, however. Saumaise knew this (even if the authorities did not), because somehow he had found out that "all of his equi-
page for daytime and night was found in his house." Moreover, Saumaise
knew that the gates of the town were closed at 7 p.m. because of the hostili-
ties raging in the nearby countryside between French and Imperial troops.
Giroux had alleged that the gates had stayed open until 9 because of the
wine harvest beginning that day, but Saumaise pointed to the registers of
the town council which showed that the wine harvest did not begin until
9 September, three days after Baillet's disappearance. Saumaise trotted out
as much evidence as he could to prove the guilt of Giroux. He recounted

the testimony of such key witnesses as Claude Lucia, the lackey in Giroux's household who had so much to say about the murder. Saumaise minimized Lucia's account of the murder (he was not an eyewitness, having heard of the murder from Eleanore Cordier), but made a great deal of the items that the lackey claimed to have seen (and that the reader is left to assume belonged to Baillet and his valet): a hat, a knife, a rapier, a boot. Of course, Saumaise said nothing of Cordier's (or anyone else's) refusal to confess to any first-hand knowledge of the murder. It was an embarrassment to Saumaise and to the prosecution that to date, four and a half years after the supposed murder, not a single eyewitness could be found, nor the bodies of the presumed victims.

Ultimately all that Saumaise had as proof was what the prosecution had —circumstantial evidence. Like the prosecution, he tried to make the most of it, telling his readers that scarcely a fortnight after Baillet's disappearance, Giroux, passing through Paris on his return to Dijon from Rennes, had an audience with his protector, the prince of Condé. What source Saumaise had for the ensuing conversation he does not divulge, but he wrote in his factum that Condé had angrily demanded, "What have you done to your cousin Baillet?" Giroux reportedly was taken aback and sputtered in confusion that he "hadn't seen him at all." Condé exploded, shouting, "You killed him! Where are your servants? Will they tell everything?"

Saumaise piled more circumstantial evidence on top of his account of this dramatic encounter. He laid before the reader a list of witnesses who might have been in a position to know something about the murder, and recounted their fate. The lawyer Humbert, a very intimate friend of Giroux who Giroux contended was in his home on the night of 6 September, died shortly thereafter. La Valeur, Giroux's servant and alleged accomplice in the crime, was a fugitive. Saint Denis, Giroux's most trusted valet, died "most strangely" shortly after the first investigation into the murders began. The lawyer Joubert, who was quite familiar with Giroux's affairs, died the day after Baillet's disappearance. The solicitor Fichot, "the most loyal of his servants," also died suddenly, as did a servant in the household of Baillet's mother, Jeanne Burgat. Saumaise told his readers that poisoning was never the official cause of death, but by even mentioning the possibility he aroused suspicion of it, and he concluded sardonically that even though the official cause of the deaths was "natural," one must admit that they "certainly [were] quite punctual" for someone interested in removing possibly incriminating evidence from the prosecution.

The careful reader would have noticed in Saumaise's factum that although he filled forty-five printed pages with evidence supporting conviction, all of it was circumstantial. If the reader was aware of Giroux's factums he would have known that much of this evidence was second- or third-hand—that is, hearsay—and not particularly compelling for judges without at least one or preferably a few eyewitnesses. He would also have known that convicting a man for a capital offense without eyewitnesses, a confession by the accused, or above all, corpus delicti (the body of the crime, the evidence that a crime had even been committed) would be highly irregular in French law. Saumaise too must have known that he was on thin ice procedurally, for toward the end of his factum he tried to justify conviction without having any of these conditions met. In the most erudite and arcane part of the factum (and, one might assume, the most deliberately obfuscating), Saumaise trotted out precedent and writings of legal theorists as far back as Roman antiquity which seemed to support his position. Presumably Saumaise did not dare place this material at the beginning of his factum because it would have lodged doubt in the mind of the reader about the legitimacy of the conviction that Saumaise so desperately wanted (despite the textual juridical authority called upon to prop it up). Surely, everyone must have assumed, we need a dead body, a confession, or an eyewitness or two to justify hanging or beheading a man for murder. Saumaise's rhetorical strategy was to put his dramatic material up front, win his readers' emotional sympathies, and then tell them why, juridically, it was possible to go ahead and convict Giroux even if the usual requisites of a conviction were lacking.

Saumaise as much as admitted that he knew his case against Giroux was tenuous, and this no doubt is why he argued that Giroux, noble status notwithstanding, should be tortured to extract a confession. He also argued that since this case involved an "exceptional crime," minors under the age of fourteen could and should be tortured as well (this would mean, Saumaise said explicitly, LaQuille, the lackey in Giroux's household, and the little girl who accused Saumaise of raping her, Hilaire Moreau). By the end of his factum, Saumaise must have seemed desperate for at least one of the three important conditions for conviction to be met. Weighing his factum along-side that of Giroux, something many readers must have done, there would have been very good reason to find Giroux's the more compelling. Neither they nor the principals could have foreseen in late March that in just two weeks the tide would turn dramatically in Saumaise's direction.

CHAPTER 12

The King of Spades

Even as the circumstantial evidence of his guilt in the murder of Pierre Baillet and Philibert Neugot piled up, Philippe Giroux forever protested his innocence. He never missed a chance to accuse the commissioners Antoine Jacquot and Michel Millière of corrupting justice, of turning the law over to the enemies of the house of Giroux. The Giroux family had risen from the ruins of the Wars of Religion, which ripped France apart in the late sixteenth century, and as the family accumulated political power in Burgundy during the first three decades of the seventeenth century it incurred envy and made enemies. To be sure, the Giroux had powerful friends and allies too. No family stood alone in the constellation of power, and the Giroux could count as friends many of the most distinguished families in the province. And for a time, they could count as a friend and protector the ally who mattered most, Henri de Bourbon, the prince of Condé. As long as Condé championed the house of Giroux and its illustrious son Philippe, there was little cause to worry about enemies. But the loss of a patron and protector would spell disaster, and after 1640 both Benoît Giroux and his son became increasingly sure that such a disaster had visited their house. All they could do was hope that the prince would recall them from disgrace, then all would be well. Meanwhile, Philippe's life hung in the balance.

Long before the winter season was upon Dijon in 1642, when Philippe supposedly plotted an escape from the castle, a cold wind was blowing against the fortunes of the Giroux. Philippe had good reason to doubt that he would get a fair trial. When he first came under suspicion of the crime and proceedings were initiated against him, there were established legal safeguards. When cases came before a Parlement in which clear conflicts of interest were evident, for example, the law of France provided for a procedure called an évocation. By this means the king's Conseil Privé, at his behest, could call the case before it and either issue a ruling or remand the case to another Parlement in France for judgment. In 1640, the year Philippe was arrested, there were eight such sovereign courts in the kingdom, all autonomous. Philippe must certainly have expected that his case would be evoked, for he was a sitting judge on the court initially charged with bringing him to trial. His colleagues could hardly be expected to judge him fairly and impartially, since he had worked on the same bench with them since 1627 and was allied through marriage or patronage to a great majority of them (fifty-nine of seventy-three). And if the case were evoked, the most logical place for it to end up, given its notoriety, was the Parlement of Paris, the most prestigious of the eight Parlements and the one with the largest geographical jurisdiction. Philippe may have reasoned that if Burgundy's Parlement could not hear his case then Paris was the best alternative, because the Giroux counted important and powerful friends there too. Unfortunately for Philippe, he would have been mistaken: eventually all judges with a conflict of interest were recused from the proceedings altogether, leaving a rump of fourteen judges — two imported from the Parlement of Metz — to preside over the trial. And none of these were friends of the Giroux. Yet there was nothing that Philippe or anyone else could do, since evocation was a royal prerogative, and a king's decision not to exercise that prerogative could not be gainsaid. Now something had to be decided about what role Philippe himself would play, not just in his own trial but in the normal business of the court. There were laws on the books that addressed precisely this problem: a royal ordinance from 1560 decreed that a judge accused of a crime would be suspended from his duties and not be permitted to enter the courthouse at all. On 7 December 1641 all the judges of the Parlement of Dijon assembled and decided that the ordinance would be enforced. Giroux, by then imprisoned for almost a year and a half, was officially suspended from hearing cases.

Little by little, the tide was turning against Giroux. Assuming that Le Gaucher was telling the truth about Philippe's plot to break jail in November

1642, one could hardly blame him for contemplating such a desperate measure. He was sure that his enemies had captured the court and that Condé had deserted him, and despaired that a fair trial vindicating him would ever take place. Giroux must have feared he would spend the rest of his days in prison, that he would never see freedom again. His father wrote to the family lawyer Pierre Bouvot de Lisle that he was outraged at the hatred his enemies were directing toward his son, and he had heard that Philippe's archenemy, Pierre Saumaise de Chasans, had found yet another false witness to testify against him. After Le Gaucher blew the cover about the planned escape and Benoît returned from Paris with the catastrophic news that Condé was decidedly lost, both Benoît and Philippe Giroux became even more despondent. Benoît also wrote to Bouvot that his son's trial totally consumed his thoughts, and he was doubly concerned for Philippe because his son had told him that he did not believe in the immortality of the soul. A father's heart was now made all the heavier: added to the physical loss of a son was the certainty, in that religious age, of his damnation for eternity.

Still, no bones had yet been found, and to convict a man of murder without corpus delicti would usually be a miscarriage of justice of the sort that only the most venomous enemies of the Giroux would contemplate. And yet Saumaise's factum of 25 March had tried to justify the legality of such a bold move, and on 6 March 1643 he had done the same in a legal brief filed with the court. Citing examples from Roman and canon law as well as opinions of French jurists, he argued that the weight of evidence could be so great (especially if the criminal were accused of several capital crimes) as to justify conviction even if the body of the victim never turned up. For example, he concluded logically, if a criminal burned the body of his victim and so destroyed the corpus delicti, this would not mean that the criminal was innocent and should be set free. The court refused to heed Saumaise's plea, but it did increase the pressure on those who might know more than they were willing to share with the authorities. Just about the time when Philippe Giroux allegedly plotted an escape from the castle, the Parlement felt that it had reached an impasse and so informed the king that torture of the prisoners was perhaps the next logical step toward reaching the truth in the trial. Torture was legal in France, although it was not employed lightly. An accused person could only be tortured once, so hardened criminals knew that if they could withstand the pain, they were likely to go free. This led the popular and acerbic seventeenth-century pundit La Bruyère to question how effective torture was in ascertaining the truth, and prompted him to quip that "torture is a marvelous invention, absolutely guaranteed to condemn the innocent of feeble constitution and save the guilty who is born robust." Still, to "apply the question" legitimately, as torture was euphemistically called, enough circumstantial evidence (called *indices*) mounting to a "half-truth" had to be gathered. It was at the discretion of the judges to decide when that threshold of evidence for a half-truth had been reached. By November 1642, they apparently decided that it had been.

When the question was applied, the law stipulated that no accused could be permanently maimed as a result. Faint consolation to the one being tortured, but such a stipulation was there, as odd as it sounds to modern ears, to protect the innocent. Legal officials took this seriously. The royal prosecutor general Pierre Lénet, the man who had led the case against Giroux since 1641 along with the royal advocate general Pierre de Xaintonge and the two commissioners Antoine Jacquot and Michel Millière, wrote to the king protesting that the means of torture customarily used in Burgundy, the *moine de camp*, or leg boot, risked crippling the accused, who might eventually be found innocent. Moreover, Lénet reasoned, such an overly harsh treatment was counterproductive even if the accused were found guilty, since a permanently disabled person would not be of much use rowing in the king's galleys, an increasingly common sentence for capital crimes handed down by the king's courts as the seventeenth century wore on.

Lénet's pleas were heard, although that was of no help to those doomed to be tortured by other means. The *brodequins* (a hideous device consisting of wooden shivs driven between the shin and a boot laced to the knee), the recommended implement of torture in the Giroux trial, were horrific enough. In any case, on 3 January 1643 the Parlement of Dijon received word from the king to proceed with the torture of the accused "in such way or manner that is practiced in the Parlement of Paris and other sovereign courts of the kingdom." His majesty added that the judges of Dijon's Parlement would be left "to decide what is the most appropriate [torture] for the carrying out of justice."

Giroux feared that he would be subjected to torture, although there was some precedent in France for exempting nobles from such painful indignities. Predictably, Saumaise asked the court to ignore the precedent and torture Giroux anyway. As in so much else, the gray area of legal procedure was colored in by the discretion of the judges. Giroux was never tortured, though the judges apparently deliberated on this matter and came only to a majority, not a unanimous decision. Two of his suspected accomplices were not so lucky. Eleanore Cordier and Devilliers were put to the question, probably in February 1643. We know this not because the official court records have survived—they have not, although we know by law that court clerks were required to be present and to record the interrogations verbatim. Rather, we know because an unofficial witness was present. How Jeanne Desfourneau, the wife of the Lord of Freste, gained entry to the torture chamber—or why she wanted to be there—remains a mystery; the fact remains that she did. This oddly curious woman, perhaps sadistically curious, tells us that she heard Cordier, the governess to Philippe Giroux's son Henri, break under the pain of the brodequins. She screamed that someone had thrown bloody blankets out the window of Giroux's house the night of the supposed murder and that Devilliers, Bouvot de Lisle, and Saint Denis were all there at the time. Cordier added cryptically, Desfourneau informs us, that she would be shocked "if Devilliers got out of this without a rope around his neck."

Desfourneau morbidly listened in on Devilliers's misfortune too. If Cordier was one of those whom La Bruyère described as having "feeble constitution," Devilliers seems to have been one of those "born robust." This man was as tough as he was defiant. When Jacquot and Millière asked him whether he saw blood on Giroux's shirt on the night when Baillet disappeared, he ignored the question and instead lashed out at them, shouting, "By the death of God! You buggers and thieves! If I get out of here I'll give [you] a hundred blows with my club!" Later in the interrogation he said that Bouvot de Lisle "was as guilty in this as he was so why don't they torture him just like the others?" Evidently no friend of Bouvot, Devilliers stopped short of fingering Giroux, however, elusively saying that "if Giroux did [it] he did it only if [Bouvot] de Lisle was present."

Some of the judges on the bench wanted to torture a third witness, Giroux's former lackey LaQuille, but the boy was mercifully spared because of his tender age (he was only fourteen). Whether he would have incriminated his former master we cannot know, but neither Cordier nor Devilliers did. The point of torture, as far as the judges were concerned, was "to hear the truth from the mouth" of the witness. Our modern sensibilities cause us to recoil from such "barbaric" treatment, and we find it ludicrous that any judge could honestly believe testimony given under the duress and pain of torture. Seventeenth-century judges could be dubious too, and so sought corroboration from other witnesses. If there was a convergence of testimony, the judges would be inclined to accept its truthfulness. Moreover, the law demanded that testimony given under torture be later confirmed willingly by the victim outside the torture chamber and beyond the sight of the implements used. And no witness could be tortured more than once about the same crime.

So in the judges' view, the case against Giroux was no further along after Cordier and Devilliers had been put to the question than before. The break that the judges needed came not from their own or the commissioners' investigative efforts but from Giroux's implacable enemy, the ever-vigilant Pierre Saumaise de Chasans. Since the spring of 1640 he had been a partie instigante in the case. Remember that Marie Rousselotte, the household servant, came forward in the autumn of 1639 with testimony supposedly incriminating Giroux—strange that a defenseless, terrified young girl would take the initiative to testify against one of the most powerful lords in Burgundy. We discover now why she was so bold: it was Saumaise who first encouraged her, promising her protection from an even higher source, and who personally escorted her in December 1639 to the chambers of the prince of Condé, to whom she told her story. Therefore it was probably no accident that shortly afterward Condé began backing away from his former client Giroux, and that only three months later a new, unfriendly team of investigators took over the case. Had Giroux known that Saumaise had such access to the prince's chambers and thus closeness to his person, he would have had good reason to fear that the power constellation in Burgundy was changing dramatically, and not in his favor. Once he had enjoyed such grace from his prince that he had nothing to fear, and he was comforted then by knowing that his deadly foe Saumaise decidedly did not. Now, however, the wheel of fortune was turning (to use an image common in the seventeenth century for the fickleness of fate), and Saumaise was rising to the top as Giroux spun helplessly toward the bottom.

The Giroux were convinced that Saumaise had shamelessly bribed and suborned witnesses to testify against Philippe. Moreover, had they known of it, they certainly would have suspected skullduggery on his part when he came to the royal advocate general Pierre de Xaintonge in early April 1643 with information potentially leading to the crucial break in the case that de Xaintonge and the commissioners had been seeking. It is not clear where Saumaise got this information, but when he notified de Xaintonge on Thursday 9 April about "some papers and other things" that had been hidden in a closet in the home of a certain Madame de Vigny, de Xaintonge at once notified the commissioners Jacquot and Millière that he wanted them to join him in the investigation. De Xaintonge's suspicion that something important had been stowed away there must have been heightened by knowing that Madame de Vigny was Philippe Giroux's godmother. At 1 p.m. that day de Xaintonge and the commissioners marched to her house.

The delegation (including two armed huissiers and a clerk who wrote a report on the spot) arrived at de Vigny's. Before so much as informing her of the purpose of the visit, they asked her to swear to the truthfulness of whatever she had to say to them. She so swore, and the commissioners then asked her if Benoît Giroux had given her "some papers and other things" for safekeeping. She replied that shortly before last Christmas he had given her something, but she had not known—and still did not know—what it was. All she could tell the commissioners was that it was locked in a trunk inside a salting tub which was currently in a large storage closet. When the officials asked who had the key, she told them that Benoît Giroux did. One of the huissiers was quickly dispatched to find Benoît and bring him, and the key, to the home of de Vigny. It took an hour or so for the huissier to find him. Benoît then went to de Vigny's, and promptly upon entering he was asked to take an oath to tell the truth. He was then informed by Millière why they had called him there. With Madame de Vigny, the clerk Claude Barbier, Antoine Jacquot, Pierre de Xaintonge, and the two huissiers intently looking on, Millière wasted no time in pointedly asking Giroux three questions. Was it true that he had left a trunk with Madame de Vigny in the house where they now stood? If so, was it still here? And did he have the key to it?

Giroux responded evasively, first offering that about three months ago—he did not clearly remember on what day—he had given Madame de Vigny a locked trunk, which he had since retrieved and taken back to his house. He muddied the waters a bit by then volunteering that he had also left her a small pine box, which he had also since retrieved. Both the trunk and the box contained some papers and some money, and if the authorities wanted to, they could go now to his house and have a look at them. Instead of leaving de Vigny's premises, the commissioners sent only the huissiers. As it turned out, the trunk and the box contained what Giroux had said they would. By suggesting that all the commissioners go to his home to open the boxes, Benoît had no doubt hoped to divert the whole entourage away from de Vigny's home. Perhaps he hoped that someone could be found to remove and hide elsewhere whatever it was that was in her storage closet. When the officials refused to take the bait and leave the premises, Benoît Giroux was forced to try a different, more desperate tactic.

While the huissiers were off on their meaningless journey to Benoît's home, Giroux, now sure that it was just a matter of time before everyone had a look at whatever was in the closet, told a most remarkable tale. Eight or ten days before he stored whatever it was in de Vigny's house, he began, he awakened at his home very early in the morning. When he walked into his courtyard behind the house he spied two small sacks at the foot of the wall that completely enclosed the courtyard. Puzzled, he walked over to them and surmised that they must have been thrown over the wall (which was at its lowest there) by someone on the outside who had approached the Giroux property by means of the stream running just behind the wall. Surprised to see the sacks there, he was naturally also quite curious about their contents. So he opened them.

Imagine Giroux's surprise—he told the commissioners he was "flabbergasted"—when he found bones inside both sacks. On quick reflection, it was clear why someone might have tossed these sacks of bones into his backyard, and what he should do with them. If they were the bones of Pierre Baillet and Philibert Neugot, whom his son, in jail, was accused of murdering, the real murderers were trying to frame him and had laid a devastating trap. He could not expect the law to vindicate his son if he came forward and gave the authorities the one thing they lacked for conviction—corpus delicti. The absence of the bodies of the victims was, up to this point, the one thing that had kept his son from the gallows. Surely, Benoît desperately thought, he must tell no one, not even the servants, and hide the sacks. The authorities would understand that that was his only choice and that his actions should not be construed as an admission of the guilt of his son. If his son were guilty, would he not have buried the bones or otherwise disposed of them, which would have been easy enough? The father knew, he told the commissioners, that the bones would be needed eventually to convict the real murderer, so he hid them with a trusted friend, the godmother to his son, Madame de Vigny.

Madame de Vigny knew nothing of what was in her storage closet, nothing of what was in the locked trunk inside a salting tub. No one but Benoît Giroux knew (except perhaps his son?). The key to the trunk, he confessed, he kept in a small armoire in his own bedchamber. Upon hearing this, the commissioners and the advocate general asked Giroux to lead them to the key, and so off they went to Giroux's house. The key was where Giroux had said it would be, hanging from a hook in an armoire in his bedchamber. Once the key was handed over to the authorities, they all marched back to the home of de Vigny to open the trunk. Millière, Jacquot, and de Xaintonge stood in front of the storage closet with Giroux. Millière then asked Benoît if this was indeed the closet that contained the salting tub that held the trunk that contained the sacks of bones. Yes, said Giroux. Upon opening the closet, Millière asked if the salting tub before them was the same that Giroux had previously mentioned. Yes. And the trunk? Yes. These sacks? Yes. And sure enough, when the commissioners opened the sacks, they found "a quantity of bones."

Now the business before the authorities was to identify them, to ascertain whether they were the remains of Pierre Baillet and Philibert Neugot. Forensic analysis proceeded according to an established procedure, so the sacks were closed again and taken to Millière's residence for formal identification. By now dusk had fallen over Dijon, but the authorities were too hard on the trail to stop. They sent the huissiers for three master barber-surgeons, summoning them to examine the contents of the two sacks. Shortly the men arrived and set about inspecting the bones and the bits and pieces of clothing that they found in the sacks. Mixed with the bones were a broken pair of spurs and the partial remains of boots, shoes, and items of clothing. The surgeons first scrutinized the clothing, but it was by now dark and, working under candlelight, they could not determine its color. Nonetheless they were reasonably sure that it was what was left of a doublet stitched with lace and bearing a row of buttons on the sleeve. Turning to the bones, they were certain that they were human remains and that they appeared to be complete. The commissioners wanted to know if there were signs of scarring on the bones that would indicate violent death. The surgeons replied that it was too dark for them to know, and that anyway the bones were obscured by mud and would have to be cleaned first. De Xaintonge then ordered the surgeons to return to Millière's house in the morning to continue their work. He also summoned the master tailor Jean de Loigny, Nicole Cuyer (the wife of the cloth merchant Guillaume Canabelin), and the master shoemaker Bénigne Rebourg.

At 6 the next morning, Friday 10 April, Millière's house filled up with the tailor, the merchant's wife, the shoemaker, the three surgeons, Benoît Giroux, the advocate general de Xaintonge, the two commissioners Jacquot and Millière, the two huissiers, and the clerk charged with recording everything. The surgeons reported first, declaring that after having washed the bones they could now inspect them more closely, and they found no evidence of scarring on them. They also told the authorities that they had no way of determining whether the remains were those of Pierre Baillet and Philibert Neugot. This was troubling news for the prosecutor, and Benoît Giroux's heart must have lifted if only for an instant. The authorities were prepared for such a conclusion from the surgeons, however, and that was why the shoemaker, the merchant's wife, and the tailor had been summoned. The shoemaker, the commissioners knew, had been the one favored by Neugot to make his footwear. So he was asked whether the boots or shoes found in the sacks had been ones that he had made for Neugot. Rebourg admitted that he had made shoes for Neugot, and that the ones in the sack were his size, but he could not say for sure whether the shoes before him were ones he had made for Neugot.

The wife of the cloth merchant was questioned next. It was quite normal for the wives of merchants to keep the books of the family business, and so the authorities believed that the wife rather than the husband would be a more fruitful witness to call. The commissioners asked her whether she had sold Baillet the material for the clothing, the remains of which had been found in one of the sacks. She presented a large account book which listed all the sales of cloth made by her husband between 1 January 1637 and 31 December 1639, and soon found the entries of sales made to Baillet. Sure enough, there she found a record for the sale of some cloth that corresponded to the material of the part of the doublet found in the sack. The authorities were getting close.

Then the tailor, Jean de Loigny. Asked whether he was the personal tailor of the late president Baillet, he said yes. When asked when he last made any clothing for Baillet, he cautiously replied, "A month before his disappearance, or his death." The commissioners asked what the clothing was made of. De Loigny replied in detail, and revealed that he had made a doublet and had stitched it with lace. He also recalled that he had accompanied Baillet to the shop of the cloth merchant Canabelin to purchase the material. The authorities then presented de Loigny with the remains of the doublet found in the sack, and asked him if it was the same doublet of which he had just spoken. The tailor inspected the doublet closely and turned it over in his hands, examining first the trim along the front, then the sleeve (which was almost intact and decorated with lace), and finally the collar. Then, looking up at the crowd gathered around him, he said he was reasonably sure that this was indeed the doublet he had made for President Baillet. He added, however, that there was one way to be absolutely sure: when he was making this doublet for Baillet, he was having difficulty making the collar stand firm. So he cut to size and inserted in the collar a playing card—a king of spades, he pointedly remembered. Hearing this, the commissioners took up the doublet. We can imagine the tense, hushed anticipation of the gathered crowd, especially that of Benoît Giroux, who must have feared that the fate of his son Philippe had come down to this. All eyes followed the knife as the collar was cut open; then, dramatically, the king of spades fluttered silently to the floor.

CHAPTER 13

Life or Death?

The Day of Reckoning Draws Near

Ever since his son's imprisonment in the summer of 1640, Benoît Giroux was tormented daily by the darkening prospects for Philippe. His despair must have reached its nadir on 9 April 1643, when he personally watched the commissioners Antoine Jacquot and Michel Millière open the trunk in the home of his friend Madame de Vigny — Philippe's godmother — and pull out a sack of human bones which he knew to be those of his nephew Pierre Baillet and his valet, Philibert Neugot. In the afternoon of the following day, 10 April, he could hardly have been surprised to find a squadron of sergeants at his door delivering to him an order from the Parlement that placed him under house arrest. Two armed huissiers were then posted at the entrance to the Giroux mansion and given explicit instructions not to allow him to leave the premises under any circumstances nor to receive any information or visitors. Benoît was further commanded to gather all his servants and send them to the court for interrogation. Armed now with the remains of the victims of the crime, the court promptly ordered that all of the accused (including Philippe Giroux) be interrogated yet again.

Not surprisingly, the first to be heard was Philippe Giroux himself. The commissioners did not, however, bring him to the Parlement for questioning — at least not yet — and so Giroux was spared for a time an unnerving confrontation with the bones, which were displayed in the room in the courthouse where prisoners were interrogated. Instead, on the 11th Jacquot and Millière visited Giroux in the castle and informed him of something he probably already knew, the recent discovery of the bones of Baillet and Neugot. Giroux promptly declared his innocence. He did not kill Baillet or his valet, nor did he have his servants do the deed for him. He repeated this two or three times, and closed his plea with a warning amid a resignation to his fate: the prosecutors were making a grave mistake and would recognize the truth and his innocence after his death. Meanwhile that same day, Baillet's mother, Jeanne Burgat, wasted no time in requesting that the court turn her son's remains over to her for final obsequies in a church and a Christian burial. Her interest in gaining a conviction of her nephew Philippe Giroux for the murder of her son had been tepid all along, but her daughter-in-law Marie Fyot—the rumored lover of Philippe Giroux—had dropped out of the prosecution altogether. On the 13th, however, two days after Burgat's request, Fyot came forward, asking the court to reinstate her as a partie instigante in the case. She also requested that her husband's bones be turned over to her, rather than Burgat, for burial. How the judges and the commissioners Jacquot and Millière felt about Fyot's sincerity we can only guess, but the advocate general de Xaintonge apparently had his suspicions. De Xaintonge asked the court to call Fyot before the commissioners "to respond to certain facts that had come to light during the trial." Fyot, curiously, was never brought forward.

One week after the discovery of the bones, Giroux's plight worsened even more. On 16 April Denise Gentilhomme, the wife of the gardener Bernard D'Ostun, and Françoise Pailley, Saint Denis's widow, reversed their earlier testimony supporting Giroux's innocence. Gentilhomme began a lengthy interrogation by confessing to perjury, saying that she must "clear her conscience" and tell the truth now, adding that if she did not she feared her soul would be damned. She then threw herself on the mercy of the court, begging the judges "to pardon her." Gentilhomme's pleas fell on deaf ears. The rest of what she had to say, however, did not. First, she told Jacquot and Millière that Giroux had tried to get her to testify falsely in his behalf to save his life. If she did not, he would accuse her of stealing silver plate from his home and see her hanged for it.

To make matters worse for Giroux, Gentilhomme also brought up the mysterious circumstances surrounding the death of Giroux's wife, Marie Le Goux de La Berchere, in 1636. She reported that Philippe Giroux's doctor Lazare Rhodot had treated Marie, and recalled that Marie's own doctor Sineau (who died mysteriously shortly after his patient did) had warned Marie that she should take no food outside her own home for fear of being poisoned. After Marie fell ill, Gentilhomme reported, the doctor realized that his counsel had been in vain because Marie's blackened lips testified that she had been poisoned in any case. Denise Gentilhomme's testimony was damaging to Giroux's chances for acquittal, but that of Françoise Pailley, Saint Denis's widow, hurt him even more. Like Gentilhomme, she reversed earlier testimony that had been favorable to Giroux, admitted perjury to clear her conscience and save her soul, and confessed that Giroux had intimidated her "by his authority." Giroux threatened, she added, to buy false witnesses "for a pistolle" who would testify that she was a public whore. For such a charge Pailley might not hang, but if convicted she would certainly have expected at least a public flogging and perhaps banishment from Dijon.

Now, after the discovery of the bones, Pailley must have thought that Giroux's fate was sealed and, like Gentilhomme before her, may have been emboldened to offer incriminating testimony against him. When asked about the circumstances of the death of her husband in May 1639, Pailley retreated from her earlier testimony that had cleared Giroux of suspicion of poisoning. She had said that her husband had been sick for a fortnight before dying. She had also testified—falsely, she now admitted—that she had ordered the autopsy and signed the report verifying its validity (that is, ascertaining that poisoning was not the cause of death). Now Pailley confessed to the court that none of this was true. Her husband fell ill only five days before he died (about what would be expected if he had been fatally poisoned), just after returning from a trip to Chalons-sur-Saône that Saint Denis had made with his master Philippe Giroux. Her husband then knew that he had been poisoned, she recounted, and that he would die from it. Pailley then implicated Marie Fyot, Baillet's widow and Giroux's reputed lover, saying that while in Chalons Saint Denis had been among a group, including Fyot, who raised a toast to Fyot. Saint Denis's cup must have been laced with poison, for it was just after that toast that he became ill. According to Pailley, Saint Denis blamed the "worthless" Fyot for the whole mess—the murder of Baillet and Neugot as well as his own impending death. He had told his wife that he was ashamed of how Giroux and Fyot carried on, and was shocked that they would murder a man so they could be married.

Pailley was not finished. She told the court that her husband had called her close to him as he lay upon his deathbed and asked her to go to Marguerite Brulart, Giroux's mother-in-law, and beg her to forgive him for trying to poison her. Saint Denis wanted Brulart to know that Giroux had ordered him to do so, and he hoped that if he gained her pardon now his soul might not be damned. He also asked Pailley to summon a priest, fearing that he might die before receiving the last rites. As for Giroux, he feared that Saint Denis might confess to the murders on his deathbed: accordingly he intercepted Pailley and assured her that there was no need for a priest because her husband was not about to die. Pailley rambled on, turning now to the death of Baillet and his valet. Giroux's lackey Mathieu Clodon told her, she recounted, that he had been posted outside the door of Giroux's bedchamber on the evening of 6 September 1638. He was ordered to allow no one to enter. Then she recounted how her husband had told her that Baillet and Neugot had been killed (she avoided saying who did it) and that their bodies had been pitched into the latrines in Giroux's courtyard. Saint Denis told his wife that the remains had been retrieved and moved about four months later to a cellar next to the house of a huissier named de Losnay. At the time of their removal from the privy, Saint Denis had noted that the bodies seemed to be whole, but when he clutched at the head of Baillet and came away with a tuft of hair, he realized that they had decomposed more than he had at first suspected.

Pailley then returned to Marie Fyot, implicating her yet again in the murder of her husband, Pierre Baillet. Pailley said that Fyot had summoned her in the late winter or early spring of 1639 while Saint Denis was away, asking her "to guard well the keys to the closet in her cousin's home" (Madame de Vigny was Marie Fyot's cousin). Apparently the keys had been entrusted for a time to Saint Denis before they ended up with Benoît Giroux. No one was safe from Pailley's confession: now she dragged Giroux's attorney, Pierre Bouvot de Lisle, into the matter as well. Shortly after Fyot had told her to guard those keys, she said, Bouvot, apparently not fully trusting Pailley, came to her house demanding that she turn the keys over to him. Pailley said she did not have them. Not believing her, Bouvot then brushed her aside and searched her house. He came up empty and stormed out.

While testimony was turning against him, Philippe Giroux remained jailed in the castle, apparently having lost all hope that his life could be spared. His responses to the commissioners' questions on the 11th betray a depressed mood, and another much more extensive document, of nearly five thousand words, leaves little doubt that in Giroux's mind all was lost. A monk belonging to the order of Minims named Father Larme preserved for posterity an eyewitness report of Giroux's doings between 10 April and 8 May. Larme's recollection of Giroux's actions and words is detailed and explicit, especially on 2 and 8 May, the times when Giroux was summoned to the Parlement for hearings and eventual sentencing. In Larme's account, Giroux requested that he and the curé of the parish of Notre Dame (Giroux's home parish), Father Thomas Chaudot, be with him constantly for what seemed to Giroux to be "this final passage." Larme emphasizes how he and Chaudot prepared Giroux for what looked to be certain death. As with some-one terminally ill, Giroux was expected to adhere meticulously to a highly ritualized script of behavior, to play the part necessary to ensure what was called at the time "a good death." A "good death" was one that prepared the soul for life everlasting. To arrive at such a state one needed to pass from penitence through expiation to absolution. As far as the priests were con-cerned, Giroux played his part well in every way but one: he never confessed to the crime. This cast doubt upon the "goodness" of his imminent death and the prospects for his soul, because if he had murdered his cousin (and the priests certainly thought he had) and was lying about it, he faced certain damnation. The frustration that Larme felt about Giroux's stubbornness in not confessing is evident on almost every page of his text. In Larme's words Giroux "recognized quite well that he could not escape death," and he im-plored the priests to instruct him in the ways that a soul can be prepared for death and merit salvation. This preparation required, as Larme put it, the "profession of several acts in the presence of the holy sacrament and a com-plete abnegation" of oneself, eventually arriving at a "perfect resignation to the will of God."

Although these preparations went on for most of April, the first dramatic moment in Larme's narrative comes on 1 May, when Giroux was expected to confess his sins and ask forgiveness for any wrongs that he had inflicted upon his enemies. Larme does not say what he confessed, and given the con-fidentiality of confession between priest and sinner we should hardly expect that he would, but we do know that he did not admit to the murder of Baillet and Neugot. Given Giroux's pride and heightened sense of honor, we might

also well imagine that he would have found it deeply painful and humiliating to ask the forgiveness of his enemy Pierre Saumaise de Chasans. In any
case, after offering confession to the priest, Giroux approached the altar to
receive the host. At this point Chaudot pointedly asked Giroux, "Well, monsieur? Do you not realize that this is your true and real savior . . . that I hold?"
To which Giroux replied, "Yes . . . God will not pardon me if I have done
or had done directly or indirectly the murder of Monsieur Baillet." Giroux
was then informed that he had been summoned to appear before the Parlement on the following day, 2 May. Fearing that final sentence might then be
passed and execution immediately follow that very day (this was standard
procedure for capital crimes), Giroux spent a fitful night. Upon rising in the
morning, Larme tells us, "he threw himself to his knees and made an ardent
prayer to God not to turn away from a heart as contrite as his." He then was
led by Chaudot to the chapel, heard Mass, and took communion again, in
Larme's words, "repeating his act of faith . . . of the preceding day."

What Giroux did not know is that the judges were agonizing over his case.
Philippe Giroux had sat at the highest perch of the social and judicial hierarchy, and possessed honor and power commensurate with that rank. A very
practical but difficult set of decisions therefore confronted the judges about
how to treat this once exalted man. On 30 April they deliberated over how
Giroux would be interrogated and even what he might be allowed to wear
during the questioning. All of this related directly to the matter of honor.
Should Giroux be allowed to wear a long coat, a short coat, a hat, his scarlet
judicial robes, or his bonnet carré (the square hat of the judge)? The judges
compromised, giving him his choice of long or short coat, hat or no hat,
but they specifically forbade him to wear the almost sacred symbols of his
office, the scarlet robes and the bonnet carré. They also deliberated over
whether Giroux should be questioned in private, "behind the bar" in the
Grand'Chambre of the Parlement, as was typical when any judge was reprimanded by the court, or rather, like all his suspected accomplices, be seated
in front of the assembled judges like a common criminal on the shameful
three-legged stool, the selette. Ultimately, the judges decided that a specially crafted, four-legged, armless chair that sat higher than the ordinary
stool would be used. They had this chair placed upon a carpet rather than
the bare floor, and brought it closer to the judges' bench than the normal
selette would have been.

Thus on Saturday, 2 May, the stage was set. Giroux was led from the castle at 5 a.m. by its commander, the Prince of Condé's trusted man Antoine Comeau. Comeau had received instructions from the Parlement that Giroux was to be brought across town in a carriage, with two hundred armed soldiers posted every step of the way to control what the judges feared might become an unruly crowd. As Giroux made his way to the chapel in the castle that morning, he was not alone in suspecting that this might be his last day on earth. Over a hundred people—soldiers, jailers, cooks, huissiers, servants—gathered in the castle to watch him pass, although few besides the priests Larme and Chaudot saw him throw himself to his knees before the altar and, as Larme reported, "beg God not to desert him."

As Giroux emerged from the chapel and walked across the bridge of the castle toward the carriage, he turned to the crowd of townsfolk who had gathered across the moat and twice bowed deeply and respectfully to them. He then mounted the steps of the carriage, and as it rumbled slowly across town he showed himself at its window several times, again for the benefit of the people who were thronging the streets to catch a glimpse of this once-in-a-lifetime spectacle. Then, upon arrival at the courthouse, he strode up its steps, turned to face the crowd that had jammed into the square, and as he stood between the columns of the portico, bowed yet again to the people, three times. He was then led into the courthouse through the "Great Door" in the front, again a concession by the judges to Giroux's honor (an ordinary criminal would have been hustled in shamefully through a side door). Giroux was then held in the huissier's anteroom until called before the judges. Security was tight, since the judges had ordered Comeau to post guards at every door to the courthouse.

Giroux emerged from the anteroom clad in a long black robe and a soutane, and though he brought a hat, he respectfully held it in his hands. He quaked and his legs trembled, Larme tells us, but he gathered himself and bowed three times before his former colleagues, so deeply that his head almost touched the ground, and so lugubriously that many of the judges, emotionally moved, had to cover their faces with the sleeves of their robes. As he approached the special chair he caught sight of the remains of his cousin Pierre Baillet and his valet Philibert Neugot, whose bones had been arrayed between the judges' bench and the chair for the accused. The neatly placed skeletons were intended to terrify the most hardened criminals, to

The Palais de Justice in Dijon as it appears today. It was in this courthouse that the trial of Philippe Giroux took place. The Chambre des Comptes, Pierre Baillet's place of employment, originally stood adjacent to this building but no longer exists. Photograph by author.

instill such fear that the accused would speak the truth. Then yet another interrogation began, this one led by the président de La Mothe.

Larme reports that de La Mothe was so shaken by Giroux's entrance and demeanor that he could not easily gather himself. When he finally did, he began his questioning by perfunctorily asking the accused to state his name, age, condition, family, and place of residence. "I have the name Philippe Giroux, age 38, son of My Lord Benoît Giroux, President in Parlement, and Lady Madeleine Baillet." De La Mothe then followed, "Do you recognize these bones?" Giroux replied, "No, my Lord." "These are the bones of the President Baillet your first cousin and of his valet whom you assassinated," de La Mothe countered; "Can you really deny this after all of the convincing and conclusive evidence presented in this trial by irreproachable witnesses . . . ? Is it not true that you poisoned your wife in order to marry the wife of Baillet after the death of her husband, and is it not true that you have poisoned ten or twelve people who were your accomplices to these murders? Have you not maliciously and slanderously charged My Lord Pierre Saumaise, a judge in this Parlement, with raping Hilaire Moreau?"

It took all the strength and presence of mind that Giroux could muster to respond, Larme says, but when he spoke he unhesitatingly proclaimed his innocence. He knew well that the trial had turned against him, but he continued to believe steadfastly that the intent of it all was to blacken his name, destroy his reputation, and ultimately kill him. For four years, he reminded the judges yet again, his enemies had guided this trial against him. As false testimony mounted, Giroux admitted that he became increasingly doubtful that his words might defend his life, but he remained resolute to this day that they could defend his honor. Never would he allow the calumnies of his enemies or his own misfortune to lead to a reproach of his father or his son. He admitted now that he feared death, but not because he murdered his cousin. He denied that he killed anyone. The only thing to which he did confess pertained to the alleged rape of Moreau: he admitted using "illegal means to gain the conviction of Saumaise of a crime he did not commit."

De La Mothe then pressed Giroux about the circumstances in which the bones were discovered, reading to him the reports of the commissioners detailing the process as well as the identification of the bones. Giroux was consistent with his father's confession in admitting that they had hidden the bones in the closet of Philippe's godmother, Madame de Vigny, and that they had done so because to have surrendered the bones to the authorities would have seemed an admission of guilt. Benoît had told in this report how early one morning in late 1638 or early 1639 — a time when rumor was already pointing a false finger at his son for the murder of his cousin — Benoît had discovered two sacks of bones in their courtyard. Giroux father and son assumed that someone and no doubt the true murderer — obviously one of the enemies of the House of Giroux — had tossed the sacks over the wall with the intention of framing Philippe. The Giroux decided to hide the bones until the true murderers were discovered, and then present them to the authorities to gain conviction.

De La Mothe then turned to the suspected accomplices (most of whom were Giroux's servants), and following standard procedure he "confronted" Giroux with each in turn. De La Mothe asked Giroux if he wished to discredit these witnesses or their testimony (which again according to procedure Giroux would not have seen). During the confrontation the judge also gave each witness an opportunity to say something of Giroux's alleged guilt. Giroux had nothing negative to say about any of them except Françoise Pailley, Saint Denis's widow: "My lords, this woman is well known for having no credibility for she leads a rather scandalous life." Outraged at such an assault upon her sexual honor, Pailley "impudently" (as Larme put it) blurted out that she was an honorable woman and that Giroux was "an evil man who had killed his first cousin . . . !" This insult touched Giroux little: he calmly and simply replied, while only slightly nodding his head and keeping his hands folded in his lap, that such "insults made by a tart" meant nothing to him. None of the others who were accused breathed a word against Giroux, leading him to conclude the confrontation with a magnanimous plea to the judges to spare them. They were not criminals, but merely good servants doing the bidding of an admittedly harsh master, Giroux himself, out of fear and respect for his authority. And this only in the whole business with Saumaise and Moreau. Of the murders of Baillet and Neugot, since these were not committed by him, they too were entirely innocent.

Giroux's fate was not sealed on Saturday, 2 May. After years of collecting evidence and even after the bones of Baillet and Neugot had been found and identified, the judges still were not certain enough of his guilt to execute him that day. Plainly troubled that none of the accomplices besides Pailley and Gentilhomme would incriminate Giroux and instead remained silent about his guilt, the judges decided that torture might resolve the case. On 5 May the court issued an order that all of the suspected accomplices be "applied to the question" using the escarpins, or "laced boot." By use of torture the judges hoped to hear "from their own mouths the truth of the crime, how it was committed, and who the accomplices were." Four witnesses were to be so interrogated: Mathieu Clodon, Eleanore Cordier, Devilliers, and Suzanne Odinelle. Young age would again spare Philippe LaQuille, although after deliberation the judges decided that he was not to be made aware of this decision but instead would be hauled into the torture chamber and prepared as though he would be put to the question. Perhaps, the judges hoped, fear would elicit a spontaneous confession from the boy.

As for the others, Cordier and Devilliers had already been tortured in February of that year and had offered the judges nothing new, and nothing incriminating. To torture them again was a breach of procedure, but the judges evidently suspected that they knew more than they were revealing, so they brushed illegality aside. As the commissioners Millière and Jacquot and the judges Joly and Moisson looked on, the executioner tightened the boot fastened to Cordier's foot five times, with each application crushing the foot and evoking "terrible cries" of pain from her, as Larme reports, but no confession of guilt—hers or anyone else's. All the authorities heard was this: "Executioners! I have very little flesh to burn, but finish the job and let me die!" Cordier did not die, but the torture was so excruciating that the bones in her foot and shin were crushed and she had to be dragged from the torture chamber back to her jail cell.

Devilliers, Clodon, and Odinelle suffered the agony of the "laced boot" too, but like Cordier they confessed nothing. LaQuille, as planned, was led to believe that he would be tortured like the rest. The authorities shaved his head in preparation, escorted him into the chamber, showed him the implements of torture, and strapped him down. However, rather than the truthful confession for which they had hoped, what they got was a warning. With Jacquot and two other judges standing by, Millière asked LaQuille, "My friend, you see the torment that the others have endured. Are you not afraid?" To which LaQuille replied, "My Lords, there is greater torment in another life for those who coerce innocent people against their consciences to confess to something they know not to be true." He then added in prayer, "Holy Virgin, give me the strength to endure what is to come and allow only

This woodcut, from Jean de Milles de Souvigny, *Praxis Crimins*
(Paris, 1541), depicts the "brodequins" or "escarpins," a
torture that was in use at the time of Giroux's trial and was
administered to his servant, Eleonore Cordier.

to escape my mouth what is not against my conscience." The judges ordered the straps loosened and the boy released.

Despite the suffering they had caused in the name of justice, the judges were no nearer the truth than they had been before they decided upon torture. There was one more prisoner, however, who had not been put to the question, Philippe Giroux himself. There is no record of the deliberation by the judges, so we cannot know how they arrived at their decision that Giroux would not be tortured, but Giroux certainly feared that he would be. Speaking to the wife of his jailer early in the morning of 8 May, Giroux said, "Madame, I believe that today they are preparing the laced boot for me. I fear the prospect of death less than this torment." Just then Father Chaudot entered the room. Giroux turned and asked, "Ah well, Monsieur, what news?" Scant comfort, but probably a relief to Giroux to hear from the priest, "I believe that your judges will assemble today to either condemn or absolve you." The day of reckoning had finally arrived.

Before leaving the castle and returning by carriage to the courthouse on Friday, 8 May, by the same route that he had taken on the previous Saturday, Giroux was led by his priests through yet more rituals preparing him for death. "If this day is to be the last of your life," Chaudot asked, "ought you not return thanks to your God?" An eternity of bliss or torment hangs in the balance, he warned, so "prepare yourself gently and courageously for whatever it pleases God to decide." Giroux replied appropriately, "I abandon myself entirely to the will of God." He then added, "However, according to the order of human justice, I must now only await death. The only thing I would wish for is that it would please my judges to soften the means." Giroux was hoping that the judges would not choose to impose humiliating and dishonorable forms of punishment, which as a former judge he knew was in their discretion in criminal cases. The customary mode of punishment for heinous crimes like those of which Giroux was accused would have been, despite his noble status, burning at the stake or breaking on the wheel. Breaking on the wheel was most hideous, humiliating, and painful. Understandably, Giroux was terrified that this might be his fate, and he knew that the judges needed good reason to depart from custom.

Giroux then went to the chapel in the castle, and again, according to Larme, who stood at his side, heard Mass "with the most tender devotion." In a state of profound sadness, crying and sobbing, he confessed his sins, took the host, and prayed movingly. He emerged from the chapel and went back to his chamber to write three letters, one to his father and one to his sister Barbe, but first one to his former patron and protector, the prince of Condé. None of the letters have survived, but there is good reason to suspect that in the letter to the prince Giroux made an eleventh-hour plea for his life. Giroux was ordered to appear before the court at 12:30 p.m., and so he spent the rest of the morning in prayer, reciting the psalms and the lamentations of Job and of the prophet Jeremiah. As the hour approached for his passage from the castle to the courthouse, he asked the priests Chaudot and Larme to precede him to the court and await him in the holding cell there. He then turned to Antoine Comeau, the commander of the castle and someone with whom Giroux had become friendly during nearly three years of imprisonment, and said, "Let's go, Monsieur, finally you will accompany me to my death." As they walked toward the carriage, Giroux passed several soldiers and said to them, "I'm upset that I have nothing to give you, but I beg you that that will not prevent you from praying to God for me." Then, as he emerged from the gate of the castle and before he climbed into the carriage, a large crowd of townsfolk caught another glimpse of one who had been among the most powerful men in their town and province, caught now in the clutches of the same law he used to administer.

The carriage trundled again across town toward the courthouse. Inside, seated next to Comeau, Giroux was certain that the verdict would be death. He arrived at Parlement, again was led through the Great Door in the front and into the holding cell, again met Larme and Chaudot, and walked with the priests into a room adjoining the holding cell for yet another confession. Incredibly, Larme spied two men hidden beneath a table there, whom he collared, questioned, and then threw out of the room. Larme tells us that the men were sent there by the judges to eavesdrop upon Giroux's confession. If Larme's suppositions are true, then the judges were still unsure of Philippe Giroux's guilt and wanted to hear from his own mouth that he had murdered his cousin.

The judges were frustrated in their plans, as Giroux held fast to his declaration of innocence. He asked Larme and Chaudot, "Ah well, my fathers, what must I do to prepare myself for death and to draw upon me the grace and mercy of God?" Larme replied, "Monsieur, the greatest act of humility that you could do and that would draw on you the benedictions of heaven, is to give satisfaction to your judges and to the people by affirming if it was you who murdered Monsieur Baillet your cousin." "Let's speak no more of that, my father," Giroux retorted. "You would not want me to affirm something that I never did. . . . My father, I tell you the truth without equivocation." Giroux was then led before the assembled judges. De La Mothe, the presiding judge, read the sentence: "The Court . . . declares the said Giroux duly attained and convicted of cruelly and premeditatedly assassinating the said . . . Pierre Baillet, President in the Chambre des Comptes, his first cousin, and Philibert Neugot, servant of the said Baillet." Upon hearing the word "convicted" Giroux uncontrollably blurted out, "Ah, convicted? Innocent it should be!" Giroux was condemned to death. He was also convicted of a host of other crimes: the poisoning of his wife Marie Le Goux de La Berchere; betraying the security of the castle to an "enemy of the state"; attempting the murder of Jacques Simon, Sieur Du Magny (Le Gaucher); contempt of court for the dishonor and disrespect he showed toward the commissioners Antoine Jacquot and Michel Millière by slandering them at various times during his trial; suborning witnesses to conceal the murder of Baillet and Neugot and in attempting to gain a false conviction of rape against Pierre Saumaise de Chasans; and plotting to murder Marc-Antoine Saumaise, the son of Pierre.

As punishment for these crimes Giroux was ordered to pay "damages" of 20,000£ each to Pierre Saumaise, Jeanne Burgat (Baillet's mother), and Marie Fyot (Baillet's widow), 10,000£ in fine to the king, 4,000£ in alms to the poor, 4,000£ in damages to Marc-Antoine Saumaise, 600£ in damages to Neugot's sister, and 300£ in charity to various convents in Dijon. Giroux was also ordered to pay court costs, including the épices, or supplementary salary paid to the judges and commissioners, a substantial charge amounting to 15,000£. The remainder of his estate was to be confiscated by the king. These monetary penalties and confiscations of course mattered less to Giroux than they would to his survivors, especially his son Henri, who found himself now dispossessed at the age of eight: only through the subsequent good graces of the king was he granted a small marquisate which allowed him to retain the title of nobility. Philippe Giroux was condemned to be taken that day to the scaffold for execution, but first he was ordered to perform the amende honorable. In this case, the wronged parties were God, the king, justice, and perhaps worst of all for Giroux, his implacable enemy

Pierre Saumaise de Chasans. Larme tells us that Giroux "was less sensitive to death than to this humiliating and dishonoring action" because he feared "losing honor even more than life."

After hearing the sentence of death, Giroux was led into the holding cell of the courthouse and prepared for execution. He was stripped of the symbols of his presidential office — ritually divested of his bonnet carré and his scarlet robe, which in any case he had not been permitted to wear since his incarceration. Such a ritual officially cast the felon into the dishonorable netherworld of social disgrace. Execution everywhere in early modern Europe "imported infamy" upon the condemned, and this was made visible by the physical treatment of the criminal's body. The body in those days was not thought of as simply the integral possession of the individual human being but rather as a socially defined entity that signified status and standing in a highly stratified system. This system, as Giroux knew as well as anyone, was held together and given meaning by that pervasive notion of honor that so preoccupied men like him. The loss of honor could ruin a family, most directly by ending descendents' prospects of marrying. It was undoubtedly because of this fear of dishonor that upon being led into the holding cell, Giroux turned to Comeau and said with tears in his eyes, "I beg you to assure my Lord the Prince [of Condé] that I remain his servant, and I beg him that this poor innocent who is my son and who has the honor to carry [Condé's] name must not suffer from the disgrace of his father. Perhaps he will be more fortunate than I." The fear of dishonor is also why Giroux was so relieved at what he heard in the holding cell moments before the sentence was pronounced. After he asked Chaudot and Larme, "My fathers, do you know how I shall die?," Chaudot replied, "We cannot know for sure, but I believe that you will be beheaded." Giroux knew that if convicted he could not escape the infamy of capital execution, but he hoped that his judges would attenuate as much as possible the dishonorable accompanying rituals. Spared both the humiliation and the pain of being broken on the wheel, Giroux gasped, "God be praised! These men have much charity and mercy, because according to the crimes of which I have been accused, I ought to be more rudely treated." Opting for beheading was one indication that the judges were trying not to dishonor Giroux. Another was that they withheld a customary phrase in the sentence of death. Usually death sentences called for actions that would obliterate the memory of the convicted felon and destroy in posterity the honor of his or her family. The body might be burned and its ashes scattered to the wind, or dismembered and buried in an unmarked grave, or documents from the trial declaring the innocence of the accused, such as factums, might be destroyed. The judges ordered none of these steps.

But although the judges apparently had no interest in obliterating Giroux's memory, they were not of a mind to dispense with the amende honorable. The first stop on the long, slow march to the scaffold which stood permanently in the plaza called Morimont was between the columns of the portico of the courthouse. There, before an enormous crowd jammed into the square, Giroux performed this humiliating and dishonoring ceremony of public apology and penitence. Forced to his knees, bareheaded and clad in a black doublet cropped at the waist, Giroux had a four-pound taper thrust in his hands. Before uttering the shameful words, he cried out, "Ah, my father! My son! My kin! My friends! What will you not suffer from this affront that will burst upon you all!" After begging forgiveness of God, king, justice, and Saumaise de Chasans, Giroux was lifted to his feet, a crucifix replacing the taper in his bound hands, and forced to continue the lugubrious procession to the site of execution, about a quarter-mile away.

The streets were lined with a hundred armed men who held in check a crowd "so numerous" and packed so densely, according to Larme, "that one could suffocate among them." Giroux apparently regained his composure, for he now strode between the two priests "with constancy and firmness," as Larme reports. The former president had the presence of mind to bid adieu to several people whom he recognized along the way. He even smiled, showing no evidence that he was suffering inside. It was in this state that he entered the chapel beneath the scaffold where, still clutching the crucifix, he bade a final goodbye to his son and asked him always to remember his father with respect and love. He then prostrated himself before the altar, saying, "Receive, O Lord, my death in expiation for my sins." He rose, turned to the priests, and asked them to promise to take his body to the family estate at Marigny for burial. He emerged from the chapel and climbed the steps of the scaffold. He faced the crowd, and bowed deeply three times. Then, his back to the executioner, he dropped to his knees. He heard his sentence of death read to him yet again, this time by an assistant to the royal prosecutor general named Deschamps, and then recited a series of litanies. After

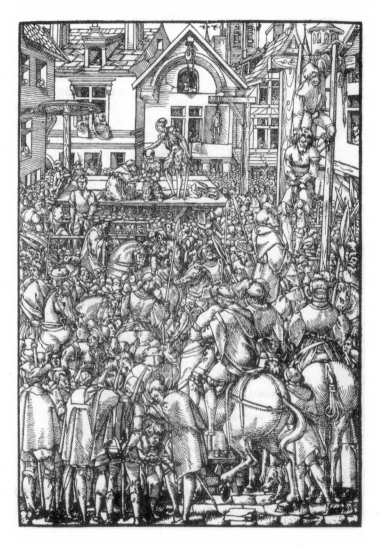

"A Crowded Square on Execution Day." The Place du
Morimont in Dijon, where Philippe Giroux met his end, would
have appeared quite similar in his day. From Jean de Milles
de Souvigny, *Praxis Crimins* (Paris, 1541).

A detail from Bredin's map showing the scaffold where Giroux
was executed. Note the raised platform. There was a chapel in the
small enclosure beneath. To the right of the scaffold is a raised
wheel where the bodies of criminals condemned to be
"broken on the wheel" would be thrown.

that, Deschamps drew close and said that he had orders to ask Giroux one
last time whether he had killed Monsieur Baillet, whether Marie Fyot was
involved in the conspiracy, and who his accomplices were. Giroux, steadfast
in his innocence to the end, replied, "I have told you everything I know."

Giroux was confessed a final time by Father Chaudot, received absolution, and awaited the approach of the hooded headsman. The executioner
removed Giroux's flowing wig to blindfold his eyes. Giroux clutched the crucifix and drew it close to his heart just before the executioner's sword flashed
toward Giroux's exposed neck. The first blow did not sever the former president's head, nor did the second. The crowd gaped in horror and then erupted
in sympathy for Giroux while he was being hacked to death. Larme too
looked on horrified, and reported that many in the crowd tried to storm
the scaffold and wanted to tear the executioner limb from limb, shouting,

The Château de Marigny-en-Charolais, the Giroux family's
principal country estate in the seventeenth century and the site
of Philippe's burial. Photograph by author.

"Death to the headsman!" And they would have done so, Larme assures us,
if the soldiers posted all around the gallows had not kept them at bay. It ultimately took the headsman five blows of the broadsword to cut off Philippe
Giroux's head.

Later that evening a group of nuns retrieved the body from the chapel
beneath the scaffold. The executioner had rolled it through an opening and
let it tumble to the ground beneath, a morbid symbol of how far this once
powerful and honored man had fallen. The head, which remained above on
the scaffold, was then collected by the nuns. Head and body were taken to
Saint Esprit hospice for the night. The next day, as Giroux had requested,
the remains of this former president of the most powerful sovereign court
in the entire province of Burgundy made their journey to their final resting
place at Marigny.

Epilogue

In this maelstrom of intrigue where guilt and innocence could be captive to power and influence, what happened to the main characters of the story after Philippe Giroux perished on the scaffold on 8 May 1643? Sentenced with Giroux was his footman Claude Bryot, known as La Valeur. He was on the lam at the time, and so was sentenced in absentia. Lucky for him, because if apprehended he would have been broken on the wheel. On 12 May Parlement convicted Hilaire Moreau and all the other accomplices who trumped up the false charges of rape against Saumaise. Moreau was flogged and fined 50£, bad enough for the girl, now sixteen, but others received still harsher treatment. One, Saumaise's bastard nephew de La Tour, was a fugitive like La Valeur and was sentenced to hang for perjury. Another accomplice was sentenced to six years' hard labor in the king's galleys, while two others were banished for five. All the culprits were fined in varying amounts, and several paid damages to Saumaise (he cleared about 1,500£ in all).

The next day the court turned its attention to the accused accomplices in the murders of Baillet and Neugot. Lazare Rhodot, Philippe Giroux's personal physician and renowned poisoner, was condemned to spend the rest of his days chained to oars and rowing in the king's galleys. His assistant Hugues Reposeur was luckier: his case was dismissed. Claude Froul, one of Giroux's most trusted servants, joined Rhodot in the galleys, if only for nine years. Rhodot and Froul were also fined: the doctor paid 300£ to the crown and 500£ in damages to Baillet's mother Jeanne Burgat, while Froul paid 100£ to the king and 200£ to Burgat.

The fate of the other accused accomplices was determined by the court on 16 May. For her loyalty to Giroux, Eleanore Cordier was not only crippled for life as a result of the torture she suffered but now banished from France forever. Before being thrown upon the road to hobble homeless for the rest of her days, she was branded and fined 300£ payable to the king and 500£ in damages payable to the victim's widow, Marie Fyot. Other servants were treated as harshly. Mathieu Clodon was sentenced to life in the galleys, 150£ in fine to the king, and 200£ in damages to Saumaise and an equal amount to Fyot. The gardener Bernard d'Ostun and his wife Denise Gentilhomme were banished from Burgundy for five years, while the servant Suzanne Odinelle, the girl who allegedly opened the door and admitted Baillet and Neugot into Giroux's mansion on the night of the murders, was banished from Burgundy for nine years. Saint Denis's widow Françoise Pailley was treated leniently, as were the young lackeys LaQuille and Didier: all three were released from custody and only made to pay court costs. While the judges were tidying up the case with these sentences, they also turned to the weighty matter of paying themselves for it. In the same court order that doomed so many men and women to the galleys or banishment, the judges appropriated 5,000 écus (or 15,000£) from Philippe Giroux's estate and divided it among themselves, the commissioners Millière and Jacquot, the advocate general de Xaintonge, a host of clerks and bailiffs, and even the jailers.

Most of the men and women suspected of involvement in the murder had been dealt with within a week or so after Giroux's beheading. One who had not was Benoît Giroux, Philippe's father. Seventy-four years old when his son died, this leader of the Giroux clan must have suffered greatly during the travails of the son in whom he had entrusted the family's future. Benoît was a suspect in the murder conspiracy (he was formally accused of concealing evidence by hiding the bones of the victims), but when his fate was decided on 20 May 1643, his former colleagues on the bench spared him. His case was dismissed (*hors de cour*). This must have seemed small consolation for this broken man who would die six years later, since the sentence against his son had plundered the family's wealth and ruined its prospects. From Philippe's estate was extracted a total indemnity of nearly 100,000£, a huge sum. And since Giroux was a condemned criminal, the remainder of his estate was confiscated by the Crown. Benoît Giroux must have seen this as the death knell not just for his son but for his clan as well.

As for Philippe's eight-year-old son and sole heir Henri, the king, on the recommendation of Condé, granted him a *brevet du roy*, in effect a royal gift. This brevet restored to Henri his father's confiscated estate, but only in the amount of what remained after all the indemnities had been paid. Henri's grandfather Benoît served as his guardian, and what wound up in Henri's hands was the fief of Vessey and some undisclosed amount of cash. Vessey was a rural estate of modest size, returning to its owner about 1,000£ annually. As the lord of his small realm, Henri could contemplate what he would have owned had his father lived. Philippe had owned several estates, some larger than Vessey, and above all the office of president at the Parlement. With his conviction all that disappeared. Philippe's office was sold in October 1643 to Claude Fremyot for 120,000£, but it is unclear how much of this wound up in Henri's pocket. Probably very little. One thing we do know is that Henri was ennobled in 1666 when his estate of Vessey became a marquisate, but this status did not result, as one might expect, in advantageous marriage. Henri, who became an aide de camp in the king's army, never married at all. Given the dishonor attached to his name as well as his reduced financial circumstances, he was at a severe disadvantage in finding a bride in the status-conscious world that he inhabited. He was the last of his line to carry the name of Giroux.

The fate of Marie Fyot was bound with that of Pierre Saumaise de Chasans. Saumaise, convinced of her complicity in the conspiracy to murder her husband, wasted little time in contesting the legitimacy of her claim to be a plaintiff in the case and thus to be awarded damages from it. On 19 June 1644 Saumaise submitted a declaration to the court alleging that Marie had been an accomplice in the murder of Pierre Baillet. This was not a formal accusation, but it might as well have been. Outraged by this defamatory charge, two months later Marie countered with a request to the Parlement that Saumaise be condemned to appear before the court and to declare on his knees, torch in hand and in the presence of Marie and her kin, that he had falsely accused her, that he begged forgiveness from God, from her, and from her family, and that he held Marie to be a woman of honor.

She also requested that Saumaise's defamatory declaration be pulled from the court's register, torn up, and burned and that Saumaise be required to pay 50,000£ in damages.

Saumaise simultaneously countered with a demand of his own, asking the court to order Marie to beg forgiveness of God, justice, and him and to pay him 30,000£ in damages, and to have the request that contained these "atrocious charges" be burned by the high executioner in the street in front of the courthouse. Perhaps angered that the court did not act on his request and still furious at Fyot's affront, on 14 August 1645, just over a year later, Saumaise formally filed charges against Fyot for her complicity in the murder of her husband.

Just after the new year in 1646, a fugitive was apprehended and hauled before Parlement to be interrogated. On 6 January La Valeur began to tell the court what he knew about the murders of Baillet and Neugot, and as we have seen, he claimed to know a great deal. Saumaise must have thought that he now had the break in the case to prove Marie Fyot's guilt and send her to the gallows. La Valeur launched his confession with a defense of his innocence. He admitted that Giroux's manservant Saint Denis had tried to recruit La Valeur to commit a murder, telling him that their fortune would be made "for this service to their good master." La Valeur balked, however, telling Saint Denis that he would defend his master with his life if he were attacked, but would not kill a man who had done nothing. Curious, La Valeur asked if the intended victim was Saumaise de Chasans, whom Giroux hated so much and with whom he was in litigation. Saint Denis said no, and later when he tried again to persuade La Valeur to come aboard, he revealed that the intended victim was Pierre Baillet, adding that a year after Baillet's murder their master would marry his widow Marie Fyot.

La Valeur must have had good and attentive ears: he reported having "heard here and there in the Giroux house" that Fyot had pleaded with Saint Denis to "stab" her husband with a dagger. While standing outside Giroux's bedchamber "about ten or eleven days before the murder" he also overheard (with ear pressed to the door?) Giroux, Saint Denis, and Devilliers lay the plans for the assassination. Then, three days later, La Valeur lurked in the shadows as he watched and heard a conversation between Baillet and a lord named Pouffier when they were leaving the Giroux house. As Baillet was about to climb into his carriage, Pouffier, "trembling all over," pulled him aside under the gallery behind the carriage and whispered that he had something to tell that Baillet must not breathe a word of to Giroux. Baillet nodded and then heard Pouffier warn him, "Guard yourself well, and go nowhere without two good, trustworthy manservants with you, because someone has an evil design on you." Baillet thanked him, and the two men embraced before they departed. The commissioners Millière and Jacquot had their interest piqued by La Valeur's mention of Fyot, and they asked him pointedly if "the Lady Baillet knew something of the conspiracy." He answered that he could not say for sure. He volunteered, however, that he had asked Saint Denis the same question, and Saint Denis had nodded his head and said matter-of-factly, "Of course. She gave 10 pistoles to Devilliers to kill him."

La Valeur's testimony about the murder is the centerpiece of the "tales of two murders" that open this book. La Valeur admitted that he had not seen the killings but only stumbled into the room in their immediate aftermath. On the way to Rennes the next day in Giroux's entourage, Devilliers had filled in La Valeur on the gory details of how the deed was done. Upon their return to Dijon, La Valeur now recounted, Saint Denis confirmed what Devilliers had said.

La Valeur claimed to know a great deal, and he told the commissioners that because of this Giroux had intended to silence him forever. Or at least that is what Devilliers and Saint Denis told him. Devilliers said that he had orders from Giroux to throw La Valeur from the walls of the town into the moat, while Saint Denis said that Giroux had instructed him to throw La Valeur under the wheel of a water mill or poison him. Dodging this fate, La Valeur was spirited out of Dijon on the eve of the second investigation, which began in March 1640. Benoît Giroux whisked him off to the family estate of Marigny in the Charolais for four or five months and then on to Avignon, where he was placed as an apprentice in a surgeon's shop. Some months later he was moved again, this time into service on the rural estate of the Marquis de Venosque, a friend of the Giroux in faraway Provence.

La Valeur's testimony could be deadly for Devilliers and Marie Fyot. Devilliers had been released from custody on 4 May 1644, the Parlement judges deeming that there was insufficient evidence of his involvement in the conspiracy to murder Baillet. He was released jusqu'à rappel, however, and when La Valeur's testimony provided incriminating evidence the authorities picked him up again on 11 January 1646. On the 18th the court turned its attention to Marie Fyot, and given that she was the daughter of one of Burgundy's illustrious sons and cousin of one of the eight presidents currently sitting on that court, these deliberations must have been every bit as delicate as those involving Giroux. The commissioners, the advocate general, and the judges debated whether to file charges against her on the basis of La Valeur's testimony or simply dismiss the case against her (initiated by Saumaise several months before). An argument for dismissal was that Marie was no longer even in the province and therefore was beyond the court's jurisdiction. On the recommendation of the advocate general de Xaintonge and at the insistence of Saumaise, the court opted for ordering Marie's arrest. She was never apprehended, however, even though, and perhaps because, it was known where she was. She was on the estate of Coudray, a day's ride south of Paris, safely protected by her new husband, noble of the sword and a captain of a regiment of light horse cavalry, Robert de Barville, whom she had married on 29 September of the previous year.

The court, meanwhile, made short work of Devilliers, convicting him of murder on 23 March 1646 and ordering the executioner "to break his arms, legs, thighs and hips" at Morimont, the same square in Dijon where Giroux's head had been hacked from his body almost three years before. Where Giroux had been dispatched relatively quickly, the court treated the commoner Devilliers much more cruelly: his body, broken but still alive, was then to be thrown face upward "toward heaven," on a wheel raised from the ground on a long spike and positioned horizontal to the ground, and left to die an agonizing death.

Saumaise cared little about Devilliers, but he pressed hard for the conviction of his enemy Marie Fyot. It had become a vendetta, and much like Saumaise's feud with Giroux it centered on the defense of honor and the pursuit of monetary damages. In the summer of 1646 Saumaise rained seven requests upon the Parlement for the conviction of Fyot, each time laying out "proofs" of guilt and reasons for conviction. Finally, on 2 August the court acquiesced and issued a conviction and a sentence of death, but in absentia. For reasons never stated, the sentence was never recorded in the official register of the Parlement. Whether Marie was guilty, as in the Giroux case, we can only speculate. Circumstantial evidence suggests that she was, but as with her reputed lover Giroux, it was not possible for the judges to know if this evidence was impartial or true, and neither is it possible for us. We hear from a witness, for example, that at the very hour when Philippe Giroux was walking through the crowded streets toward the scaffold at Morimont on 8 May 1643, Marie had taken refuge in a nearby convent, shrieking hysterically. Was she quaking from fear that Giroux might implicate her in the murder of her husband? Giroux was asked that very question on the scaffold only moments before he lost his head. If in fact she were guilty, could she be sure that he would say nothing against her? Perhaps Marie sought sanctuary in the convent to escape the arrest that would follow immediately if Giroux did implicate her, since in the seventeenth century the secular power—in this case the Parlement—could not apprehend someone who was within the arms of the church. Or perhaps she was distraught over what was about to happen to the man for whom she had such strong feelings.

Whatever she may have felt, we know that Pierre Saumaise de Chasans, convinced of her guilt and harboring an unquenchable hatred for her and the entire Fyot clan, would pursue her in court for over a decade. Saumaise went to great lengths in trying to bring down Marie and tar the Fyot with an infamous conviction. His victory was seemingly won on 2 August 1646 with the sentence of death against Marie. How shocked and outraged he was when she and her family began to maneuver for a reversal of this devastating decision. Even a year before the death sentence Marie had petitioned the chancellor of France, Pierre Séguier, requesting that her case be evoked from the Parlement of Dijon to the Parlement of Paris. The chancellor was a very powerful royal officer who was the personal liaison between the king, the royal Conseil Privé, the prime minister Cardinal Mazarin, and the royal courts. All petitions for hearings in the Privy Council or in those courts were channeled to him and had to be approved by him, including all requests for evocations like Marie's. Evocations were especially requested by the rich and powerful, because the court system of France was staffed by men from those great families, and also because the courts were primary battlegrounds where the families competed for interest, wealth, prestige, and vengeance.

Marie's request for an evocation was therefore far from unusual. Yet Chancellor Séguier denied it, even though her petition had been supported by several unnamed princes and princesses of the royal family, the Bourbons. Marie and the Fyot may have had distinguished friends in high places, but if Séguier was not among them, then her only immediate recourse after he turned down the petition was flight. Political winds shift, however, and families like the Fyot must read them well to survive and prosper in the viciously competitive world of the powerful. In 1650 Séguier was replaced, a victim of the Fronde, a rebellion against his protector Mazarin which erupted in 1648. On 10 May Marie Fyot again filed a petition for evocation with the Parlement of Paris that would, following procedure, first be routed through the chancellor: with Séguier gone, Fyot and her allies must have sensed that his replacement Chateauneuf would be sympathetic to her cause, and so he was. This time the petition was approved.

The Parlement of Paris promptly evoked the case from the Parlement of Dijon, and after a hearing, reopened it. Then, by an order from the Parlement of Paris on 13 May 1653, Marie was brought to Paris in person. To surrender to the authorities with a death sentence outstanding against her, Marie must have been either desperate or confident that her case would turn in her favor. On 13 June 1655 she heard from that court what she had longed to hear for nearly nine years. The Parlement of Paris overturned Marie's death sentence of 1646 and restored to her all property and privileges that had been taken from her as a result of that sentence. Exactly one month later Marie's inveterate enemy Pierre Saumaise de Chasans, incredibly, filed his petition with the same Parlement to reopen the case yet again.

Saumaise, as in his attack on Giroux, posed now as the champion of justice "moved by the hand of God to exterminate such monsters" who would murder a husband and corrupt justice. He hoped to dredge up new evidence, first from a monitoire, and then from an investigation. It was in this heated atmosphere that a torrent of factums written by Saumaise and painstakingly laying before the reader all of the indicators of Marie Fyot's guilt flooded Dijon and most likely Paris. In these factums Saumaise alleged that the reason why such an illustrious court as the Parlement of Paris could even consider overturning Fyot's conviction was that it did not have all the incriminating information. The reason it did not have this was that the legal record had been tampered with. He claimed that evidence proving Fyot's guilt had been expunged from the legal proceedings of the trial held in 1646 in Dijon. Moreover, the perpetrators had done this knowing that the official procedure of evocation required all proceedings from the previous trial to be forwarded to the Parlement of Paris for renewed consideration. How could such a miscarriage of justice happen? Ill-directed power and influence, Saumaise wrote, and it was directed against him. This conspiracy, Saumaise declared, was secretly hatched by "cruel enemies" of Saumaise "in the sepulchral cellars of their powerful houses" with the intention of destroying him.

Through their connections, Saumaise accused, the Fyot had driven justice off its rails to save one of their daughters. Saumaise never tired of repeating that "all of the court [the Parlement of Dijon] is filled with its name," that the court is packed with the "house" of Fyot, and that because of this Marie Fyot was "all powerful." He had a point, even if he exaggerated its extent. One of the eight presiding judges in the 1640s actually bore the name and wore the family coat of arms of Fyot (Philippe, a cousin of Marie), as did one of the conseillers. Moreover, in one of his factums Saumaise pointed out that the Fyot were closely allied by blood and marriage to the first president Jean Bouchu, to seven conseillers, to the dean and subdean of the court, and to the royal prosecutor general. If we extend the family alliances to cousins and other kin, Saumaise claimed, he could count "infinite others." Indeed, the Fyot influence stretched beyond the Parlement and into the countryside. During Marie's trial in the mid-1640s she was held under house arrest in a chateau guarded by fourteen archers. And yet she still escaped, disguised and spirited away one night "under the cloak and upon the horse" of one of the Fyot family's trusted clients. Riding double with this unnamed noble accomplice throughout the night, this "beautiful fugitive" fled eastward, beyond the boundaries of the court's jurisdiction, through the dark forests and over the hills of the Morvan into the province of the Nivernais in central France. There she was given shelter on an estate of another Fyot friend, the first president of the Parlement of Aix-en-Provence.

The Fyot influence transcended Dijon and even Burgundy, but it was the family's tight grip on the Parlement of Dijon that most directly vexed Saumaise. Above all, Saumaise pointed an accusing finger at Michel Millière, who had been one of the two rapporteurs assigned to the case in the 1640s. Millière was therefore entrusted with organizing the prosecution and was privy to every scrap of evidence it turned up. He was also well placed to tamper with the proceedings if he was so inclined. Saumaise suspected that Millière would intrude upon the proceedings to remove traces of Marie's guilt because, as he pointed out more than once, Michel Millière was the son of Michelle Fyot, who was herself an aunt of Marie. In other words, Michel

Millière was Marie Fyot's cousin and therefore could hardly be expected to remain impartial. Moreover, Saumaise counted Millière as one of his inveterate enemies (he seemed to have many). It was therefore unsurprising, Saumaise contended, that when the Parlement of Paris evoked the case and therefore expected all the proceedings from the trial to be sent along, Millière and several subservient clerks had already altered or even simply withheld the twenty-four most damning pieces of evidence against Marie. They did so deliberately, Saumaise bitterly railed, to throw the Parisian judges off the track, to "throw dust in their eyes."

Not only had Millière been corrupted by the Fyot family's power, according to Saumaise, but this redoubtable family also got to the king's advocate general at the Parlement of Dijon, Pierre de Xaintonge. This especially pained Saumaise because at one time he and de Xaintonge had been fast friends and intellectual colleagues. There was a time when these two men would meet and discuss books, forming a small "society of letters." Indeed, Saumaise lamented, at one time both had been driven by "the zeal for justice," even though taking this high road had brought upon them the anger of fellow judges who were less driven by this noble ideal. How tragic that de Xaintonge turned from the just path and against his former friend. And how monumental a betrayal it was in Saumaise's eyes, because de Xaintonge deviated from the path of justice during a trial between Marie Fyot and Saumaise about the attempted murder of Saumaise's sons. Now we uncover the real motivation for Saumaise's dogged pursuit of Marie Fyot: beneath his almost shrill and self-righteous pose as a disinterested champion of justice was something less noble, a vendetta against the Fyot insatiably driven by vengeance and by naked familial and self-interest.

Saumaise was enraged that Marie Fyot had "outrageously," in his words, filed suit against him in 1645 seeking monetary damages. Marie alleged in her suit that Saumaise had no legal right to the monetary damages he had been awarded in the Baillet and Neugot murder trial, and she was demanding that he turn over to her the damages he had been awarded. Marie's suit, however, was a counterthrust responding to an earlier one that Saumaise had lodged against her. He had already claimed in court in 1643 that she had had no legal right to be a claimant in that earlier trial (since she was complicit in the murder), and had demanded that she repay her share which, he added, should rightfully go to him.

Money therefore accounts in part for the animosity between Saumaise and Fyot, but there was also vengeance. Saumaise alleged that in an effort to intimidate him into abandoning his case for damages and ending the vendetta, the Fyot had some of their kin, two men from the Siredey family, attempt to kill two of Saumaise's sons. Although the circumstances surrounding these attempts are murky (there may have been duels, common although illegal practice among France's nobility at the time), Saumaise points out more than once in his factums that only one of his sons escaped the plot, the other dying in his arms in 1644, victim of a sword thrust from one of the Siredeys. We can now imagine Saumaise's pain and rage, and why he vowed to pursue the Fyot (and Marie in particular) for the rest of his days. How much more vexed he must have been when he watched his former friend Pierre de Xaintonge, the advocate general in league with the Fyot, decline to investigate the murder of Saumaise's son. So Pierre Saumaise de Chasans was locked in a bitter and deadly feud with the Fyot and their allies, and his immediate target was Marie. Sometimes the war between these families spilled over into outright violence, but usually and not surprisingly, given that these families were nobles of the robe and not of the sword, it was fought in courts of law like Parlement. Thus Saumaise and Fyot engaged in lengthy and expensive legal proceedings, which in the end could be just as deadly as battles of the sword.

The feud lasted until 1658. In April of that year, nearly twelve years after Marie's conviction and almost fifteen after that of Philippe Giroux, Marie at last received the news for which she must have waited for years. She was informed that her nemesis, who would pursue her as zealously as he had Giroux in his quest to see her humiliated and dead, was himself now dead. Pierre Saumaise de Chasans, a man probably in his sixties, died in Paris, and his remains were quickly taken back to Dijon for funeral and burial in the family chapel of the parish church of Saint Pierre. With Saumaise now gone, the case against Marie was quickly concluded. On 3 June 1658 the Parlement of Paris definitively overturned the sentence of 1646 and in so doing officially restored to Marie all her privileges and property.

Now approaching her fiftieth birthday, Marie was and would remain childless, and thus, like Philippe Giroux's son Henri, without direct heir. In late November she formally claimed her lands, hers by "right of succession." These included two fiefdoms, those of Marigny-le-Cacuhet and Barain, rural holdings of moderate size near Semur-en-Auxois, a day's ride northwest of Dijon. Marigny-le-Cacuhet was nearly five times the size of Henri Giroux's Vessey; amid woods, orchards, vineyards, and arable soil sat a substantial manor house flanked by a moat on one side and surrounded by stables, a dovecote, and barns, one of which held a wine press. Barain, less commanding and smaller than Marigny-le-Cacuhet, sat in a fertile valley and produced a substantial quantity of wheat and oats which generated an annual revenue of about 1,600£ for its mistress.

Like many a seventeenth-century French lord or mistress, Marie seemed to have had little taste for managing rural estates, or even residing on them. Perhaps this was because she was once again widowed, Barville having died sometime between late 1658 and early 1665, or perhaps she simply could not bring herself to reside in Burgundy because it stirred so many painful memories. Instead Marie opted for Paris, and by 1665 she had sold both her estates. The buyers were family, her niece Marie Morin and her rich husband François Bretagne, the lord of Nansoutil and a judge in the Parlement of Dijon. There is no record of what Marie Fyot obtained for the sale of Marigny, but for the less substantial Barain she was to be paid 20,000£ in annual installments of 2,000£. Moreover, for the remainder of her life she was to have usufruct of the estate (which meant that she would continue to receive the revenues it generated). Despite the terms of the contract, the buyers paid Marie only sporadically. She must have been financially comfortable in spite of this, for she resided on the fashionable rue de Garantière in Paris within sight of Luxembourg Palace, the home of a royal princess. From the windows of this residence in 1676 she could have gazed upon the swarms of people pressing toward the bridges spanning the Seine in hopes of catching a glimpse of the notorious poisoner the Marquise Marie de Brinvilliers, bumping in a tumbrel over the cobblestoned street on her final journey to the Place de Grève, where she would soon be burned at the stake.

In 1684 a bourgeois financier in Paris agreed to pay Marie the remaining 9,000£ still owed her by her niece and her husband in exchange for the right to collect the principal and interest from them. A visitor to the archives in Dijon today can hold this document and read the crabbed signature of Marie Fyot, then seventy-five years old. This mundane financial transaction is the last trace of her. And it is our final glimpse into that foreign yet in many ways familiar world of law and power, of justice and influence, of human passions. In the dust of archives and libraries, buried in the vast silence of the past, are all those extraordinary men and women with such colorful names and singular personalities — the blindly loyal Saint Denis, the foolish La Valeur, the pitiable Eleanore Cordier, the somber Benoît Giroux, the august and haughty prince of Condé, and above all the vengeful Pierre Saumaise de Chasans, the beautiful Marie Fyot, and the proud and arrogant Philippe Giroux — the remarkable cast of characters that once strode so confidently, so bitterly, and at times so fearfully through this tale of intrigue, revenge, honor, blood, and death.

Analytical Essay

The Paradoxes of Power, Law, and Justice

In February 1645, not quite two years after Philippe Giroux was beheaded, a book was published in Paris that told a familiar — yet in crucial ways different — tale.[1] The book carried the title *L'Illustre Amalazonthe*, and in its fourth section it began a story about the *Histoire des Sénateurs Rufinius et Balisthène*. Right from the start the author tells the reader, who he assumes is "already fully informed about the subject of the story that he is nonetheless obliged to recount," that Balisthène "always lived in a marvelous probity and an assiduity in his work that was little common among those of his profession." Suddenly, this man disappeared "like a flash of lightning." His wife, the "beautiful and virtuous Bérénice," with her friends employed every effort to find him. The senator Rufinius hated Balisthène and loved his wife Bérénice. So venomous was his hatred that he plotted to kill Balisthène (his cousin) only two years after he had poisoned his wife Kéralie (with the help of his personal physician Toxaris of Rhodes). "As an evil man hides for a long time his malign inclinations, Rufinius could not prevent his vicious habits from eventually surfacing." Balisthène is dispatched, and at the end of the novel, Rufinius is convicted of the murder and, after confessing to the deed on the scaffold, is beheaded.

This of course is the story of the Giroux and Baillet affair, and all of the main characters in the real episode appear with fictional, sometimes Latin names in the novel: Pierre Baillet becomes Balisthène, Marie Fyot becomes Bérénice, Philippe Giroux becomes Rufinius. Lazare Rhodot the convicted poisoner cleverly becomes Toxaris of Rhodes, Condé is Caesar, Pierre Saumaise de Chasans a tribune of justice named Cusanus, St. Denis and Devilliers become Rufinius's "slaves," and so on. Hilaire Moreau, the prepubescent girl whom Saumaise was accused by Giroux of raping, is cast in this story as Morélie.

There are so many correspondences between the "fictional" Histoire and the Giroux and Baillet affair that it is as obvious to us after exploring the historical evidence of this lurid trial as it was to readers in 1645 that the fictional tale seems "true." However, there are two highly significant departures from the historical record. First, we find in the historical evidence that Giroux did not confess to the crime on the scaffold, or at any other time. After careful weighing of every piece of evidence available to us, we cannot be as sure as the author of the Histoire that Giroux was in fact guilty of the murder of Baillet. But even if Giroux was guilty, the historical record leaves traces suggesting that he did not act alone, and here is the second important departure in the novel. Giroux has his henchmen, to be sure, but there is reason at least to suspect that Marie Fyot was also involved in a conspiracy with Giroux to murder her husband. After all, the common rumor in town (a rumor recounted by more than a dozen witnesses) was that she and Giroux were passionate about one another—sexually—and so she had a motive. In the Histoire, however, Bérénice rebuffs the passionate overtures of Rufinius and is horrified that he would murder for passion—hatred and affection. Marie Fyot, by contrast, was reported in the trial records to have tried to poison her husband, to have paid an assassin to do the deed when poison failed, and to have ordered that the bodies of her murdered husband and his servant be removed from the privy in the courtyard of her lover's mansion.

So which story is true? Or perhaps we should ask, Is any of this true? And if so, how can we know? If we still cannot answer these questions definitively at the end of this book, after all the evidence has been found, read and reread, and pieced together like some gigantic jigsaw puzzle without benefit of a picture, then we probably never will. Clearly the novel intends to challenge the implications in the trial that Marie Fyot was complicit by portraying her fictional counterpart Bérénice as virtuous and loyal. When we explore who the author of this book was, we begin to understand why. The author listed on the title page is Le Sieur Des Fontaines, but this is a pseudonym for a Jesuit priest named René de Cerisiers. All books published at the time carried a dedication, and this one is dedicated to "His Royal Highness," Henri II de Bourbon, the prince of Condé. Authors dedicated tracts (fictional or not) to distinguished men and women in an attempt to curry favor, or to thank patrons for past patronage. Cerisiers (Des Fontaines) was in the latter category. In his dedication he lavishes praise on the prince while also making self-depreciating pleas to remain in the prince's entourage, writing that although he "merits it the least he desires most passionately to be for the rest of his life . . . the most humble, most obedient and most faithful servant" of the prince.

As we have discovered in our scrutiny of the Giroux and Baillet affair, Cerisiers was not alone in his attempt to win and keep the favor of this powerful prince. The influence of the prince of Condé throughout Burgundy cannot be overestimated, but he exerted this influence through a network of other powerful families. Men and women struggled to become part of that network because by doing so they guaranteed privilege and power to themselves. The Giroux were one such powerful family. The Fyot were another. Cerisiers was linked with both Condé and the Fyot, and he states openly on the first page of his novel that he had had a "longstanding friendship with the house" of Fyot. Thus his depiction of Bérénice as innocent of the murder of her husband was an attempt to curry favor with both the prince and the house of Fyot.

That house of Fyot, every bit as much as that of Giroux, was one to be reckoned with in the seventeenth century. The Fyot of Burgundy had by then split into three branches, each descended from Jean Fyot, a close advisor in the 1460s to Philip the Good, duke of Burgundy. Each branch for the next two centuries amassed landholdings and placed its sons in some of the most prestigious offices that Burgundy had to offer and its daughters in marriages of equal grandeur. Marie's father François was a man of great wealth and distinction, as would be some of his children. Marie's eldest half-brother Philippe became a canon at the royal chapel of Sainte Chapelle (the most powerful and esteemed religious house in Dijon) and from 1625 until his death in 1640 was the grand vicar general for the bishop of Langres. One of her full brothers, Jacques II, was trained in the law and became a conseiller du roy at the Parlement of Dijon from 1621 until his death in 1645. It was her father François Fyot de Vaugimois, however, who brought the greatest power to this branch of the Fyot. The lord of the fiefs of Vaugimois, Barain,

Couches, and Boussernois and a judge in Parlement beginning in 1593, he became dean of the court in the mid-1620s and thus the conseiller with the greatest seniority. The crowning achievements of an illustrious career came in 1624 and 1625, when King Louis XIII successively named him a commissioner in the newly created Chambre de Justice and a conseiller d'état in the king's Conseil Privé. Marie's father continued to enjoy the close confidence of the king and remained close to the seat of power until his death in 1636.

It is within this tangled thicket of power and influence that legal judgment took place. Judgment was supposed to be based on the weighing of evidence, but evidence had to be interpreted, and interpretation requires a context in which pieces of evidence acquire their meaning. But "context" comes to us, as it did to judges, in a variety of forms, "narratives" sometimes complete with plots and motives. As we have amply seen in this trial, narratives about what happened varied widely, and often conflicted. Depositions of witnesses, evidence so important in the telling of this story, are one form of narrative, factums (those biased legal briefs that Giroux and Saumaise published) another, interrogations of prisoners yet a third.[2] All of these legal documents have something in common, and they are not as far from a "fictional" account like the Histoire as we might at first assume. Each of these "narratives" is about persuasion, is an attempt to convince the reader or listener that the "story" being recounted is "true." In part, our task in getting the story right about the affair of Giroux and Baillet is similar to the task before the judges weighing the guilt of Philippe Giroux. As historians, we are not primarily concerned with proving the guilt or innocence of Philippe Giroux, Marie Fyot, or any other suspects in this case, but we do sift through evidence and decide which pieces correspond most closely to a "reality" that none of us were present to witness. How can we know what is true, and what not? What is fiction, and what is history? Is our understanding of the past—or of the present, for that matter—just the product of competing narratives, each striving to convince us of the truth of its story?

As we sift through these rival narratives—depositions, interrogations, factums, petitions, monitoires, and so on—we ask ourselves the question the judges posed to themselves: What can we believe, and why? And upon what can we base our judgment? To answer these questions judges were supposed to follow certain procedures. By the time of this trial in the mid-seventeenth century, a clear body of legal procedure and practice had built up in France over the previous century or so.[3] Therefore, practitioners of the law (judges, prosecutors, lawyers) by now had guidelines—sometimes explicit, sometimes tacit and simply understood—that they knew they were expected to follow for a trial to be legitimately concluded.[4] This does not mean that procedure was invariably uncontested. As we have seen, Giroux based much of his defense upon the claim that the law had been captured by his enemies and procedure manipulated to frame him. For procedure even to be contested, however, it was necessary for there to be an assumption among litigants, attorneys, and judges that it even could be corrupted, and the potential for corruption required an existing assumption that legitimate guidelines should be followed. This of course rings obvious in modern ears, but assumptions of the supremacy of the abstract rule of law were just beginning to take hold systematically in the sixteenth and seventeenth centuries. Legal procedures, as we have seen in this book, were still directly challenged by the more traditional means of score settling—vendetta.

Most of the evidence gathered for this trial came in the form of depositions by witnesses (hundreds of them) and factums (dozens of them). Judges were required by accepted, customary procedure and by the king's law to accept as valid evidence only depositions offered by impartial and unimpeachable witnesses. Factums, on the other hand, were deliberately tendentious rhetorical attempts at persuasion. These documents summed up a case from the perspective of the litigant and so told a particular story about the case, and in assembling the story litigants wrested, as the historian Sarah Maza has put it, "snippets of 'truth' and pressed these into the service of their own emplotting of the past."[5]

Many factums gathered around the Giroux trial, and even a cursory reading of them shows that they were conflicting versions of the same story. Less obvious is what audience the author-litigant was trying to reach and persuade. Certainly the judges hearing the case. But who else? Determining this audience goes to the heart of understanding the legal process and the role of influence within it. Factums were being printed, which means that more were generated than those simply needed to pass around to judges. All other trial documents, after all, were copied longhand. When Giroux and Saumaise published and distributed scores or even hundreds of factums, they targeted an audience beyond the judges hearing the case and even beyond the boundaries of Burgundy. These pamphlets in fact played a pivotal role in the workings of the judicial system, for they were a nexus between official judicial procedure and power relations among the great, in other words a link between the judicial system and the political system. Trusted clients passed these pamphlets around and talked about their contents in corridors and drawing rooms inside the splendid chateaux of the high French nobility, or while strolling in the gardens that so elegantly graced their grounds. Politics and the law in the seventeenth century were viewed by these people as processes whereby one gained or lost influence through managing the perceptions of others. These same people believed that the printed word in general (and this would include the factum) was especially effective in this management of perceptions, and therefore could be perilous and must be taken seriously.[6]

Gaining or losing influence was of supreme importance to these men of the robe, and so we should hardly be surprised that factums — like novels, elegies, or political treatises — also included appeals for favor. Consider Philippe Giroux's factum rebutting one by Saumaise, undated but published after 17 March 1641 (the latest date mentioned in the document). Giroux assaults Saumaise's character and case for twenty-seven pages, asserting along the way that Saumaise's factum is an unreasonable releasing of "bile." It is not only false but boring, written by "an impudent schemer" of "insupportable pride" who seeks to ruin Giroux so that he may ascend the social and political hierarchy. Giroux concludes his assault upon Saumaise's case by appealing directly to "S.A.," abbreviation for "Son Altesse," or in this context His Highness Henri II de Bourbon, the prince of Condé. Giroux writes: "If it pleases his highness to believe that [Giroux's] debt has been paid, and that this iron that has been so long in the fire has lost its rust, to deign to bestow the favorable regards upon him that in former times had ignited his courage, [then Giroux] will not despair from reentering into the enjoyment of favor that he believes gone astray rather than lost." Giroux here acknowledges that by 1641 he has lost Condé's favor, and that he is in hopes of recapturing it. But how to convince Condé to come back? Use this factum to rally to Giroux's cause people who matter to Condé, those men whom Condé needs to govern Burgundy. Giroux appeals explicitly to a "public" that in reading his factum will see the reasonableness and verity of his case: "The public knows well the falseness of [Saumaise's] factum and that Giroux's is very true."

Guilt and innocence may therefore not have mattered more than power and influence. Or perhaps more accurately in cases like this one, guilt, innocence, power, and influence could not be separated. Patrons like Condé had to heed the loyalties and opinions of the men who mattered, the men through whom the prince governed Burgundy. This included the nobility of the robe, that increasingly important office-holding, magisterial class made up of clans like the Giroux, the Baillet, the Fyot. They are the primary "public" that Saumaise and Giroux are referring to, and they curry favor with it as much as they do with Condé, sometimes, as in Giroux's factum, in the same document.

This book has demonstrated how power could be exerted in a particular murder trial. It also shines a rare light upon a dark corner of history. There are few modern studies of the dynamics of the legal system in its day-to-day workings. True, thanks to the work of Alfred Soman, Nicole Castan, and Christiane Plessix-Buisset,[7] among others, we know about crime and criminality, and from Adhémar Esmein, Richard Andrews, John Langbein, and Arlette Lebigre, to name but a few, we learn of procedure in the criminal justice system.[8] But their studies tell us little about how, in David Parker's words, "vested interests might be at work within France's highly complex legal structures," how the mechanisms of the law might be manipulated for private, or more accurately familial, interest.[9] Our examination of this episode helps to fill that gap. The trial of Philippe Giroux for murder was the continuation of a deadly feud between Giroux and his archenemy Pierre Saumaise de Chasans, and the law became a public tool for family vengeance and private interest.[10]

Our close analysis of this trial also locates it at a pivotal moment in the emergence of the rule of law in European polities, the mid-seventeenth century.[11] During the seventeenth century law was increasingly perceived by the ruling classes as the elemental substratum of a well-ordered state. The chaos of civil and religious war in the previous century prompted many French men and women of the upper classes to welcome a more authoritarian form of governance that historians somewhat uncomfortably call "absolutism." This authoritarianism reflected a change much deeper and broader than mere governance, however, for it grew from a reorientation of how men understood the meaning of order in general and their place in securing it. As Michel Foucault suggested, men of the seventeenth century cast the very meaning of order in a more hierarchical mold, as a new epistemology took hold that emphasized differentiation within an overarching order, supplanting the previous one that grasped meaning through similitudes within a "total system of correspondence."[12]

The chaotic events of the sixteenth century were evident everywhere— from a sundering of the universal Christian church to economic dislocations caused by population growth, inflation, and conquest overseas to poverty, pestilence, and dearth—and brought a sweeping sense of anxiety to Europeans. This sense of a collapse of the traditional world was accompanied by an intellectual reorientation in which men recast the very meaning of order itself. The result was an epistemology of differentiation and hierarchy. As William Bouwsma has perceptively pointed out, men in power felt compelled to renew "a sense of limit in the social universe," and exerted considerable energy in constructing and maintaining a new authoritarian definition of the nature of the polity, and of the role that king and magistrate would play within it.[13] Public law and royal justice would be among their most important tools in the building of the new edifice.

This new epistemology of order and hierarchical authority conditioned thinking about political and social relations, never more pointedly than among the class of magistrates who were the ministers of the law and who are the central characters of this book. These men (representatives of great families) assumed increasing political and social importance during the seventeenth century, and jealously defended their heightened status.[14] They never tired of proclaiming their special role as dispensers of justice, nor of the exalted, even sacred nature of their supposedly disinterested and impartial task. No one spoke of equality before the law in the mid-seventeenth century, and so no one assumed that peasant and noble should be treated the same in the eyes of the law. Men did believe, or claim to believe, however, in the need for justice to be free from the taint of corruption. Nicolas Brulart, a first president of the Parlement and a contemporary of Giroux and Saumaise, intoned that "among the presents that God has given to man, that of justice is without doubt the most august and the most divine . . . It communicates the knowledge of good and evil; it inspires the love of one and the hatred for the other; it makes known to man his duties and obligations."[15]

Like Brulart, both Saumaise and Giroux repeatedly postured as vessels of divine justice. Giroux vilified Saumaise for disrespecting justice, calling

Saumaise's patent attempt to frame Giroux "a perfidy toward God." He contrasted himself with his opponent by styling himself as an awestruck agent of the grand application of God's law. Before such "an exalted enterprise . . . he confesses his feebleness, [but] he deploys his conscience in his words, and the experience of eighteen years [on the court guides] his ministry." Saumaise's rhetoric was no less high-flying. He repudiated Giroux's tactics as ineffective "human diversions" that nonetheless could not stop "divine justice from . . . slowly descending from heaven upon Giroux." And in case anyone missed Saumaise's role in all of this, he added that he was "the minister of this imminent vengeance."

Magistrates girded themselves for the duty to dispense justice by embracing what could arguably be taken as their byword of the century—"discipline"—and they sought to apply it to themselves no less than to the world around them. Consequently, they internalized the emergent philosophy of neostoicism, which demanded self-discipline and thus a control of the passions that increasingly were viewed during the seventeenth century as the primal source of discord and disorder.[16] In the sixteenth century "passion" connoted emotions like shame, sadness, fear, suffering, pain, and affliction, but during the seventeenth century in France it came to mean an emotional impulsion toward disobedience and indiscipline. Commonly it was narrowly cast by moralists, theologians, tragedians, and political philosophers as concupiscent appetite, or lust.[17] All men naturally felt this, but magistrates in particular, as guardians of the new order, were expected to shield themselves from it by reason and self-control. More than one judge must have felt deep misgivings, therefore, about Philippe Giroux's reported passion for a woman that may have driven him to murder.

While justice was voiced in a lofty rhetoric of public impartiality girded by self-discipline, we learn from historical episodes like the Giroux murder trial that justice was also patrimonial. Patrimonial justice was an awkward sibling to the ideal child of impartial disinterest, for it brought familial, private interest into the equation of administering the law and rendering judgment. Here lay the core of the paradox of power. Many magistrates, even judges at the Parlement, were venal officeholders, which meant that they had property rights to their office that could be bequeathed to heirs. Possession of parliamentary office—a judgeship or above all a presidency—was a mark of the highest social distinction among the nobility of the robe, of preeminent importance in this vertiginously hierarchical and increasingly status-obsessed society. Indeed, as a way for judges to justify their position at the top of the social pyramid, they continuously pointed to their divinely inspired and royally sanctioned task of dispensing justice. In short, their social persona was legitimated by the impartiality of their task, and their claim to high social status in turn rested upon this legitimacy.

Most of the time, as near as we can tell from the underdeveloped state of current research into this fundamental contradiction, this paradox of power, judges could go about their work, safely ignoring the conflicted relationship between patrimonial and public justice that resided at the heart of this system; the tension between familial interest and public interest usually remained quietly in the background. Only a case like the Giroux murder trial laid the paradox bare. Suddenly entire families were thrust into a crisis, and their social and political survival along with their honor hung in the balance.

Within the narrative through which this story of intrigue, revenge, honor, blood, and death is told, many voices have been heard, each with its own internal logic and objectives. Of course there is the official voice of prosecution and the voice of defense, but there are also hundreds of witnesses testifying about what they "know" about the case. All these voices often contradict one another, and so the absolute "truth" of Giroux's guilt or innocence will never be known. As Natalie Davis so perceptively points out, fiction often rules in the archives.[18] But for readers interested in discovering the sinews of power—law, patronage, ambition, interest, vengeance—that defined political culture in this age of absolutism, the story of the Giroux affair offers a dramatic opportunity for them to do so.

Notes

Preface

1   Bibliothèque municipale de Dijon (henceforth BMD), Ms 328, f. 45r.

CHAPTER 2   Passion and the Beautiful Cousin

1   Compare this figure to the 300,000 livres that the bride of Henri II de Bourbon, the prince of Condé, brought to their marriage in 1609, or the 600,000 livres that Cardinal Richelieu dowered his niece in the marriage in 1641 with the prince of Condé's son, Louis II, the future Grand Condé. See Katia Béguin, *Les Princes de Condé: Rebelles, courtisans et mécènes dans la France du grand siècle* (Seyssel, 1999), 29, 45. Contrast these sums with the average dowry of a master artisan for his daughter in Dijon between 1600 and 1650: 357 livres. See James R. Farr, *Hands of Honor: Artisans and Their World in Dijon (1550–1650)* (Ithaca, 1988), 96.

2   Quoted in E. de La Cuisine, *Le Parlement de Bourgogne depuis son origine jusqu'à sa chute* (Dijon and Paris, 1864), 1:155–56.

3   Jacques-Paul Migne, ed., *Collection intégrale et universelle des orateurs sacrés du premier ordre* (Paris, 1845–), 36:1143.

CHAPTER 5   The House of Giroux

1   Pierre Lénet, *Mémoires* (Paris, 1838), 209.

CHAPTER 9   A *"Minister of Vengeance"*

1   Pierre-François Muyart de Vouglans, *Instituts au droit criminel* (Paris, 1757).

Analytical Essay

1   René de Cerisiers (Le Sieur Des Fontaines), *L'Illustre Amalazonthe* (part 4 is *L'Histoire des sénateurs Rufinius et Balisthène*) (Paris, 1645). On the history of the novel, see Thomas DiPiero, *Dangerous Truths and Criminal Passions: The Evolution of the French Novel, 1569–1791* (Stanford, 1992).

2   On the use of legal records in historical research, see J. H. Baker, *Legal Records and the Historian* (London, 1978). For suggestive observations about the study of law and history, see Sally Falk Moore, *Law as Process* (Cambridge, Mass., 1977); and June Starr and Jane Collier, eds., *History and Power in the Study of Law* (Ithaca, 1989). On the interpretation of legal records and the assessment of evidence, see James Chandler et al., eds., *Questions of Evidence: Proof, Practice, and Persuasion across the Disciplines* (Chicago, 1994). On the "story telling" in law, see Peter Brooks and Paul Gewirtz, eds., *Law's Stories: Narrative and Rhetoric in the Law* (New Haven, 1996); Daniel Farber and Suzanna Sherry, "Telling Stories Out of School: An Essay on Legal Narratives," *Stanford Law Review* 65, no. 4 (1993): 807–57; and "Legal Story-telling," *Michigan Law Review* 87 (1989) (special issue). On the role of language and power in jurisprudence, see James Boyd White, *Heracles' Bow: Essays on the Rhetoric and Poetics of the Law* (Madison, 1985), and John M. Conley and William M. O'Barr, *Just Words: Law, Language, and Power* (Chicago, 1998).

3   The royal edict of Villers-Cotterests, published in 1539 by King François Ier, attempted to codify criminal legal procedure throughout the realm. For the text of the edict, see François Isambert et al., *Recueil général des anciennes lois françaises*, vol. 12 (Paris, 1833).

4   For an exceptionally clear and concise description of criminal legal procedure in sixteenth-century France, see William Monter, *Judging the French Reformation* (Cambridge, 1999), chapter 1: "Criminal Justice in Sixteenth-Century France."

5   Sarah Maza, *Private Lives and Public Affairs: The Causes Célèbres of Prerevolutionary France* (Berkeley, 1993). On factums, see, in addition to Maza, Lise Lavoir, "Factums et mémoires d'avocats aux XVIIe et XVIIIe siècles," *Histoire, économie et société* 7, no. 2 (1989), 221–42, and David A. Bell, *Lawyers and Citizens: The Making of a Political Elite in Old Regime France* (New York, 1994), 31.

6   See Jeffrey Sawyer, *Printed Poison: Pamphlet Propaganda, Faction Politics, and the Public Sphere in Early Seventeenth-Century France* (Berkeley, 1990).

7   The bibliography on early modern crime and criminality is huge; for introductory references see "A Note on Sources" under "Prologue: Looking Back."

8   See Adhémar Esmein, *Histoire de la procédure criminelle en France* (Paris, 1882, 1978); John Langbein, *Prosecuting Crime in the Renaissance* (Cambridge, Mass., 1971), chapter 9; Richard Mowery Andrews, *Law, Magistracy, and Crime in Old Regime Paris, 1735–1789*, vol. 1 (Cambridge, 1994); André Laingui and Arlette Lebigre, *Histoire du droit pénal*, 2 vols. (Paris, 1980). See also John A. Carey, *Judicial Reform in France before the Revolution* (Cambridge, Mass., 1981).

9   David Parker, "Sovereignty, Absolutism and the Function of the Law in Seventeenth-Century France," *Past and Present* 122 (1989): 36.

10 On blood feuds in another microhistorical context, see Edward Muir, *Mad Blood Stirring: Vendetta and Factions in Friuli during the Renaissance* (Baltimore, 1993).

11 See James R. Farr, "Honor, Law, and Custom in the Renaissance," *A Companion to the Worlds of the Renaissance*, ed. Guido Ruggiero (Oxford, 2002), 124–38; Gerald Strauss, *Law, Resistance, and the State: The Opposition to Roman Law in Reformation Germany* (Princeton, 1986); Julius Kirshner, "Introduction: The State Is 'Back In,' " *Journal of Modern History* 67 (1995), supplement; and Aldo Mazzacane, "Law and Jurists in the Formation of the Modern State in Italy," in Julius Kirshner, ed., *The Origins of the State in Italy, 1300–1600* (Chicago, 1995), 62–73.

12 Michel Foucault, *The Order of Things: An Archeology of the Human Sciences* (New York, 1973), 54–55.

13 William Bouwsma, "Anxiety and the Formation of Early Modern Culture," in Barbara Malament, ed., *After the Reformation* (Philadelphia, 1980), 237. See also Bouwsma, "Lawyers and Early Modern Culture," *American Historical Review* 78 (1973): 303–27.

14 Ralph Giesey, "State-Building in Early Modern France: The Role of Royal Officialdom," *Journal of Modern History* 55, no. 2 (1983): 191–207; James R. Farr, *Authority and Sexuality in Early Modern Burgundy (1550–1730)* (New York, 1995), esp. part 1; Robert Descimon, "La Haute noblesse parlementaire parisienne: La Production d'une aristocratie d'état aux XVIe et XVIIe siècles," in Philippe Contamine, ed., *L'État et les aristocraties* (Paris, 1989), 357–86.

15 BMD Ms 319; Nicolas Brulart, "Discours et harangues prononcées par Mgr. Nicolas Brulart . . . premier président au Parlement de Dijon, 1657–1692."

16 See Gerhard Oestreich, *Neostoicism and the Early Modern State*, trans David McLintock (Cambridge, 1982); Nannerl Keohane, *Philosophy and the State in France* (Princeton, 1980); and J. H. M. Salmon, *Renaissance and Revolt: Essays in the Intellectual and Social History of Early Modern France* (Cambridge, 1987).

17 See Guido Ruggiero, *Binding Passions: Tales of Magic, Marriage, and Power at the*

End of the Renaissance (New York, 1993), esp. chapter 1; James R. Farr, "The Pure and Disciplined Body: Hierarchy, Morality, and Symbolism in France during the Catholic Reformation," *Journal of Interdisciplinary History* 21, no. 3 (1991): 391–414; Ioan Couliano, "A Corpus for the Body," *Journal of Modern History* 63 (March 1991): 61–80; and Robert Muchembled, *Sociétés et mentalités dans la France moderne, XVIe–XVIIIe siècles* (Paris, 1990).

18   Natalie Z. Davis, *Fiction in the Archives: Pardon Tales and their Tellers in Sixteenth-Century France* (Stanford, 1987). See also Malcolm Gaskill, "Reporting Murder: Fiction in the Archives in Early Modern England," *Social History* 23, no. 1 (1998): 1–30.

A Note on Sources

Readers interested in the documentation upon which this book is based will find the references here, as well as a list of secondary literature on various aspects of seventeenth-century France. I have organized this material by chapter.

This book centers upon a murder trial that began in 1639 and was concluded in 1643. The proceedings of that trial were lengthy, extensive, and seldom organized in coherent chronological order or paginated consistently. I have tried to be as explicit as possible in referencing this material. Most of the documentation for this book is preserved in the Bibliothèque Municipale de Dijon (henceforth abbreviated BMD) and in the Archives Départementales de la Côte d'Or (henceforth abbreviated ADCO). The proceedings for the trial are scattered in both of these repositories, but most of them can be found primarily in the following places: the manuscript collection of the Dijon library, in manuscripts 328, 1356, and Fonds Saverot 19 (a collection of nine sources relative to the Giroux trial); and in the archives in series B, boxes 12175 and 12175bis. Tucked in B12175 is the *Journal de ce qui s'est passé en Parlement au procez criminel de Monsr Le Président Giroux, 5 mars 1640–16 juillet 1646*, an important journal of several hundred pages describing in detail the unfolding of the trial from the perspective of the prosecution. Information on the trial can also be gleaned from BMD Ms 766, "Delibérations secrètes du Parlement de Dijon" (January 1641–December 1651), 903; BMD Ms 781, "Pièces originales relatives au procès du President Giroux;" BMD Ms 1346; BMD Ms 3330, "Notes concernant le procès de Philippe Giroud, Président du Parlement" (manuscript notes compiled by an eighteenth- and nineteenth-century Burgundian scholar named Gabriel Peignot); ADCO 1 F 458; and 1 F 459.

Research in the Parlement's archives is made easier and more systematic thanks to the important article by Jean-Claude Garretta, "Les Archives du Parlement de Dijon, étude des sources," *Mémoires de la société pour l'histoire du droit et des institutions des anciens pays bourguignons, comtois et romands* 23 (1962): 203–44.

Prologue: Looking Back

On law, crime, and criminality in early modern Europe, see James R. Farr, "Honor, Law, and Custom in the Renaissance," *A Companion to the Worlds of the Renaissance*, ed. Guido Ruggiero (Oxford, 2002); Bruce Lenman and Geoffrey Parker, "The State, the Community, and Criminal Law in Early Modern Europe," *Crime and the Law: The Social History of Crime in Western Europe since 1500*, ed. V. A. C. Gatrell et al. (London, 1980); Alfred Soman, "Deviance and Criminal Justice in Western Europe, 1300–1800," *Criminal Justice History* 1 (1980): 3–28; Alfred Soman, "Criminal Jurisprudence in Ancien Regime France: The Parlement of Paris in the Sixteenth and Seventeenth Centuries," *Crime and Criminal Justice in Europe and Canada*, ed. Louis Knafla (Waterloo, Ont., 1981), 43–75; Nicole Castan, *Justice et répression en Languedoc à l'époque des lumières* (Paris, 1980); Christiane Plessix-Buisset, *Le Criminel devant ses juges en Bretagne aux 16ᵉ et 17ᵉ siècles* (Paris, 1988); and A. Abbiaticci et al., *Crimes et criminalité en France, 17ᵉ et 18ᵉ siècles* (Paris, 1971). For material about Marie-Madeleine Dreux d'Aubray, the Marquise of Brinvilliers, see Arlette Lebigre, *L'Affaire des poisons, 1679–1682* (Brussels, 1989).

CHAPTER 1 Tales of Two Murders

This chapter is based primarily upon the riveting testimony of Claude Bryot, called La Valeur. It came to light on 6 January 1646 and can be found in ADCO B12175, f. 170r–174v.

CHAPTER 2 Passion and the Beautiful Cousin

BMD Ms 328, f. 163–68; ADCO B12175, *Journal de ce qui s'est passé en Parlement au procez criminel de Monsr Le Président Giroux, 5 mars 1640–16 juillet 1646*; and ADCO B12175bis, *2–10 September 1655*. On the Fyot family, see BMD Ms 1915, 1921, 1923; 1449 (Fonds Juigné). On the Baillet, see BMD Ms 1331, 1443, and 1915.

On morality, passions, neostoicism, and civility, see Anthony Levi, *French Moralists: The Theory of the Passions, 1585–1649* (Oxford, 1964); Gerhard Oestreich, *Neostoicism and the Early Modern State*, trans. David McLintock (New York, 1982); Maurice Magendie, *La Politesse mondaine et les théories de l'honnêteté en France au XVIIᵉ siècle, de*

1600 à 1650, 2 vols. (Geneva, 1970); and Robert Muchembled, L'Invention de l'homme moderne: sensibilités, moeurs et comportements collectifs sous l'Ancien Régime (Paris, 1988).

CHAPTER 3   The Trial Opens: Jean-Baptiste Lantin's Investigation

ADCO BI2175, f. 47r–123r; BMD Ms 328, f. 27–56.

On criminal procedure in early modern France, see Andre Laingui and Arlette Lebigre, Histoire du droit pénal, 2 vols. (Paris, 1980); Jean Imbert and Georges Levasseur, Le Pouvoir, les juges, et les bourreaux (Paris, 1972); Edmond Detourbet, La Procédure criminelle au XVIIᵉ siècle (Paris, 1881); Adhémar Esmein, A History of Continental Criminal Procedure with Special Reference to France, trans. John Simpson (Boston, 1913); John Langbein, Torture and the Law of Proof (Chicago, 1977); and Prosecuting Crime in the Renaissance (Cambridge, Mass., 1974). Giroux's contemporaries and colleagues would certainly have been familiar with the royal ordinance of Villers-Cotterests of 1539, an edict by King François Iᵉʳ which sought to regularize and standardize procedure in criminal law. It was only partially successful, and several legists from the sixteenth and seventeenth centuries wrote books either interpreting and clarifying the ordinance or presenting what had been customary procedure. Among some of the more important were Jean de Mille, Pratique criminelle (n.p., 1541); Joost de Damhoudere, Pratique judiciare et causes criminelles (Antwerp, 1564); Pierre Ayrault, L'Ordre, formalité et instruction judiciaire (Paris, 1576); Jean Imbert, La Pratique judiciaire, tant civile que criminelle . . . (Coligny, 1615); and Claude Le Brun de La Rochette, Le Procez civil et criminel (Paris, 1623).

On French law in general, see Jean Brissaud, History of French Public Law (New York, 1969); and more recently, Philippe Sueur, Histoire du droit public français, XVᵉ–XVIIIᵉ siècle: La genèse de l'État contemporain, 2 vols. (Paris, 1989). On men of the law see William Bouwsma, "Lawyers and Early Modern Culture," American Historical Review 78 (1973): 303–27.

CHAPTER 4   A Hat, a Rapier, a Knife, and a Dagger

BMD Ms 328, f. 62–76, 96–108, 119–21 (depositions of witnesses, spring and early summer 1640); f.175–82, "Extrait sommaire du régistre sécret et particulier des deliberations de messiurs les juges du procès de M. le Président Giroux du 5 Mars 1640"; ADCO BI2175, Journal de ce qui s'est passé en Parlement au procez criminel de Monsr Le Président Giroux, 5 mars 1640–16 juillet 1646; Bibliothèque de France in Paris (henceforth BdF), Fonds français 1994, "Les deux titres des deux procès du Président Giroux," f. 1–25v.

CHAPTER 5 *The House of Giroux*

Piecing together the building blocks of family wealth and political and social connections takes the researcher into vast amounts of disparate archival material. I have culled thousands of notarial records (housed in the ADCO) to locate marriage contracts, credit arrangements, property devolutions, and last wills and testaments of many of the key figures in this drama. To gain some sense of the extent of their landholdings, I have plumbed the registrations of fiefs at the Chambre des Comptes in the ADCO, B10668–B10888, "Dénombrements et reprise de fiefs," 1575–1700; in the BMD Mss 1433–1442 [microfilm 65–74], "Fiefs de Bourgogne," compiled by M. le Baron de Juigné; and in the BMD Ms 780: "Extraits de divers régistres de la Chambre des Comptes de Dijon concernant les fiefs mouvans du duché de Bourgogne et particulièrement du bailliage de Dijon." Also extremely useful is the survey of landholdings by the royal intendant Bouchu in 1666, ADCO C2887, and BMD Ms 926–28, "Recherches de la noblesse de Bourgogne en 1669: Copie des minutes déposées au greffe de la Chambre du Trésor, des procès-verbaux et jugements rendus par M. Bouchu . . . contre les usurpateurs de titre, le tout rangé par bailliage." To explore clientage networks among the important families of Burgundy I have waded through thousands of baptismal records from 1600 to 1650 (Archives Municipales de Dijon, État Civil, series B), which list the parents and godparents of every child baptized in the seven parishes of Dijon.

Some of this research is genealogical. On French and Burgundian noble genealogies see de La Chenaye-Desbois et Badier, *Dictionnaire de la noblesse* (Paris, 1858); Henri Beaune and Maublon d'Arbaumont, *La Noblesse aux États de Bourgogne de 1350–1789* (Geneva, 1978); Jules d'Arbaumont, *Les Anoblis de Bourgogne* (Paris, 1867); and BMD Ms 1443–1458; Mic 134–49; Fonds Juigné (organized alphabetically by patronym): On the Giroux family, see especially BMD Ms 1450 (Fonds Juigné). On the Le Goux de La Berchere family, see the book by Albert Bissey, *Précis historique sur les Le Goux de La Berchere* (Beaune, 1887); and BMD Mss. 1698, 1903, 1915.

On the nobility of France in general, nobility of the robe in particular, and clientage networks within nobility see Jay M. Smith, *The Culture of Merit: Nobility, Royal Service, and the Making of Absolute Monarchy in France, 1600–1789* (Ann Arbor, 1996); Jonathan Dewald, *The European Nobility, 1400–1800* (Cambridge, 1996); David Parker, *Class and State in Ancien Regime France: The Road to Modernity?* (London, 1996); M. L. Bush, *Rich Noble, Poor Noble* (Manchester, 1988); H. M. Scott, *The European Nobilities in the Seventeenth and Eighteenth Centuries*, 2 vols. (London, 1995); Jean-Pierre Labatut, *Noblesse, pouvoir, société en France au XVIIᵉ siècle* (Limoges, 1987); Daniel Dessert, *Argent, pouvoir et société au grand siècle* (Paris, 1984); Robert Harding, *Anatomy of a Power Elite* (New Haven, 1987); Sharon Kettering, *Patrons, Brokers and Clients in*

Seventeenth-Century France (Oxford, 1986), Jonathan Dewald, The Formation of a Provincial Nobility: The Magistrates of Rouen, 1500–1610 (Princeton, 1980); Robert Descimon, "La Haute Noblesse parlementaire parisienne: La Production d'une aristocratie d'état aux XVIᵉ et XVIIᵉ siècles," L'État et les aristocraties, ed. Philippe Contamine (Paris, 1989), 357–86; Denis Richet, "Élite et noblesse: La Formation des grands serviteurs de l'état (fin XVIᵉ s.–début XVIIᵉ s.)," Colloque franco-polonais sur la noblesse, XVI–XVIIIᵉ s. (Lublin, 1975). On Burgundy in particular see James R. Farr, Authority and Sexuality in Early Modern Burgundy (1550–1730) (New York, 1995); Gaston Roupnel, La Ville et la campagne au XVIIᵉ siècle: Étude sur les populations du pays dijonnais (Paris, 1955); and Pierre de Saint Jacob, "Mutations économiques et sociales dans les campagnes bourguignonnes à la fin du XVIᵉ siècle," Études rurales 1 (1961): 34–49. On the venality of offices see Bernard Barbiche, Les Institutions de la monarchie française à l'époque moderne (Paris, 1999); and William Doyle, Venality: The Sale of Offices in Eighteenth-Century France (Oxford, 1996).

Specifically concerning Henri II de Bourbon, the prince of Condé, see Katia Béguin, Les Princes de Condé: Rebelles, courtisans at mécènes dans la France du grand siècle (Seyssel, 1999); Henri, duc d' Aumale, Histoire des princes de Condé pendant les XVIᵉ et XVIIᵉ siècles, 8 vols. (Paris, 1863–96); Arlette Jouanna, Le Devoir de Révolte (Paris, 1989); the memoirs of Pierre Lénet in Joseph-François Michaud, ed., Nouvelle Collection des mémoires pour servir à l'histoire de France depuis le XIIIᵉ siècle jusqu'à la fin du XVIIIᵉ, 3e série ii (Paris, 1838): 183–632; Pierre Lefebvre, "Aspects de la fidélité en France au XVIIᵉ siècle: Le Cas des agents des princes de Condé," Revue historique 250 (1973): 59–106; and Christian Jouhaud, "Politique des princes: Les Condés (1630–1652)," L'État et les aristocraties (France, Angleterre, Écosse), XIIᵉ–XVIIᵉ siècles, ed. Philippe Contamine (Paris, 1989), 335–55. On Condé's entry into Dijon in 1632 see Pierre Malpoy, ed., Entrée du prince de Condé à Dijon en 1632 (Dijon, 1632).

On godparentage and clientage see John Bossy, "Blood and Baptism: Kinship, Community and Christianity in Western Europe from the Fourteenth to the Seventeenth Centuries," Sanctity and Secularity, ed. Derek Baker (New York, 1973).

On state building and the magisterial office-holding class see Ralph Giesey, "State-Building in Early Modern France: The Case of Royal Officialdom," Journal of Modern History 55 (1983): 191–207; Albert Hamscher, The Conseil Privé and the Parlements in the Age of Louis XIV (Philadelphia, 1987); and Sarah Hanley, "Engendering the State: Family Formation and State-Building in Early Modern France," French Historical Studies 16, no. 1 (spring 1989): 4–27.

On the French Parlements in general see Jacques Poumarède and Jack Thomas, Les Parlements de province: Pouvoirs, justice et société du XVᵉ au XVIIIᵉ siècle (Toulouse, 1996). On the Parlement of Dijon see E. de La Cuisine, Le Parlement de Bourgogne depuis son origine jusqu'à sa chute, 3 vols. (Dijon and Paris, 1864); Jean Richard, "Le Parlement de Bourgogne et la monarchie aux deux derniers siècles de l'ancien régime," *Annales de Bourgogne* 49 (1979): 107–19; Heide Gronau-Chenillet, *Le Parlement de Dijon et la Fronde: Un Corps face à la crise* (Dijon, 1991); BMD Ms 1330 (Mic 101), which includes a "Tableau des officiers du Parlement . . . suivant l'ordre de création de chacun des offices" (109 pp.), followed by a "Table des officiers du Parlement . . . depuis son origine jusqu'à sa suppression" (26 pp.); BMD Ms 740, "Liste des Présidents, des Conseillers, des Procureurs-Généraux, des Avocats-Généaux, avec notes généalogiques" (229 pp.).

On ideas about justice and the judicial vocation see BMD Ms 319; Nicolas Brulart, "Discours et harangues prononcées par Mgr. Nicolas Brulart . . . premier Président au Parlement de Dijon, 1657–1692."

CHAPTER 6 *Prison*

BMD Ms 328, f. 109–19 (interrogation of Philippe Giroux, 10 August 1640); *Journal de ce qui s'est passé en Parlement au procez criminel de Monsr Le Président Giroux, 5 mars 1640–16 juillet 1646*.

CHAPTER 7 *Poison*

BMD Ms 328, f. 76–78, 91–93, 123–30 (procès de Maistre Lazare Rhodot); Fonds Saverot 19, f. 61v; *Journal de ce qui s'est passé en Parlement au procez criminel de Monsr Le Président Giroux, 5 mars 1640–16 juillet 1646*. On infanticide in Burgundy see James R. Farr, *Authority and Sexuality in Early Modern Burgundy (1550–1730)* (New York, 1995), 126–33. On the conflict over sovereignty between king and judiciary see James R. Farr, "Parlementaires and the Paradox of Power: Sovereignty and Jurisprudence in *Rapt* Cases in Early Modern Burgundy," *European History Quarterly* 25, no. 3 (July 1995): 325–51. On poisoning as a crime see Arlette Lebigre, *L'Affaire des poisons* (Paris, 1989), and Anne Somerset, *Unnatural Murder: Poison at the Court of King James I* (London, 1997).

CHAPTER 8 *Jailbreak*

BMD Ms 328, f. 78–89.

CHAPTER 9 *A "Minister of Vengeance"*

ADCO B112175, *Journal de ce qui s'est passé en Parlement au procez criminel de Monsr Le Président Giroux, 5 mars 1640–16 juillet 1646*; ADCO 1F459, "Table générale chronologique

et alphabétique . . . des choses plus importantes tirées des registres du Parlement"
(28 April 1636); petition, n.d. [after December 1636], *Instance criminelle introduite au
conseil du roy . . . par Me Pierre de Saumaise Chazans*; ADCO B12175, 181r–v and 193r;
BMD Fonds Saverot 19, 74r–80v; BdF, Fonds français 1994, *Les deux titres des deux
procès du Président Giroux*, f. 1–25v; BdF Factum 29615(3), 1635, *S'ensuit la foible response
du sieur Giroux au roy* . . . [Giroux's petition dates from 1635, but printed gloss in the
margin is by Saumaise, after 22 May 1636]; petition for evocation, 24 November
1636, *Plainte adressée à la personne du roy sur l'oppression du sieur de Saumaize-Chazans*.

On the Saumaise family see the flawed but useful book by Jules Du Bard de
Curley, *La Maison de Saumaise* (Chalon-sur-Saône, 1894); and BMD Mss 1457 (Fonds
Juigné), 2053, 2164. Among Pierre Saumaise de Chasans's writings see Pierre
Saumaise, *Discours de consolation a Mgr le duc de Bellegarde, sur la mort de M. de Termes*
(Dijon, 1621), *Discours d'honneur sur les vertus eminentes de tres haut et tres puissant prince
Henri de Bourbon, Prince de Condé, Premier Prince du Sang, Premier Pair de France, etc.* (Dijon,
1627) and *Panégyrique de Louis le Juste* (Dijon, 1629).

On honor see James R. Farr, "Honor, Law, and Custom in the Renaissance," *A
Companion to the Worlds of the Renaissance*, ed. Guido Ruggiero (Oxford, 2002), and
James R. Farr, "The Death of a Judge: Performance, Honor, and Legitimacy in
Seventeenth-Century France," *Journal of Modern History* 75, no. 1 (spring 2003).

CHAPTER 10 *Rape?*

BMD Ms 328, n.p., 9 December 1642 (Extrait de la procédure criminelle faite à
l'instigation et poursuite de M. de Chasans contre M. le Président Giroux fils);
Fonds Saverot 19, 26–52v; *Réponse au titre du factum du Sieur De Chasan*, 56r–78r *Factum
du procez des sieurs Giroux et Chasan*; factum, 25 mars 1643, *Bref inventaire des principales
charges des deux procez criminels joints pour estre jugez ensemble . . . contre Monsieur le Président Giroux*; BdF, Fonds français 1994 *Les deux titres des deux procès du Président Giroux*,
f. 1–25v; Fonds français 8251 *Extrait du registre des délibérations du Parlement*, 142v–61r,
20 May 1635–14 August 1643.

On rape in early modern Europe see James R. Farr, *Authority and Sexuality in
Early Modern Burgundy (1550–1730)* (New York, 1995), 97–110; Guido Ruggiero, *The
Boundaries of Eros: Sex Crime and Sexuality in Renaissance Venice* (New York, 1985); Nazife
Bashar, "Rape in England between 1550 and 1700," *The Sexual Dynamics of History*, ed.
London Feminist History Group (London, 1983), 33–40; Miranda Chaytor, "Hus-
band(ry): Narratives of Rape in the Seventeenth Century," *Gender and History* 7, no. 3
(1995): 378–407; Garthine Walker, "Rereading Rape and Sexual Violence in Early
Modern England," *Gender and History* 10, no. 1 (1998): 1–25.

CHAPTER 11 Attack, Counterattack

BMD Factum, 25 March 1643, S'ensuivent les convictions et faits permanents de l'assassinat du feu Monsieur le Président Baillet, et de Philibert Baudot [Neugot] son valet de chambre; factum, 25 March 1643, Bref inventaire des principales charges des deux procez criminels joints pour estre jugez ensemble . . . contre Monsieur le Président Giroux; BMD Fonds Saverot 19, 56r–78r (Factum du procez des sieurs Giroux et Chasan); Factum (no title), 25 March 1643; factum, n.d. [after 10 April 1643], Supplement des preuves des deux procez crimnels . . . à la poursuite du Sieur de Saumaise Chasans; BdF factum 34346, n.d. [after 9 December 1642, before 9 April 1643], Par ce que au procez criminel . . .; factum, n.d. [before 10 April 1643], Factum du procez criminel fait au Président Giroud [sic].

CHAPTER 12 The King of Spades

Journal de ce qui s'est passé en Parlement au procez criminel de Monsr Le Président Giroux, 5 mars 1640–16 juillet 1646; BdF, Fonds français 1994, Les deux titres des deux procès du Président Giroux, f. 1–25v.

On torture see John Langbein, Torture and the Law of Proof (Chicago, 1977); Lisa Silverman, Tortured Subjects: Pain, Truth, and the Body in Early Modern France (Chicago, 2001).

CHAPTER 13 Life or Death? The Day of Reckoning Draws Near

BMD Ms 328, f. 132–49, and ADCO B12175, 123r–37r (depositions, confessions, April–May 1643); Journal de ce qui s'est passé en Parlement au procez criminel de Monsr Le Président Giroux, 5 mars 1640–16 juillet 1646; BMD Ms 328 f. 150–51 (conclusions of advocate general Pierre de Xaintonge, 7 May 1643), f. 153–57 (death sentence against Philippe Giroux, 8 May 1643), 157–75, 183–90 (Relation de la mort de Mr le Président Giroux, account of Giroux's last month, from 10 April–8 May 1643, by the Minim monk father Larme); BdF, Fonds français 1994, Les deux titres des deux procès du Président Giroux, f. 1–25v. For another copy of the death sentence against Philippe Giroux and his accomplices see BdF, Fond français 1994, 26r–50v.

For an extended analysis of Giroux's execution see James R. Farr, "The Death of a Judge: Performance, Honor, and Legitimacy in Seventeenth-Century France," Journal of Modern History 75, no. 1 (spring 2003). On the significance of the amende honorable see James R. Farr, "Honor, Law, and Sovereignty: The Meaning of the Amende Honorable in Early Modern France," Acta Historiae IX 8, no. 1 (Capodistria, 2000): 129–38. On capital punishment in early modern Europe see Richard J. E. Evans, Rituals of Retribution: Capital Punishment in Germany, 1600–1987 (Oxford, 1995).

On the king's galleys see Paul Bamford, *Fighting Ships and Prisons: The Mediterranean Galleys in the Age of Louis XIV* (Minneapolis, 1973), and Andre Zysberg, *Les Galériens: Vies et destins de 60,000 forçats sur les galères de France, 1680–1748* (Paris, 1987).

Epilogue

Journal de ce qui s'est passé en Parlement au procez criminel de Monsr Le Président Giroux, 5 mars 1640–16 juillet 1646; BdF, Collection de Bourgogne 105, Mémoires et observations des choses plus remarquables tirées des registres du Parlement de Dijon . . . f. 407r, 7 décembre 1641.

The sources for the disputes between Marie Fyot and Pierre Saumaise can be found in ADCO B12175, f. 270r ff; B12175bis; BMD Ms 328, f. 19r–57v (including factum, *Convictions de Dame Marie Fyot* and *Reponse aux dernières passions de la Damoiselle du Coudray* . . .); f. 191–95; BMD Ms 1356, f. 267r–75r; BMD Ms 766, "Delibérations secrètes du Parlement," 625ff and 768ff, (21 and 23 April 1650, 30 January 1651); BMD Fonds Saverot 19; and the BdF, Manuscript Collection, Fonds français 8251, "Extrait du registre des delibérations du Parlement," 162r–180r (27 January 1644–16 March 1650); BdF factum 14927, 1656, *Dixiesme et XI partie du tragique procez du feu Président Gyroux et de Damoiselle Marie Fyot*, one of thousands of factums housed in France's national library. For a guide to those factums see Augustin Corda, *Catalogue des Factums* . . . *antérieurs à 1790*, 10 vols. (Paris, 1890).

Index

James R. Farr is a professor of history at Purdue University

Library of Congress Cataloging-in-Publication Data

Farr, James Richard, 1950-

A tale of two murders : passion and power in seventeenth-century

France / James R. Farr.

p. cm.

Includes bibliographical references and index.

ISBN 0-8223-3459-3 (cloth : alk. paper) — ISBN 0-8223-3471-2 (pbk. : alk. paper)

1. Giroux, Philippe, d. 1643—Trials, litigation, etc.

2. Trials (Murder)—France—Franche-Comté—History—17th century.

3. Law—Social aspects—France—Franche-Comté—History—

17th century. I. Title   KJV130.G575F37 2005

364.152'3'094445—dc22

2004030133